THE VOICE ACROSS THE BORDER

THE VOICE ACROSS THE BORDER

MEHTAB ALI SHAH

GYAN

Views and responsibility are of the authors only and not of the Publishers or any associate of the Publisher

The Voice Across The Border

ISBN:978-81-212-1054-6

Rs. 750

Published in 2011 in India by
Gyan Publishing House
23, Main Ansari Road, Darya Ganj
New Delhi-110002
Phones : 23282060, 23261060
Fax : 011-23285914
E-mail: books@gyanbooks.com
Website: www.gyanbooks.com

Laser Type Setting by: Rudra Computer Graphics, Delhi
Printed at : Chawla Offset Printers, Delhi

Contents

PART III: FOREIGN POLICY OF PAKISTAN

PART IV: TRIBUTE TO EDWARD SAID

PART V : HIGHER EDUCATION IN PAKISTAN

Foreword

The book *Voices from Across the Border* by Mehtab Ali Shah is an important contribution to promote be3tter understanding between the two countries. There are great misunderstandings between peoples of the two countries thanks to subcontinental politics and unhealed injuries inflicted by partition. We judge each other by stereotypes promoted by media on one hand and politicians on the other. There is very little available to read which is authentic.

Such books as this one helps to promote people to people understanding. Mehtab Ali Shah hails from Sindh and it is Sindh which bore major impact of partition. The Indian immigrants (still known as muhajirs) mainly settled down in Karachi and not in Punjab. Also, the muhajirs, mainly Urdu speaking, had supremacist attitude towards Sindhis and since they began to outnumber them (Sindhis) in their own capital, it led to tensions.

According to the author Sindh produces 70 per cent of economic resources as Karachi happens to be the industrial hub of Pakistan and these resources are used by military to pursue its own military agenda and more the tension between

India and Pakistan, greater the misuse of resources for military confrontation. This inflicts more suffering on the people of Sindh.

Also, Karachi has attracted migration from Punjab as well as North West Frontier Province as it is industrial hub and Ziaul-Haq's regime encouraged formation of Muhajir Qaumi Movement which Mr. Shah describes as neo-fascist movement and at one point of time, Karachi became battle ground between Muhajirs and Sindhis on one hand and between muhajirs and Pathans, on the other.

The author also deals with the problem of religious sectarianism in Pakistan as well as of communalism in India. Ziaul-Haq promoted religious sectarianism by declaring Pakistan as' an 'Islamic state' encouraging Ulema to indulge in politics. Also, the ISI trained militants and various outfits like Lashkar-e-Tayiba, Lshkar-e-Jhangvi and others came into existence. Apart from infiltrating into Kashmir, these lashkars also attacked Muslims of other sects in Pakistan.

Books like these explode the, myth that all Pakistanis are one and hostile to India. It is sheer myth, as much of a myth. as that all Hindus in India are hostile to Pakistan. It is right wing forces such as the BJP in India and Jamat-e-Islami and other rightwing parties including Pakistani Taliba~ who promote hostility between the two countries to benefit politically.

The essays in the book, though written from time to time and published in Pakistan make a useful collection in this book and since it is being published in India, will be within the reach of Indian people and would help dispel many myths about Pakistan. As these essays were read in Pakistan, they must be read in India too, to promote better people to people understanding.

Asghar Ali Engineer

Acknowledgements

Sometime ago, the Gyan Publishing House, New Delhi, very kindly invited me to send my menuscript for considering it to republish the informed me that they were ready to publish it. I was enthralled on this good news. So were my family members, especially my wife, Malika, son, Zulfiquar and daughter; Kiran. My other children and indeed, my colleagues in the department of International Relations who desired that my second book should also come in the market were also pleased to know this.

I am grateful to the Gyan Publishing House for publishing the book. Dr. Asghar Ali Engineer, the Director Centre for Society and Secularism, Mumbai, very kindly agreed to write the preface of the book, and grateful to him for this great favour. Like Zulfiquar and Kiran, some departmental colleagues, acted as my advisers. I appreciate their keen interest and support in completing this book My benefactor, Dr. Peter Lyon, the reader emeritus, the University of London, despite feeling unwell, from time to time telephonically guided me on different aspects of this volume I am beholden to him. Similarly, my time tested friend and guide, Dr. Charles Jones of Cambridge University, sent an advice about the legal aspects of reproducing my papers into a new volume. I am thankful to him for his usual "firm and polite worded" advise.

Mr. Kashan Narejo, the Computer Programmer, Department of International Relations, remained a source of support. Without his expertise in the computer technology, and assistance in formating the document, converting it from one programme to other, the publication of this volume might have been difficult. Kashan thank you for your patience and assistance.

I have deep gratitude for all those friends in Pakistan, India, and England, who either helped me in completing me this book or blessed me to do so.

Mehtab Ali Shah
Sindh University, Jamshoro, Sindh.

Introduction

After long sessions with my son Zulfiquar, and daughter, Kiran, me came to conclusion that sufferings of the contemporary Sindh have significant imprints of the partition of India and creation of Pakistan in 1947. And these marks can be traced directly or indirectly in each of these chapters. Thus, the events analysed in them should be primarily perceived from a Sindhi point of view.

Keeping in mind this scheme of things, the major theme has been divided into five sub-themes and correspondingly, in five parts. First, deals with Sindh and its problems in the post-partition era. The second part, examines the curse of sectarianism in Pakistan. The third part, investigates foreign policy of Pakistan towards other states, especially India. The fourth part containing only a chapter pays tribute to the Palestinian scholar and peace activist, Edward Said. In the fifth part, the causes and consequences of an unsatisfactory higher education in Pakistan are discussed and the remedies to improve its quality are suggested.

The foreign policy of a given state is considered to be the extension of its domestic politics. Both of these realms of political activity are inseparable and they markedly influence by each other. When one discusses Pakistan's relations with the other states, especially with India, one finds repercussions of those particular postures of foreign policy on the provinces of Pakistan Balochistan, Gilgit-Baltistan, Khyber Pakhtunkhaw, Punjab and Sindh. Probably, biggest looser of Indo-Pak discordance are the Sindhis.

Sindh produces about 70 percent of the resources of Pakistan. The state of tension with India, on one hand, siphons off Sindh's resources in name of defence, on the other; it increases the manoeuvrability of the armed forces, intelligence agencies and their civilian proxies in subjugating and exploiting Sindh. In addition, the partition of India and the resultant creation of Pakistan markedly changed the economic, political, social and cultural landscape of Sindh. It is no longer a homogenous province inhabited by Sindhis only. A huge number of people with a different language and culture demonstrating an apparently superiority complex to local Sindhis, migrated to Pakistan, which rose tension between Sindhis and the migrants. Generally speaking, Sindhis perceive that since the migrants have roots in India and their relatives across the border have a vote bank, they enjoy India's explicit or tacit support vis-à-vis them.

It is not only the people of the Indian origin who have allegedly impinged on the resources of Sindh, but the people from the upcountry, especially Punjab, as they have numerical superiority in the armed forces and bureaucracy; help themselves with the resources of Sindh irrespective of the form of the government. Thus, Pakistan's tense relations with India are a factor or an "input" of the relations between the federation and Sindh and vice versa.

Picking up this sub-theme, Chapter One discusses the plight of the fisher-folk of District Badin, bordering the Rann of Kutch and the Arabian Sea. This fisher-folk live below the poverty line and repeatedly suffers from the cyclones. It is frequently and badly manhandled by the paramilitary forces, the Rangers and their approved *dallals* (brokers) *and waparis* (traders). Had there been friendly relations between India and Pakistan, the dispute over the maritime boundary between Sindh and Kutch would have been resolved a long ago and the fishermen would have lived a peaceful life. The Second Chapter highlights the transfer of population at the time of partition and the resultant tension between native Sindhis and the new arrivals from India that still persists. This chapter also suggests some measures to bridge the gap between the two communities within the framework of a united Sindh and a stable Pakistan. Chapter Three discusses the settlement of "stranded Pakistanis" or "Biharis" in Sindh and the reaction of Sindhis towards their settlement. Chapter Four, analyses the formation of the Mutahida Quomi Movement (MQM) widely believed to be a neo-fascist terrorist organization on the security of Pakistan and the regional stability. Chapter Five investigates the causes of the emergence of criminal gangs in the capital of Sindh, Karachi, which is the commercial hub of the country and their adverse effect on Pakistan. In the same series, Chapter Six examines the anti-Sindhi policies of Pakistan's military dictator, General Zia-ul-Haq during the 1980s.The rising level of tension between India and Pakistan at that time has also been covered in this chapter. The continuation of the Zia legacy is highlighted here as well. The summary of this part and indeed, of the book is that Sindh and Sindhis are great losers of the India-Pak tension for the prosperity of Sindh. Pakistan and India, there should have good neighbourly relationships.

Part Two of the book consists of two chapters that reflect a mirror-image relationship between India and Pakistan. Chapter Seven argues that from the 1980s onwards, the Wahabi religious outfits, like Lashkar-i-Jhangvi, Sipah-i-Sahaba, and Lashkar-i-Tayba were reportedly created and militarily trained by Pakistan's intelligence services with the purpose of supporting Mujahiden and later, the Taliban in Afghanistan and Jihadis in the Indian administered Kashmir, respectively. Now these Lashkars and Sipahs, like Taliban have turned on the sects other than Wahabis or the state institutions. And they have increased Pakistan's vulnerabilities. This chapter ends with a note taking that for a rapidly developing India as a world economic power.

Part Three contains six chapters dealing with different aspects of Pakistan's foreign policy, especially to India. It has been emphasized here that India and Pakistan cannot be de-hyphenated from each other. Their culture, traditions, history, economy, geography and security are inseparable from each other. Much of their hostility to each other originates in their domestic problems. Pakistan considers Kashmir as their core problem. It gets an added dimension of the reduced flow of water from India to Pakistan, for which Pakistan blames India of obstructing by constructing new barrages on Jhelum, Chenab and the Indus rivers.

It has been argued in this book that the undoubtedly, Kashmiris are not happy with the style of the autocratic Indian rule, especially the heavy presence of the paramilitary forces. However, Pakistan's intelligence agencies also exacerbate the situation by fomenting trouble by sending agents provocateurs, like Hizb-ul-Mjahideen and Lashkar-i-Tayeba there. It is also difficult for Pakistan to absolve the role of agencies in the Mumbai carnage of 2008. The non-extradition to India, of Hafiz Saeed, the main perpetrator of the Mumbai carnage, who is reportedly backed by the agencies, widens the trust deficit between the two states.

This psychological barrier between Indians and Pakistanis, as argued in this work can be broken by increasing people to people contact, by rising the volume of trade, reducing the postal and telephone charges, and cooperating in curbing the drug and human trafficking and other fields. Civil societies and the media have to play an active and positive role to create an atmosphere of understanding between the younger generations of the two countries. It has been further argued that the cordial relationship with India may be much beneficial to the security and prosperity of Pakistan than its host of military and economic ties with distant United States.

Part Four contains Chapter Fifteen only that pays tribute to the Palestinian scholar Edward Said, who despite enjoying the luxurious life of New York and having professorship at the prestigious Columbia University, never forgot his roots in Jerusalem. He never compromised or concealed his "national i.e. Palestinian identity" and the yearning for the creation of a secular Palestinian state, where the Palestinians will have a right to return. Edward Said was so much nostalgic about Palestinian land, that he wanted to be buried there, which Israel did not allow. His feelings are similar to several Indian and Pakistanis, especially Sindhis, who crossed the border at the time of partition and settled in India, but still wish that their ashes may be flown into the river Indus. Here Edward Said has been cast on a Sindhi canvass.

Part Five, has three chapters dealing with the state of higher education in Pakistan. Chapter Sixteen deals with the redesigning of the syllabus of International Relations. Here it has been suggested that the concept of 'human security' must have precedence over the 'military orientated national security'. States are for people not the other way round. And in the 21st century, the problems like climate change, food and, water scarcity and strong international institutions, deserve major attention in a country like Pakistan.

All these ideas are overshadows by the military and intelligence 'services' invisible dictates through their rented academics to continue with an emphasis on the traditional "state-centric" and a "military dominated, centralised theocratic state paradigm" in the study of International Relations. In the next chapter, it has been argued that intelligence services discourage the critical study of social sciences and through university administration, they harass the independent minded social scientists. Sometimes, these social scientists are either sacked or harassed. The result of this regimentation of the universities is that good social scientists leave the Pakistani universities and there is dearth of creative and innovative thinking in the universities.

The last chapter is the link of the same chain. It argues that higher education in Pakistan is in the state of shambles. The appointment of retired generals, bureaucrats and second-rate academics on the political basis, as the vice-chancellors, contributes enormously towards the degradation of higher education. The penetration of the intelligence moles in the teaching and student communities as well as in the administration, downgrades the university education system. On the basis of political expediency, the appointment of chancellor reportedly with a criminal record will encourage the trends of criminalization and gang war on the campuses within his jurisdiction. The ban on student unions will also create suffocation which will lead to the degradation of the educational system. Sindh and Balochistan Universities are the places of major machinations of the intelligence agencies so that the students of the these universities should not compete with the students of other provinces and will be left nowhere.

This chapter concludes that for the survival of country, we need a strong higher education system. Collaboration with Indian, Bangladeshi and Sri Lankan universities will help us markedly to improve our educational system. Above all, the prevalence of genuine democracy, ending the interference of the agencies in the universities, the appointment of Higher

Education Commission, of gentleman chancellors, and scholar vice-chancellors will also be conducive to improve the higher education system.

Lastly, it has been argued that the problems of India and Pakistan are intertwined. For improving our daily lives, good education, adequate medical facilities, sufficing job opportunity, security against extremisms and terrorism, we Pakistanis must press the government of Pakistan to come to terms with geopolitical realties and give top priority to improving relationships with India. We expect the similar posture of the Indian civil society towards their government vis-à-vis Pakistan. The veteran Indian journalist, Kuldip Nayyar and the senior Pakistani intellectual, I.A. Raman's columns in the *Dawn* are a case in the point in which both of them strongly advise their respective governments to improve the relationship with the other country. The Indian lawyers, A. G. Noorani and Ram Jethmalani do the same. Their efforts will not go in vain.

Indian and Pakistani should sit together and make a joint strategy to maintain their economic independence, without which political independence is meaningless. Water scarcity in Pakistan is not only a creation of India but mainly by the climate change. Let us discuss this problem of climate change, which includes the military activity of the two countries in the Siachen Glacier badly affecting the ecosystem of the high Himalayas. Let us ask Indian and Pakistani governments not to treat Kashmir as their *Jagirs* (fiefdom) but respect the wishes of the people who live there. We are not "us" and "they" but "we" with thousands of years common history, common culture and common languages. State boundaries cannot separate our hearts and minds from each other .We are basically one people. Let us sit down and talk with open minds and large hearts. Let us try to have peace within our minds, within our countries, in the region and the world at large. This is the message of Shah Latif Bhittai, the poet-saint of Sindh and other mystics of all regions and religions, and peace activists, which have been conveyed in this book and that is why it has been given the title of *The Voice Across the Border*.

PART - I
PROBLEMS OF SINDH AFTER CREATION OF PAKISTAN

1

Ferment in Sindh: Mistreatment of Fisherman in Badin District in Pakistan and its Implications

The fishermen community of Badin district in the southern province of Sindh in Pakistan faces much hardship caused by the Thar Rangers, an auxiliary of Pakistan's armed forces. They have been deprived of their principal livelihood of fishing in their ancestral habitat. These fishermen enjoy enormous sympathy throughout Sindh, which indicates the discontentment of Sindhis with Pakistan's federal structure. If the government does not address the grievances of the fishermen, in particular and the Sindhis, as a whole properly, the consequences may be horrendous.

Badin is the extreme southern district of Sindh province of Pakistan. It has a coastline on the Indian Ocean, along the Thatta and Karachi districts of Sindh and the Makran coast (in Baluchistan province) of the Persian Gulf. It makes Pakistan a littoral state of the Indian Ocean, increasing its significance in the geostrategic maritime map of south and south-west Asia. Badin district abuts the Rann of Kutch in the Indian state of Gujarat to its south and south-west. In effect, the disputed Sir Creek maritime boundary is the lingering problem of the demarcation between Badin and Kutch, which can be resolved even by low level maritime officers of the two countries, if their higher-ups wish to do so.

The location of Badin district, adjacent to the Indian border and the hitherto tense relations between India and Pakistan, are the principal reasons for the plight of the people of the area. India-Pakistan discord had given extra leverage to armed forces of the country to rule it almost perpetually, on the one hand and make poor Sindhi fishermen, worst example of their exploitation in the name of national security, on the other.

After the repatriation of Pakistan's prisoners of war from India in 1972 and their reintegration into the regular units, Pakistan army gradually started asserting itself in the politics of Pakistan. The Bhutto government's inept military action in Baluchistan enhanced the army's role in politics of the country. As a part of its expanded role during the last days of the Bhutto government, Indus Rangers, a paramilitary force deployed on Sindh-Kutch portion of Indo-Pakistani border, requested Sindh government to hand over four *dhandhs* (water reservoirs) within limit of five miles from the international border.[1] The Sindh Government of the day complied with wishes of Rangers in the name of national security and handed over these dhandhs to them for limited purpose of fishing for personal use of 'jawans' (military personnel). By staging a coup against the elected government of Zulfiqar Ali Bhutto in 1977, General Zia-ul-Haq came to power. At that time, he beat the drum of instability and external intrusion into the country. Coastal areas of Badin district were declared a sensitive area Rangers were heavily reinforced there and security zones restricted areas were created there. Besides Navy, Coast Guard Rangers were given responsibility of patrolling the coast and adjacent areas.

Initially, Rangers were allowed by the then docile Sindh provincial government to fish for the limited purpose of personal use and supplying to jawans deployed on the border with India. Subsequently, this fishing for personal use by Rangers took on a commercial dimension. Starting from the initial four water reservoirs, Rangers acquired possession of 20 such reservoirs in Badin district alone.[2] For 27 years in general and Musharraf era (1999-2008) in particular, one after the other, not only coastal lagoons but inland lakes and even drainage canals, prey to Thar Rangers, who acquired fishing contracts from the Sindh government at a nominal cost and monopolized fishing activity of the district. It is noteworthy that it was the Zia era when armed forces began getting involved in commercial activity in the country on a large scale. And now they are a business empire in their own right, having about 30 commercial concerns.[3]

The very poor and chronically cyclone-stricken fishermen have been deprived of their centuries old livelihood. They cannot sell their catch on their own in the traditional *mianis* (small spot markets) at the bargaining price to a *wapari* (trader) or *dalal* (broker) or a private contractor, but only to the Rangers approved contractors, who determine the price. A well-connected Punjabi contractor, for instance, buys one kg of prawns at throwaway price of Rs. 10 to 12. The same quality of prawns is sold in fish market of Karachi at a price as high as Rs. 250 to 300.[4] Even at the local miani, what catch the fishermen can sell at the price of Rs. 50, the *sarkari* (Rangers-approved) contractor buys at Rs. 5 only.[5] If a fisherman is caught fishing 'illegally' he is severely beaten his nets and boats are confiscated and even burnt by Rangers. A catch for personal use without permission of the Rangers is also considered illegal. Rangers frequently search huts of fishermen for seizing what they call illegal catch. They beat men and molest women.[6] Fishermen crossing the entry points of restricted areas have to wait for hours to do so. After a humiliating search of their belongings and body, they are allowed to cross. In the meanwhile, their womenfolk accompanied by them are badly harassed. Other members of civil society, particularly journalists and NGO workers, are not allowed to visit the restricted zones. Their cameras and tape recorders are confiscated.[7] Thus, Badin coast and adjoining areas have become a large concentration camp, where the inhabitants are deprived of all amenities of life and have to starve to death or leave their ancestral hearths.

Unarmed Resistance

In order to redress their grievances, fishermen of Badin district chalked out a two-pronged strategy. First, they organized themselves into a community and sought membership of Pakistan Fisher Folk Forum (PFF) with the purpose of seeking support from fishermen of other parts of Sindh, who were facing similar problems, created by various federal agencies. Second, a law suit for the ejection of Rangers from the waters occupied by them was filed in lower court of Badin. The court asked district administration to serve ejection orders on Rangers.[8] The official who was to serve the orders was not allowed by Rangers to enter their premises.[9] Various provincial governments of Sindh, especially that of late Syed Abdullah Shah of Pakistan People's Party (PPP) tried their best to eject Rangers from occupied waters but in vain. Thus, neither the provincial governments nor the law of the land were effective against the mighty Rangers.

Inefficacy of the law of land against Rangers compelled fishermen to resort to agitation for restoration of their basic right to live and work. From time to time, they staged *dharnas* (sit-ins) and *hartals* (strikes, especially hunger strikes) in their villages and in Badin town. Rangers retaliated with abuse, arrest, physical and mental torture, which further stirred up feelings of fishermen against Rangers. There was an atmosphere of mutual loathing between Rangers and fishermen. As stated earlier, fishermen also got NGOs and other members of civil society involved on their side, which evoked a bitter response from Rangers.

The simmering resentment of fishermen, turned into a furious resistance movement when, on October 20, 2004, two Rangers entered the hut of a fisherman on pretext of searching for illegal fish and retrieve an eagle that had strayed. Their real intention was to rape two women.[10] Women shouted for help and the whole village turned out against Rangers. Unarmed villagers resisted Rangers and tied them up with ropes and handed them over to a local police station, where Rangers confessed their real intention to the police.[11] On the insistence of Ranger higher-ups, Instead of any action being taken against Rangers, perpetrators were set free. Villagers were arrested, beaten and put in solitary confinement for 23 days. This heaped injury on already furious fishermen. They gave a strike call, which was observed by the fisherfolk throughout Sindh including its capital, Karachi. Members of provincial and national assemblies representing the coastal areas of Sindh, across the board, supported the cause of fishermen. Other members of civil society also expressed their solidarity with fishermen of Badin.[12] Once again on November 2, 2004, which is World Fisheries Day, fishing community of Karachi and interior Sindh expressed its solidarity with the fisherfolk of Badin district and demanded federal government to withdraw the Rangers and other similar agencies from occupied waters. The citizens of Karachi also participated in the *mela* (festival) organized by local fishermen and lent their support to them.[13]

Transformation of Struggle

Local resistance offered by poor and unarmed fishermen of Badin against military might of the state, was transformed as the Movement for Restoration of Democracy (MRD) of 1982, launched against military dictatorship of General Zia, into a symbol of resistance of exploited Sindhis against the military rule. Badin was one of the hotbeds of pro-democracy and anti-Zia MRD. Once again, it became the symbol of unarmed persons fighting for their just cause against a mighty arm of the state. PPP, representing downtrodden masses of Sindh, took the issue of plight of Badin fishing community to the parliament in Islamabad. The Awami National Party (ANP) representing, mainly the North West Frontier Province (NWFP), supported it. They jointly tabled a motion in senate, the upper house of the parliament in Pakistan for investigating causes of fishermen's plight. In order to prove itself as one of the mainstream political parties of the country, the radical Islamist alliance, Muttahida Milli Amal (MMA), also supported the PPP to requisition a session of the senate to discuss violation of the human rights of fishermen of Badin and other parts of Sindh.[14] Having enough trouble on his plate over issues of burgeoning insurgency in Balochistan and his continuing as the army chief till 2007, Pakistan's military ruler, General Musharraf, wanted to avoid yet another thorny issue for parliamentary debate. He therefore ordered the Rangers to withdraw from the waters of Badin and hand them over to their rightful owners, *ie,* the fishermen.[15]

This was the first victory of an unarmed group of poor fishermen of Badin, who by organizing themselves into a closely knit community and seeking cooperation from fishermen community of Sindh and civil society, forced armed forces to withdraw from their business concern, which they acquired in the name of security. Landless tenants of Okara in Punjab who are striving for their ownership rights in the military-owned agricultural farms, have to emulate them. Similarly, the Jahanian Sayeds of Hyderabad, Sindh, whose valuable land in middle of city had been occupied by the army, or several other families or the Sindh government, can learn a lesson from the

Badin fisherfolk. Education department of government of Sindh, 55 of whose buildings have been occupied by Rangers, must have the courage of fishermen to eject Rangers from their premises.[16] In addition, genuinely elected politicians who have been deprived of their due share in the governance of the country, may learn a lesson from the struggle of unarmed anglers.

Simmering Sindh

The repression of fishermen of Badin and their agitation against paramilitary forces, if not addressed properly, would have wider consequences for the state of Pakistan in the end. Fishermen of the coastal areas of Sindh have been badly treated by state agencies. They are deprived of their means of living by the federal government. Pakistan's territorial waters and the exclusive economic zone adjacent to the Sindh coast are, physically and historically part of (*Sindhu Sagar or Sindhu Raj)* Sindh-waters. In these waters, fishing contracts have been given to foreign fishing trawlers or settler Bengali or Punjabi fishermen, who have bigger and thinner nets which catch more fish than boats and nets owned by Sindhi fishermen. By adopting such a policy, federal government has deprived Sindhi fishermen of their principal source of income. In addition, Pakistani intelligence agencies frequently accuse some Sindhi fishermen of spying and smuggling Indian arms to Pakistan from Kutch district and interrogate them. This type of stories frequently appear in the press. For instance, see Mazhar Abbas, Al -Zulfikar, Myth or Reality, *Herald*, Karachi, June 1992, pp. 33-39 and Daily *Ibarat*, Sindhi, Hyderabad Sindh, 12 March 1999. In some cases, fishermen have been killed by state agencies and arrested. Their alleged accomplices languish in jails without trial.

Story of exploitation and persecution of Sindhi fishermen of coastal areas is tip of the iceberg. From 1947 onwards in general, and the advent of the Zia era (1977-1988) in particular, Sindhis as a whole have been deprived of their natural resources by the federation. Sindh is deprived of its due share of its only river, the Indus. Proposed construction of dams and canals upcountry on river Indus will convert Sindh into a desert. The huge tracts of fertile land in Ghulam Mohamed and Guddu Barrage areas are owned by retired military officers, principally Punjabis. Federal government, treating them as federal subjects, is exploiting oil, gas, coal and other mines of Sindh. Political deprivation is at the top of this structure. One Sindhi prime minister, Zulfiqar Ali Bhutto, was hanged (in 1979). Another Sindhi prime minister, Muhammad Khan Junejo, was unceremoniously dismissed in mid-night while returning from China in 1988. Benazir Bhutto was twice dismissed (1990 and 1996) on flimsy charges and assassinated. Thus, the overall impression of Sindhis is that they are living under internal colonialism, rather than as part of a federation, share to its decision-making processes; commensurate with their contribution to national exchequer, which is about 67 per cent of the national wealth of Pakistan.[17]

It has been argued that poor and unarmed fishermen of Badin have more than 30 years been engaged in a struggle against Thar Rangers, who had made their lives miserable. This resistance has had both symbolic and political dimensions. People of Sindh as a whole support the fisherfolk. This state of affairs, in the wake of trouble in Baluchistan, drew the special attention of power holders in Islamabad. In order to mitigate the situation, fishing activity of the Rangers in the Badin area had to be brought to an early end, as General Musharraf had announced. Following this, fishing rights in these waters should be given exclusively to the local fishermen. Those fishermen who had suffered physical or psychological losses should be adequately compensated by state. Not only in Badin district, but in coastal areas of Sindh as a whole, fishing rights in Pakistan's territorial waters should be given to Sindhi fishermen of the respective local areas.

In Pakistan's territorial waters, adjacent to coasts of Sindh and Balochistan, fishing rights should be given to local fishermen as desired by them and endorsed by civil society principles of equity.[18] Even in the exclusive economic zone, 100 out of 200 miles should be reserved for Sindhi and Baloch fishing communities of the respective coastal areas. Same formula can be applied to the continental shelf of Sindh. Huge seabed oil and gas deposits have been reportedly discovered in the Sir Creek. The Money generated from exploitation of seabed resources should also be used for benefit of local communities of both Sindh and Kutch.

These objectives can be achieved in accordance with the constitution of 1973, which was supposed to transfer subjects mentioned in the concurrent list, including fishing, to provinces. Oil, gas and mines should also be made provincial subjects. At least, the existing 12.5 per cent royalty rate should be increased to 70 per cent. By doing so, provinces will be richer, more autonomous and less dependent on the federal government in the economic and political realms.

Much of the cause of trouble in center-province relations in Pakistan is result of lack of provincial autonomy and over-centralization of the country. 1940 Resolution for Pakistan is the basic document, which provided the ideological and territorial basis of the state of Pakistan. It emphatically mentions that with the exceptions of defence, foreign policy and currency, all powers should be given to the federating units of the proposed Muslim majority state of Pakistan. If this resolution had been implemented, Bengalis would not have parted company with West Pakistanis. Learning a lesson from the separation of East Pakistan from the rest of the country the grievances of Sindhis and Balochs the two suppressed nationalities 1940 Resolution should be put into practice.

Good neighbourly relations between India and Pakistan, among numerous other things, will alleviate sufferings of the fishermen community in two countries and the people as a whole. Such a scheme of things will be markedly helpful in improving Pakistan's image abroad as a peaceful state, instead of a dictatorship, an unstable breeding ground of fundamentalists and terrorists and above all, a failing state, as it is perceived even by its friends.[19]

References

1. Seema Fazilat and Sa'adia Raza, A Battle Won, *Newsline,* (Karachi, December 2004), pp. 44-46.

2. *Ibid.*

3. Hassan Askari Rizvi, The Situation Can Be Described as the Colonization of Civilian Institutions by the Military, *Herald, (Karachi*, October 2004), pp. 56-57.

4. Ali Hassan, Villagers Try to Resist the Rangers Control of Fishing Rights, *Herald,* November, 2004, pp. 56-57, and Fauzia Wahab, Mistreatment of Fishermen Letters to the editor. *Dawn,* Karachi, November 11, 2004.

5. S. Fazilat and S. Raza, *op. cit.*

6. A series of reports by the *Sindh* television channel, October 27-November 5, 2004.

7. *Ibid.*

8. Muzaffar Haider, Fisherfolk at Finishing Point, *Ibrat* (Sindhi), Hyderabad, December 2004, p. 12.

9. Incidentally, the then district magistrate of Badin, Subhan Memon, is a former student of this author.

10. TV reports, *op. cit.*

11. Ali Hassan, *op. cit.*

12. *Kawish* and all Sindhi newspapers, October 26-27, 2004.

13. *Dawn, the Metropolitan Page,* November 3, 2004.

14. *Dawn,* November 13, 2004.

15. For Instance, see Mazhar Abbas, Al-Zulfikar, Myth or Reality, Herald, Karachi, June 1992, pp. 33-39 and Daily *Ibarat,* (Sindhi, Hyderabad Sindh, 12 March 1999) *Dawn,* November 23, 2004.

16. Rauf Sheikh, home minister of Sindh, in a statement in the provincial assembly, *Dawn, Metropolitan Page,* December 30, 2004.

17. State Bank of Pakistan and World Bank reports, *The Economic and Business Review: Dawn,* November 8, 2004.

18. Sohail Usman Ali (incidentally a former student of this author), Fishermen's Problems, Letters to the editor, *Dawn,* November 27, 2004.

19. In the annual report of the Freedom House, a Washington based human rights organization, Pakistan has been placed in the category of 192 not free states, *Dawn*, 28December, 2004. Stephen Cohen in his latest book on Pakistan, *The Idea of Pakistan,* is vague whether Pakistan is a failed state or a weakened state, surviving at the mercy of its powerful neighbours and the great powers, pp. 267-300.

(This article was published in the Economic and Political Weekly of India (EPW) Mumbai, 5 March 2005)

2

Urdu Speaking Immigrants in Sindh: Fish out of Water

From the creation of Pakistan in 1947 onwards, its southern province of Sindh has had waves of ethnic tensions between native Sindhis and the Muhajirs, the Urdu-speaking immigrants of Indian origin. Since the launch of the Muhajir Quomi Movement (Immigrants' Nationalist Movement) in 1986, rising tensions have threatened both the territorial integrity of Pakistan and regional security arrangements with India. A solution to ethnic tensions in Sindh requires an understanding and accommodation between Sindhi and Urdu sections of the population. The willingness of Urdu-speakers to gradually assimilate themselves in the host community and the devolution of power at federal, provincial and local level are crucial in bringing about harmony between these two major sections of the population of Sindh.

One of the biggest migrations in human history followed the creation of Pakistan in 1947. Sindh, the southern province of Pakistan, accepted the highest number of immigrants from India; while approximately one million Sindhi Hindus migrated to India, about 1.3 million Indian Muslims entered Sindh.[1] As a result of this enormous demographic change and its corresponding socio-economic after-effects, Sindh is witnessing tension between local Sindhis and the Urdu-speaking faction of immigrants commonly known as the *Muhajirs*.[2] Ethnic tensions in Sindh appear to be harmful not only to these two communities, but also to both the territorial integrity of Pakistan and its relations with India.

A History of Ethnic Tensions in Sindh

There has always been a strong sense of a distinctive Sindhi identity among the inhabitants of the province. In 1843, the British conquered Sindh as an independent state, not as part of the Mughal India. The principal inhabitants of pre-Partition Sindh, were Muslims and Hindus, the former comprising about 75% of the population, while the latter formed around 24%.[3] Muslims were principally agriculturists and lived in rural areas while Hindus were engaged in trade, both inside Sindh and throughout the world, and lived in cities such as Karachi and Hyderabad. Because of earlier access to the Imperial educational system, more Hindus than Muslims were in the bureaucracy, although by 1940s, the gap between educated Hindus and the Muslims was rapidly closing. However, in cultural terms, before 1947 Sindh was an homogenous province of British India. Both Hindu and Muslim sections of the population of Sindh spoke the Sindhi language. Moreover, unlike other parts of the British Empire in India, the Hindus and Muslims of Sindh demonstrated a high degree of communal harmony towards each other. For instance, they showed marked respect to the same saints: Shah Latif Bhittai and Sachal Sarmast, although the Muslims' saints, were equally revered by Hindus. The poetry of Shah Latif of Bhit conferred the status of a sacred language on Sindhi. Even after the lapse of 65 years, there will be hardly a Muslim or Hindu family of Sindhi origin settled anywhere in the world without a copy of *Shah Jo Risalo* (the verses of Shah Latif of Bhit). Similarly, Udero Lal, a Hindu saint, Sadhu T. L. Waswani, Nawal Rai Advani, and Dada Hoondraj "Dukhyal", the Hindu social reformers and educationists, were revered by Muslims.

In the 1943, Pir Pagara, the leader of a militant group, *Hurs,* waged guerrilla warfare against the British rule with an intention of establishing an independent state of Sindh. However, he did not muster much support from Sindhi Muslims as a whole and his rebellion failed. In 1943, the Sindh Provincial Assembly, under the leadership of G.M. Syed considered Sindh a Muslim majority area, passed a resolution for joining Pakistan. This historic resolution provided Pakistan with a physical, as well as a legal base.[4]

At the time of partition, the people migrating to Sindh came from Muslim minority areas of India such as UP, MP, Bihar, Hyderabad, Delhi, Rajasthan and Gujarat and settled principally in the big cities like Karachi, Hyderabad and Sukkur. The immigrants entering Sindh were principally divided into two categories. Onecomprised of Gujarati and Kutch-speaking businessmen and industrialists. Since Gujarat, especially its Kutch district, is adjacent to Sindh, this group of immigrants had a great deal of cultural similarity with native Sindhis. This affinity, along with their professional ethics, kept Gujarati-Kutchi immigrants aloof from politics and they have lived in peace with the host community to this day[5].

The second category of people migrating to Sindh from 1947 onwards was mainly Urdu-speaking. Quite a few of them were well-educated, having held government jobs in united India. These were the people who had formed the core of the Muslim League leadership in the Muslim minority provinces. Liaquat Ali Khan, the first Prime Minister of Pakistan, was their principal leader. Like Liaquat, many of the migrant leaders of Muslim League had no constituencies in Pakistan and in order to create their own constituencies, they encouraged the further transfer of population from India to Sindh.

This cross-border transfer of population became one of many bones of contention between indigenous Sindhis and the immigrant leadership of Pakistan. Another is the feeling that the historical contribution of Sindh towards the creation of Pakistan has never been fully recognised by the historians of the Pakistan Movement. If Sindh had not provided Pakistan with a physical base, the state would have not come into existence.[6] Sindhi Muslims also felt that after the creation of Pakistan, the lands which they had mortgaged to Hindu money-lenders would be returned to them, and that the major chunk of government jobs will be also given to them. Neither desire was fulfilled. To the great resentment of local Sindhis, Karachi, the capital of Sindh, was separated from it in 1948 and made the federal capital. Finally, and perhaps most importantly, Urdu, a language having no territorial base in Pakistan but belonging to north India and spoken by only 4% of the population of Pakistan, was made the national language.

Much of Pakistan's bureaucracy hailed from Urdu-speaking areas of undivided India. This 'immigrant bureaucracy', while relying on the support of the military-bureaucratic nexus, brought Punjabis and Urdu-speakers close to each other. In 1955, the military-bureaucratic coalition forcibly merged the provinces of Sindh, Punjab, NWFP, and the Baloch areas in the Western wing of the country. Among other things, the formation of the one-unit province of West Pakistan deprived the Bengalis of East Pakistan of their numerical majority in the country by imposing parity. In 1970, the one-unit province of West Pakistan was dissolved, the old provinces of the Western wing of the country were restored, and Karachi became once again the capital of Sindh.

After the creation of Bangladesh in 1971, a new configuration of forces emerged in Pakistan. Punjabis became the nation's largest ethnic group, followed by Sindhis, Pushtuns and Urdu-speakers. Very few of Urdu-speakers joined the PPP led by Zulfiquar Ali Bhutto, as his Sindhi ethic background was perceived as a threat to them and Balochs. As a result of 1970 elections, Pakistan Peoples Party (PPP) came to power both in Sindh and Punjab. During that time, Punjabis felt that it was in their own interests to forge links with native Sindhis instead of the Urdu-speakers of Sindh[7]. Yet most Urdu-speakers were inclined to reactivate their working relationships with Punjabis instead of Sindhis. Very few of them joined the PPP led by Zulfiquar Ali Bhutto; as ethnic Sindhis, they perceived Bhutto's ethnic background as a threat to them. Most supported either the Muslim League or one of the religious parties, especially the *Jamait-e-Islami,* having bases in Punjab. When the Sindhi Language Bill, aimed at reintroducing Sindhi as the official language of the province, was moved in the Sindh Provincial Assembly in June 1972, Urdu-speakers rioted. They felt that such a move was aimed at undermining their position as founders of Pakistan *(Baniyan-i-Pakistan)* in the country. As a result of these riots, a great deal of damage was done to public and private property and many Sindhis, at that time outnumbered in the big cities, were forced to leave their homes. At this time, various demands for the creation of a separate Karachi province, the incorporation of Karachi into Balochistan, or making Karachi a federal unit, were also raised by some Urdu-speaking intellectuals and politicians.[8]

Differences between Urdu-speakers and native Sindhis deepened when many Urdu-speakers joined the ranks of anti-Bhutto Nine Party Alliance, which resulted in the overthrow of his government and subsequent hanging by Pakistan's new leader Zia-ul-Haque in 1979. As a reaction to Bhutto's political murder and their persecution by the Zia regime, Sindhis launched the Movement for the Restoration of Democracy (MRD) in 1983. Before the launching of the MRD, Sindhis were usually perceived by the 'martial race' Punjabis and Pushtuns as 'docile people'. This perception changed after the MRD violently. Sindhis, clashed with Pakistan Armed forces in Sindh. Thereafter, Sindhis were perceived by the Zia regime as a serious threat to it and to the Punjabi-dominated establishment of Pakistan. The regime made a long-term plan for punishing Sindhis severely.

From 1984 onwards, in order to divide the Sindhis, Zia started associating with Sindhi separatists with the intention of pitting them against PPP supporters in rural areas. At the same time, Zia encouraged Urdu-speaking militants to form their own political party, the *Muhajir Quomi Movement* (MQM) under the leadership of Altaf Hussain with Karachi as its operational base.[9] According to its charter, MQM professed to redress the grievances of urban centres of Sindh. In order to do so, it wanted to use both legal and extra-legal methods. According to some observers, Zia's purpose in creating the MQM and providing its cadre with training and firearms was two-fold. First, it was supposed to counterpoise the PPP in the big cities of Sindh.[10] Second, and more significantly, MQM's ultimate aim of dividing Sindh along ethnic lines fitted into Zia's strategy of perpetuating his rule by creating cleavages in Pakistani society on ethnic and sectarian lines.[11] In the 1985 non-party elections, the MQM won overwhelming majorities in the big cities of Sindh. However, it remained a minority in the province as a whole, winning about one-quarter of the provincial Assembly seats. In the 1988 elections, the MQM also won in these centres with a similar position in the assembly[12], and became a coalition partner in the centre; first with the PPP government of Benazir Bhutto, then with Pakistan Muslim League-Nawaz Group, or PML (N).

In 1992, because of a clash of personalities and policies, the MQM split into two factions. The main faction was led by

Altaf Hussain; the other headed by Afaq Ahmed and named as the *Haqiqi* (original) Group. The Altaf Group retained its grip on the majority of the Urdu-speakers. For the purposes of this discussion, by MQM we mean the Altaf Group. The MQM boycotted the 1993 National Assembly elections but contested the provincial assembly elections and sat in the provincial assembly on the opposition benches.[13] In February 1997 elections, MQM received once again a mandate from Urdu-speakers, but it remained a minority in Sindh, winning just 28 out of the house of 109 members.

The Unacceptable Demands of the MQM

The successive victories of the MQM in Urdu-speaking pockets of the urban centres of Sindh, its exclusivist character, heavy-handed tactics, and its implicit and explicit agenda for the division of Sindh were anathema to Sindhis. In 1994, it presented an Eighteen-Point Charter of Demands.[14] Every year, these 18 points are reviewed and new appendixes are included in its Charter. Some of the MQM's demands appear offensive to other communities living in Pakistan, especially Sindhis, while others seem fairly acceptable, even to Sindhis. As a whole, these demands are the principal reason of tension between Sindhi and Urdu-speaking sections of Sindh province elaborated hereafter:

The Recognition of the Muhajirs as a Nationality

Both factions of the MQM claim that all those people who migrated from India form an ethnic group, the *Muhajirs* and should be recognized as a fifth nationality of Pakistan equal to other nationalities in the country.[15] Interestingly, those Punjabis who migrated from the Indian Punjab and settled down in Pakistani Punjab or in Sindh, are not recognized as *Muhajirs* by the MQM. Although some Gujaratis have been co-opted in their ranks, the definition of *Muhajir* is confined principally to Urdu-speakers. In response to this MQM demand, Sindhis argue:

The immigrants came to Sindh from different parts of united India. All of them do not speak a common language, Urdu. But they speak several languages, such as Kutchi, Gujarati, Memoni, Marathi, Tamil, Telgu, Bengali, etc. These immigrants neither have a common history nor do they have a common experience of migration. They came to Sindh for different motives. Thus, even on the basis of their own argument, the *Muhajirs* cannot be recognized as an ethnic group, let alone a nationality within Pakistan in general, and in Sindh in particular.[16]

Other nationalities of Pakistan, such as Balochs, Punjabis and Pushtuns, also do not agree to the MQM's demand for recognition of Urdu-speakers as a nationality. Interestingly enough, the MQM(A)'s erstwhile staunch supporters such as Nawaz Sharif and late Ajmal Khatak, Punjabi, and Pushtun nationalists respectively, do not recognize this demand. Probably, they felt that a recognition of Urdu-speakers as a nationality might lead to the partition of Sindh, which, in turn, would set a precedent for the division of Punjab into central Punjab, inhabited by Punjabis themselves, and the Siraikis of southern Punjab. Such a step might also lead to a similar division of the Frontier Province between its Pushtu and Hindko-speaking sections of population17. Thus, even those MQM allies of Punjabi and Pushtu leaders do not support its bid for recognition of Urdu-speakers as a nationality.

The Division of Sindh

Altaf Hussain, leader of the MQM, from time to time demanded the creation of an Urdu *Suba* (province).[18] Sometimes, he is on record of going even further and implicitly demanding the creation of a sovereign Urdu-speaking state, or *Muhajirisitan.*[19] The boundaries of a proposed Urdu province within Pakistan or an Urdu-speaking independent state are deliberately kept vague. In some maps captured by the Pakistani

Army in June 1992, Karachi is mentioned as *Urdu Suba* or *Jinnahpur*[20]. In other maps, Karachi, Hyderabad, Thatta, Badin, Mirpur Khas, Tharparkar, parts of Nawab Shah, Sanghar and Sukkur districts of Sindh are mentioned as the areas comprising the boundaries of the proposed province of *Muhajirisitan*[21] To popularize the demands of a separate province, the MQM has coined a new phrase: 'Southern Sindh'.[22] It claims that in this area, the constituents of the MQM are in a majority. While the MQM(A) sometimes tactically withdraws this demand from its agenda, the MQM (Haqiqi) faction made the idea of 'Southern Sindh' non-negotiable.

The demand for the creation of a new province by dividing Sindh is highly offensive to Sindhis. To them, Sindh is not just an administrative unit of Pakistan but an ancestral, historical, and sacred homeland. Its division is unthinkable. Besides this expression of their emotional attachment with Sindh, Sindhis argue that there is no physical or demographic demarcation line dividing the state into northern or southern zones. Moreover, citing official figures on the ethnic mix of Karachi and its suburbs, the core area of the proposed Urdu province, informed Sindhis suggest that Urdu-speakers would form about 45% of the population of this area. Thus, Urdu-speakers cannot proclaim themselves as a majority even in their proposed core area.[23]

The demand for the division of Sindh and the creation of new provinces also does not receive support from the Pakistani establishment on constitutional grounds. The four provinces of Pakistan, Sindh, Balochistan, Punjab, and the NWFP are mentioned by name in the constitution. The Pushtuns of the NWFP have changed the name of their province to Khyber Pakhtunkhaw. The new name falls into line with the names of the three other provinces, which are identified by their inhabitants. If the Pakistani establishment was unwilling to change the name of an existing province from NWFP to

Pakhtunkhaw, it will never tolerate the idea of an Urdu province, which will open a Pandora's Box of separatism as discussed earlier.

In strategic terms, Pakistani establishment is also very sensitive about the creation of an Urdu province. All those parts of Sindh, which have been earmarked by MQM as parts of its proposed province, share land or sea borders with India. Because of the proximity and cultural affinity of this proposed new province with India, the Pakistani establishment is apprehensive that the creation of this province might be a stepping-stone towards the creation of a sovereign state, *Urdu Pradesh.* One can argue that the marked proximity of this proposed Urdu Suba to India adds a new dimension to the endemic Indo-Pakistan tension. Since the creation of the MQM in the mid-1980s, which coincided with insurgency in the Indian administered Kashmir, Pakistan has persistently accused India of supporting MQM activists in their fight against law-enforcement authorities.[24]

It is debatable whether the MQM intends to break away from Pakistan or it plans to extract maximum benefits from the Pakistani Federation by raising the stakes. However, its demand for the recognition of Urdu-speakers as a nationality and the division of Sindh has created a similarity of perceptions of it by Sindhis and the Pakistani establishment. For Sindhis, Sindh is their ancestral homeland whose division they will resist tooth and nail. For Pakistani establishment, the division of Sindh might result in a civil war and disintegration of Pakistan. Thus, Sindhis and the Pakistani establishment, traditionally an odd couple, are against the division of Sindh.

An end to the Quota System

Another of the major demands of the MQM is the abolition of the quota system in Sindh and the allocation of government jobs and the admission to educational institutions on a merit basis. The quota system was introduced in Pakistan in 1949 by

Liaquat Ali Khan for candidates seeking competitive entry into official level jobs in the federal bureaucracy.[25] In one form or another, it continued until 1973 when it was revamped on the basis of the 1971 census and each province of Pakistan allocated government jobs according to its percentage of total population of the country. In the federal service structure, allocation was made on the following basis: merit, 10%; Punjab, 50%; Sindh, 19%; NWFP, 11.5%; Balochistan, 3.5%; (Pushtun inhabited) Northern Areas and Federally Administered Areas (FATA), 4%; and Kashmir, 2%.[26] The quota system was supposed to be reviewed after every 10 years. When all areas of the country stood at par with each other socio-economically, it was to be abolished.

Yet, since 1973, no significant change came in removing disparities between different areas of Pakistan, nor within Sindh itself. Because of the huge socio-economic gap between the rural and urban areas of Sindh, the federal quota for this province was divided on an 11.4 and 7.6% basis, respectively. A similar arrangement was also made for the Sindh provincial Civil Service.[27] Meanwhile, the allocation of jobs according to the level of development was not confined to Sindh only, Balochistan, Punjab and the NWFP were also divided into zones, according to the level of the development of each zone in each of these provinces.[28]

Karachi has become the financial hub of the country and much of its industry, bank headquarters, autonomous and semi-autonomous bodies and multinational corporations are located here, providing an enormous number of jobs. In contrast to Karachi, the rural areas of Sindh still suffer from abject poverty and 65% of rural Sindhis still live below the poverty line.[29] The prevailing gap of facilities between rural and urban areas, the quota system gives a chance to the children of rural areas to get some of the government jobs.

A survey of the allocation of jobs conducted by the Lahore-based English language newspaper, *The Frontier Post,* reveals that Punjab and urban Sindh are over-represented in the federal services at the expense of rural Sindh, Balochistan and Federally Administered Area.[30] This survey indicates that instead of its 50% allocation, Punjab has got 62.2% of federal jobs. Similarly, instead of its prescribed quota of 7.6%, urban Sindh has acquired 9.75% of federal jobs. Conversely, rural Sindh gets only 6.32% in contravention of its quota of 11.4%[31]. Moreover, many non-Sindhis, especially the Punjabi settlers and Urdu-speakers living in the rural areas, also get jobs on the quota of rural Sindh in the provincial and federal bureaucracy.[32] If the quota system was abolished, and the population of rural Sindh further under-represented in the civil service structure of Pakistan, national cohesion would be endangered.[33] Thus, neither Zia in 1983 nor Nawaz Sharif in 1993 abolished the quota system. On the contrary, they extended it for the next 10 years. In April 1997, the Supreme Court of Pakistan declared the quota system illegal. However, during the second term of office beginning in February 1997, Mr. Nawaz Sharif extended the quota system for a further 10 years in a new form. This continuation of the quota system has become one of the principal reasons for the discontentment of the MQM with different governments of Pakistan.

Fifty per cent of jobs for Urdu-speaking youth

The MQM claims to represent 22 million people: half the population of Sindh. On the basis of this claim, it demanded that Urdu-speakers should be given 50% of jobs in the provincial services.[34] The MQM further insisted that same formula should be adopted for the allocation of federal jobs to Sindh. In addition, MQM demands 50% representation should be given to it in provincial cabinet. The native Sindhis, for their part, argue that the Urdu-speakers could hardly comprise more than 5-6 million out of the 22.6 million population of Sindh. Moreover, Sindhis point out that since 1985, representation of MQM in Sindh Assembly has remained fairly static, *i.e.,* 26 or 28 out of 109 seats. From a Sindhi perspective, MQM's demand for a 50% share in provincial jobs and ministries is therefore untenable.[35]

The Appointment of an Urdu-speaking Chief Minister of Sindh

After every Provincial Assembly election since 1988, MQM has been demanding posts of governor and chief minister should rotate between Sindhis and Urdu-speakers. Sindhis argue that, according to parliamentary democracy, leader of the majority party forms the government. Since they (Sindhis) are in majority in the province and correspondingly in the Sindh Assembly, the chief minister should be a Sindhi. From 1971 onwards, the post of provincial governor has usually gone to a non-Sindhi, helping to maintain checks and balances in the governance of the Sindh Province. Yet, after February 1997 elections, MQM went a step further and demanded the governorship of the province for its nominee.[36] In reaction to this additional MQM demand, Sindh National Front and *Sindhi Awami Tehrik,* two Sindhi nationalist parties argued that if a Punjabi can be Governor of the neighbouring Punjab Province, or Governor of NWFP usually a Pushtun, then the Governor of Sindh should be a Sindhi, because Sindhis comprise a majority in their home province.[37] The MQM's insistence on appointment of its nominee as the Governor of Sindh, generated a new controversy between Sindhi and Urdu-speaking sections of Sindh. This controversy ended after the appointment of the Urdu-speaking, Punjab-domiciled, (retired) General, Moeenu-ddin Hyder as the Governor of Sindh in March 1997 by the President of Pakistan.[38]

The Repatriation of Stranded Pakistanis from Bangladesh

The MQM persistently demands repatriation of about 250,000 Urdu-speaking 'Biharis' living in Bangladesh, to

Pakistan. Sindhis oppose this demand on two grounds. The detailed discussion has been given in the next chapter. It is suffice to argue here that it is not only Sindhis, but Punjabi and Pashtun settlers and Balochs in Sindh are also opposed to the settlement of volatile Biharis to Pakistan in general, and Sindh in particular.[39]

Confrontation and Violence

Despite strong opposition to its demands as described above, MQM appears intent on achieving its objectives by both parliamentary and extra-parliamentary means. Zia's reign coincided with the war in Afghanistan, which brought a huge quantity of arms from all over the world into Pakistan. Anybody with money was able to buy weapons from the bazaars of the North-West Frontier Province and Afghan camps in Balochistan. Thus MQM had access to all sorts of small arms and has appeared willing to use them.[40]

In reaction to MQM's strong-arm tactics, Nawaz Sharif, then Prime Minister of Pakistan and a coalition ally of the MQM itself, was compelled to take military action in 1992 against it under the codename of 'Operation Clean-up'. From 1993 to 1996, MQM was at odds with both the first government of Nawaz Sharif and the second government of Benazir Bhutto. The pro-MQM coverage of Indian media aroused suspicion that it was acting as proxy. MQM denied these charges and accused the second PPP government (October 1993-November 1996) of committing genocide against its members. International Institute for Strategic Studies, London, in its 1995 annual report on Pakistan, considered MQM as a neo-fascist political party, because of the personality cult developed around its leader, Altaf Hussain, its opposition to any dissent within the party and its use of violence for achieving political ends.[41] This finding of the IISS about the MQM and a similar coverage by the Pakistani media, cast doubts on its credentials as a political party, functioning in democratic political processes of the country.[42]

After 1997 elections, in order to prevent the PPP from forming a provincial government in the Sindh, the PML (N) and the MQM(A) were forced to form a coalition government in Sindh. However, they could not overcome their deep suspicions about each other.[43] After the spate of violence in Karachi, which started after the MQM's return to power, even Muslim Leaguers accused it of disturbances in the city.[44] Thus, mistrust between the MQM and most of Pakistan's political parties persisted, especially the PPP and PML (N) the two largest federal parties on one hand, and MQM and establishment on the other.

The Acceptable Demands of the MQM

Despite its exclusivist nature and controversial character, MQM presented another set of demands, acceptable to other ethnic groups of Pakistan, including Sindhis. Although even this set of demands might be aimed at creating Urdu-speaking enclaves in Karachi, Hyderabad, and Sukkur in hinterland of Sindh along Bosnia-Herzegovina model, it can be tried as a base for achieving inter-communal harmony in Sindh. These demands are discussed below:

Holding a New Census

No census was held in Pakistan after 1998. The house enumeration exercise of 1991, which gave provisional figures of Pakistan was not acceptable to Punjab and Balochistan Provinces and the MQM for different reasons. Balochistan objected to the reported enumeration of Afghan refugees as citizens of Pakistan. It feared that by so doing in Balochistan, the demographic balance would be altered in favour of Pushtuns *vis-à-vis* Balochs. Before this house enumeration exercise, Sindh claimed that as result of migration from up-country to Karachi and its other parts, the province comprised about 30% of total population of Pakistan[45]. Punjab objected to this claim and suggested that there was no significant demographic change; it still comprised 57.88 instead of 54.91% of the population of

Pakistan[46]. The MQM raised objections to the increase in the rural population of Sindh as shown in house enumeration. Because of these objections, results of 1991 provisional census were declared null and void. Thereafter, the holding of a fresh census became imperative. In deference to public wishes, government of Nawaz Sharif announced a new census to be held from 18 to 21 October 1997 under the supervision of armed forces.47

While announcement of holding a new census was hailed by all political parties, Sindh based intellectual forum, the Sindh Democratic Group, suggested that it should be conducted under the supervision of judiciary instead of armed forces in order to give the census credibility at home and abroad[48]. Among other things, this census would determine the approximate number of Urdu-speakers in Sindh, as well as in Pakistan as a whole. It will also enable the urban and rural areas of Sindh to get provincial and central government jobs according to their ratio within the population of the province, as well as in the country as a whole. Moreover, the new census could help the provinces in drawing their share of income from the divisible national pool according to the ratio of their respective population.

Holding Local Body Elections

Pakistan has inherited a three-tier system of government from the British, consisting of the federal, provincial and local levels. Local bodies are supposed to provide civic amenities such as water supply, sewerage, garbage collection, maintenance of inner-city roads, etc, to the citizens at grassroots level. Unfortunately, local bodies have been neglected by successive governments of Pakistan. As mentioned earlier, MQM's major constituency is big cities of Sindh. Its demand of holding local body elections appears reasonable. The then chief minister of Sindh, Liaquat Ali Jatoi, agreed in principle to hold local body elections in September 1997. The MQM(A) was a partner of the ruling party. If local body elections were held, the MQM activists will get power at grassroots level and their grievance of being deprived from power-sharing arrangements will be redressed to a certain extent. Holding local body elections will be equally good for the rural areas.

Broadening the Tax Base of the Local Bodies

The MQM persistently insists on increasing the tax base of local bodies. The local bodies in their jurisdictions should levy taxes like vehicle, property and sales tax, and these bodies should be held responsible for the maintenance of these services. Presently, there are two lists of portfolios in the country Central and Concurrent. Under the Concurrent List, powers are shared by both federal and provincial governments. There is a need to transfer the portfolios from centre to provinces and from provinces to local bodies. Representatives of the MQM, in the government, would cooperate with representatives of other political parties from Sindh and other small provinces for increasing the amount of provincial autonomy. Autonomy, gained by the provinces, the easier it will be for local bodies to increase their tax and power base.

Creating a Special Police Force for Karachi

The MQM argues that because most of the police operating in Karachi are from up-country and do not treat the city's citizens in an appropriate manner, law and order problems are exacerbated. In order to mollify this situation, a separate metropolitan police force should be created which should be at the disposal of Karachi Municipal Corporation.[49]

There is seemingly no harm in creating a special police force for Karachi. However, in order to make it more effective, this force ought to be recruited from all ethnic groups residing in Karachi. Many unemployed youths would be happy to join and should prove enthusiastic in improving the law and order situation in the city. Since the police department is under concurrent jurisdiction of central and provincial governments, provincial government will retain control of the police force until the constitution of country is amended. Thus, the creation of a special multi-ethnic police force for Karachi is a good idea but so far constitutionally not practicable.

On its face value, MQM has formally changed its name from the *Muhajir Quomi Movement* to the *Mutahida Quomi Movement.*[50] Term *muhajir* projects the image of MQM as an exclusivist party of Urdu speakers of Indian origin. Conversely, the term *Mutahida* (united) apparently conveys a sense of a nation-wide movement of the under-class, which anybody can join. This nomenclatural change should also help bring the MQM into the mainstream of Pakistani politics.[51] As a result of this marked change of name and image, the MQM will presumably renounce its claim of a separate nationality for Urdu speakers.[52] Aftab Sheikh, one of the MQM's leaders, had indicated such a significant shift in its policies some time ago.[53] Moreover, if MQM gives up the demand for a separate nationality for its constituents, consequently, it will not implicitly or explicitly demand division of Sindh. Such a sea change will bring younger generations of Urdu speakers closer to their Sindhi counter parts. Young generation of Urdu and Sindhi speakers Professor Karar has a great deal in common. They want to live a decent and peaceful life, instead of state of confrontation.

Sindhi nationalism is not a manifestation of an exclusivist, linguistic or racial identity. Anybody can be a Sindhi, if he identifies himself with Sindh, irrespective of this mother tongue. Many Urdu speaking intellectuals such as late Professor Karar Hussain, journalist late M.B. Naqvi and the trade unionist, late Ali Mukhtiar Rizvi; considered themselves Urdu speaking Sindhis. These Urdu speakers are the 'new Sindhis'.[54] If MQM adopts this integrative mantle, the Sindhi and Urdu speaking sections of Sindh, can be brought closer to each other.

The inter-communal disharmony in Sindh disturbs the peace and prosperity of this province and poses a serious threat to the security of Pakistan. Mutual recrimination is an extra irritant in the Indo-Pakistani relationships. Inter-communal harmony in Sindh will bring about an end to this new and dangerous dimension of Indo-Pakistani rivalry and be conducive in achieving stability in South Asia. A solution to ethnic tensions in Sindh will bring about positive results for Sindh, Pakistan and South Asia as a whole.

MQM's demands for holding local body-elections or introducing a three-tiered system of government, came to fruition when in 2002, General Musharraf introduced the local government system in the country. As it will be discussed later in this book, local government system facilitated the establishment of the city-government scheme, which enabled MQM to amalgamate four districts of Karachi into a single city government, controlled by the MQM man, Syed Kamal Mustafa. Conversely, the district of Hyderabad was divided into three new districts and Hyderabad city fell into the hands of MQM man, Kuwar Naveed. Development works in these two major big cities of Sindh were carried out lopsided. Sindhi and Baloch localities were neglected. When other three provinces disbanded the local government system and reintroduced the old commissionerate system in 2009, MQM resisted the move, tooth and nail. Finding itself isolated in the country, MQM conditionally accepted the commissionerate system in Sindh which is yet to be reintroduced and the old distracts are yet to be restored. Prime Minister Yusuf Raza Gilani announced to reunite the four districts of Hyderabad into the single district.[55] But due to MQM's threats of leaving the coalition, PPP government at the expense of Sindhis, eaten its words without remorse.[56] Similarly, MQM's demand for broadening the tax-base of provinces may ultimately end up in demand for handing over these taxes to the cities, which will give the fiscal autonomy to MQM held enclaves in Sindh. Thus, MQM has neither given up its claim of a fifth nationality nor the creation of more provinces which is indirectly demanding division of Sindh. Thus, the MQM's demands and policies appear to be irreconcilable to the Sindhis. However, to be in power, corrupt and inapt governments of President Asif Ali Zardari at the centre, and chief minister, Qaim Ali Shah at Sindh province, concede to MQM's demands so as it may not use its tact of the street-power in which it masters.

References

1. Francis Robinson (ed), *Cambridge Encyclopedia of South Asia* (Cambridge: Cambridge University Press, 1991), p. 33.

2. The British and other world media use the term *Muhajirs* principally for the Urdu-speaking immigrants who came to Pakistan from India after 1947. For instance, see "Pakistan: Blood and Balloting in Karachi', *The Economist* (London), 25 January, 1997, p. 28.

3. Robinson, *op. cit.*

4. Subsequently, after creation of Pakistan, when the implications of partition on Sindh and on himself started unfolding, G.M. Syed called the tabling and passage of Pakistan Resolution, as the biggest blinder of his life. G.M. Syed, *Sindh Jaghi Thee Sindh Speaks: A Testimony of G.M. Syed in Sindh High Court, Karachi Bench*, (Sanni: GM Syed Academy, 2004) p. 28.

5. For those Gujaratis who do not share the MQM's confrontational attitude towards the Sindhis. See the interview of the president of the Karachi Gujarati Sabha, Haroon Ahmed Memon, in *Dawn* (Karachi), 7 April 1995. Moreover, as a result of the February 1997 elections, the MQM has won 12 seats in the National Assembly. Out of this number, none is a Gujarati. Similarly, out of 28 MQM Provincial Assembly members, there are only

two non-Urdu-speakers, *i.e.*, Gujaratis, Farooq Sattar and Abdul Qadir Lakhani. This marginal position of the Kutchi and Gujaratis in the hierarchy of the MQM indicates their lack of commitment towards its goals. The party aims, objectives and policies are primarily determined by its Urdu-speaking leadership. Compiled from *Dawn,* 6 February, 1997.

6. The edifice of a state rests on three bases; the territorial or physical, the institutional and the ideological. The most significant among these is the physical base. Without a piece of land, an ideology cannot be practiced nor the institutional or legal authority of the state be established. See Barry Buzan, *People, State, and Fear,* 2nd edn. (Sussex: Wheatsheaf, 1991), p. 65.

7. For details of this tactical change of mind by the Punjabis, see my book, *Pakistan, Ethnicity and Foreign Policy: 1971-1994* (London: I.B. Tauris, 1997).

8. Daily *Jang,* Urdu, (Karachi), 4 June 1972.

9. Ayeshi Jalal, *Democracy and Authoritarianism in South Asia* (Cambridge: Cambridge University Press, 1995), pp. 107-108.

10. Salamat Ali, 'Soldiers and spooks', *Far Eastern Economic Review* (Hong Kong), 10 November 1988, p. 36.

11. Daily *Hilal-E-Pakistan,* Sindhi, (Karachi), 27 September, 1992.

12. In the 1988 and 1990 Provincial Assembly elections, the MQM won 26 out of 109 seats. Their representation was 26.82% of the house. See *Dawn,* 10 October, 1993.

13. *Ibid.*

14. *Charter of Demands* (Karachi: MQM Information Department 1995).

15. Khalid Akhtar, compiler, Altaf Hussain Ki Hahani Unki Zibani, autobiography of Altaf Hussain (in Urdu), 4th edn. (Lahore: Jang Press, 1991), p. 12.

16 . *Dawn,* 27th June 1995.

17. In April 2010, when the 18th Constitional amendment was passed by the National Assembly of Pakistan and the name of the NWFP was changed as Khyber Pathtunkhaw, there were violent demonstrations in the non-Pashtun Hazara Division of the province. At the same time, the demands were raised for the creation of a Hindku speaking Hazara province. For instance see Ahmad Hassan, "PML-Q supports Demand for Hazara Province", *Dawn* 15 April, 2010.

18. Ghazanfar Hussain Hidayatullah, 'The Mohajir Qaumi Movement And Sindh', *The News International* (Karachi), 26 August, 1995.

19. *Dawn,* 27 June, 1995.

20 . See Suryanarayana, 'Crisis in Karachi', *Front Line* (Delhi), 12 January 1996, p. 13; and M. Hanif, 'Karachi: the city of death', *India Today* (Delhi), 15 July 1996, p. 42.

21 . *Jang* (London edn.), 22 July, 1992.

22. The figures about the ethnic break-up of Karachi were released by Shahid Ali Raza, himself an Urdu-speaker and the divisional coordinator of the Ministry of Human Rights. Cited in *Ibrat* (Hyderabad), 14 April, 1996.

23 . Farooq Sattar, an MQM leader, used this phrase in an interview with the *Herald,* July 1997, p. 32.

24 . Charles H. Kennedy, 'Policies of ethnic preferences in Pakistan', *Asian Survey,* Vol. XXIV, No. 6, 1984, p. 692. And *Frontier Post*(Lahore), 21 May, 1995. 14 April, 1996.

25. C H. Kennedy, *Ibid.*

26. *Ibid,* p. 693.

27. *Ibid.*

28. *Ibid.*

29. G.G.P. Rikisits, "Centre-Provincial Relations in Pakistan Under President Zia: The Government's and Opposition's Approaches", *Pacific Affairs* (Vancouver), Vol. 61, No. 1, Spring 1988, p. 81.

30. "Punjab and Urban-Sindh Enjoy Major Chunk in Civil Services", *Frontier Post,* 1 February, 1996.

31 . *Ibid.*

32 . Feroze Ahmed, "What Do We Mean by Urban? *Dawn,* 1 March, 1996.

33. See the coverage of the pro-Quota System demonstration staged by the workers of Sindhi Awami Tahrik, *Dawn,* 30 July 1997, and *Ibrat,* of the same date.

34 . Charter of Demands, op. cit., p. 47.

35. Hidayatullah, *op. cit.* According to 1992 UN estimates, Pakistan's total population is about 119,107,000: See *Whitaker's Almanack 1996,* p. 980. In the 1972 and 1982 censuses, Urdu-speakers comprise 7.6% of the total population of Pakistan. Two-thirds of them live in the Urban centres of Sindh and about one-third is scattered all over the country. Feroze Ahmed, 'Ethnic politics is a dead end street—II, *Dawn.* By these calculations, Urdu-speakers comprise about 5-6 million of the population of Sindh, which confirms Hidayatullah's estimates about them.

36. The statement of Farooq Sattar, an MQM leader, *Dawn,* 2 March, 1997.

37 . *Daily Barsat, Sindhi (Karachi),* 3 March, 1997.

38 . On insistence of the MQM, the Musharraf government in 2002 appointed Dr. Isharat Ibad Khan as the Governor of Sindh, who is allegedly implicated in several murder and other criminal cases. The PPP government, due to the MQM's heavy-handed tactics is unable to remove him despite his unpopularity with all the non-Urdu speaking sections of the population of Sindh.

39. See the statement of Ghulam Serwar Awan, the leader of Punjabi-Pushtun Etahad (alliance), in *Barsat,* 14 May, 1997, and 16 June, 1997.

40. Chris Smith, The Diffusion of Small and Light Weapons in Pakistan and Northern India (London: London Defence Studies No. 20, 1993), p. 16.

41. *Strategic Survey 1994-95* (London: Brassy for IISS, 1995), pp. 198-199.

42. G. Hussain, *op. cit.,* pp. 24-25.

43. Azhar Abbas, "Eyeball to Eyeball", *Herald,* July 1997, p. 38.

44. See the interview of Ejaz Shafi, *Herald,* July 1997, pp. 28-29.

45. Cited from the interview of Sayed Asad Ali Shah, the then financial advisor to the PPP government, *Barsat,* 22 February 1997.

46. *Ibid.*

47. *Ibrat,* 25 June, 1997.

48. *Barsat,* 21 July, 1997.

49. Farooq Sattar, *op. cit.*

50. *Dawn,* 27 July 1997.

51. MQM Seeks a New Image', *Dawn,* 29 July, 1997.

52. No such pronouncement has been made so far.

53. Daily *Ibrat,* Sindhi, (Hyderabad), 3 March, 1997.

54. Nisar Usmani, 'MQM: Crucial Days Ahead', *Dawn,* 13 October, 1993.

55. "Hyderabad' Orinal Shape to be Restored, Says P.M". *Dawn, 9th May 2010.*

56. "Restoration of the Hyderabad District : One More Broken Promise by the PPP", *Affairs*, fortnightly, Sindhi, (Karachi: 14h May 2010) p. 1.

(This paper entitled, "Ethnic Tensions in Sindh And Their Possible Solution", was published in *Contemporary South Asia*, (Oxfordshire: Carfax Publishing Ltd.) Vol. 6, No. 3, 1997. It has been slightly modified here without changing its central theme).

3

Vested Interests Wanted more Biharis in Sindh

The repatriation of the so-called stranded Pakistanis in Bangladesh" is, one of the burning issues of a political debate in this country. It is a highly sensitive issue and there are two diametrically opposite views on expressed by two communities, ironically living in the troubles stricken province of Sindh. Urdu speaking segment of the population of provinces mainly personified in the political shape of the Muhajir/ Mutahida Qaumi Movement (MQM), argues Biharis as genuine Pakistanis and they should be brought to Pakistan without any delay.[1] The native Sindhis, on the other hand, vehemently oppose such an idea. Sindhis argue, if the Biharis were brought to Pakistan, they would prefer to settle alongside their kith and kin in the big cities of the Sindh province. Otherwise that will reduce the indigenous Sindhis into minority even in their ancestral homeland, and would ultimately lead to the partition of province.[2]

Pakistan Peoples Party (PPP), which in 1988 formed a coalition government in the province of Sindh, found itself caught in the middle. Throughout its rule, PPP, whose major constituency has been the rural Sindh, remained opposed to the proposed settlement of the Biharis in Pakistan. Whereas, PPP's coalition partner, MQM, composed of the Urdu speaking community - many of them Biharis themselves - as strong supporter of their settlement in Pakistan. PPP's position on the settlement of Biharis, was to some extent, comparable with the British Mandatory Power in Palestine which (1919-45), faced a dilemma of adjusting irreconcilable interests of the native Palestinians and the waves of Jewish immigrants, both scrambling for gaining mastery over the same small piece of land.[3] The point of view of the Urdu speaking community on the issue of the settlement of Biharis has been presented by a number of politicians and intellectuals. Let us analyze the issue from its political, economic and legal aspects.

Justification for the Settlement of the Biharis

The main postulate of supporters of repatriation is that the 1940 Resolution, which envisaged the idea of the creation of Muslim homeland in the contiguous Muslim majority provinces in North West India, entitled the Muslims from all over India to settle in these provinces. Any opposition to such a settlement in the existing boundaries of Pakistan will tantamount to opposition of the very idea of creation of Pakistan.[4]

The above argument appears to be out of touch with the reality. If one looks at the very spirit of the 1940 Resolution, which did not talk about Pakistan, but a 'Muslim Homeland', composed of 'Sovereign States', will find that, the said Resolution was passed for the purpose of creation of a Muslim homeland, where Muslims would be protected from the economic and social exploitation by non-Muslims. Nothing was mentioned about immigration of religious communities from one area to another.[5] The later day historians suggested if the leaders of the Muslim majority provinces, had foreseen the biggest migration of the human history, they might had refrained from forming the grouping of 'Sovereign States', in the Muslim majority areas. It is also a widely held view that, if father of the nation, Quaid-e-Azam, had foreseen the blood bath and subsequent migration of people, he might have not insisted even on the partition of India.[6] The bloodshed and exodus of people, was a result of evil design of Muslim chauvinists. And the Biharis were victims of that conspiracy. Thus, the 1940 Resolution, the creation of Pakistan in 1947, and the secession of its Eastern Wing in 1971, does not *ipso-facto* entitle the Biharis for their repatriation to Pakistan. The term 'repatriation', according to the Oxford English Dictionary, means to restore, or return a person to his native land.[7] It is noteworthy that no part of Pakistan, especially Sindh is the native land of Biharis, who hail from the Bihar state of the Indian Union and migrated to the former East Pakistan at the time of partition.

Who is Burden on Whom?

The views of many Urdu speaking intellectuals and politicians from other provinces are not in line with the views of those who suggest that 'Sindhis' and rest of Pakistanis are a burden on the "Muhajir inhabited Karachi"[8] In fact, Karachi was built with blood, toil and sweat of Sindhis, who have been living there from the time immemorial. And today Karachi is an inseparable part of Sindh. For instance, if a demagogue of Pakistani origin claims that Birmingham and Bradford are Pakistani inhabited cities and the British are a burden on them, what treatment he would receive? He will be ridiculed or possibly brought to the book under the Race Relations Act. Similarly, if a self-appointed leader of the migrant workers in the Gulf States claims that the local Arabs are a minority and thus burden on the migrant workers, he will be immediately expelled. Demographically, the Urdu speaking community does not outnumber the natives in Karachi as a whole. On the contrary, they are a minority.

A person with deep knowledge of history, will appreciate that Karachi seaport and Air Port were built by the British, before the arrival of the Urdu speaking people, because Karachi was (and still is) a vital communication link between Europe and East. Foundation of industrialization of Karachi was laid by the government of Sindh during pre-partition era. And most of the industrialists do not use Urdu as their first language. The major determinant of the industrialization of Karachi is its coastline, which nature has bestowed on Sindh and Balochistan. Thus, the Urdu speaking community has a marginal role in the industrial development of Karachi. The second largest industrial base in Pakistan is located in the Central Punjab, where the Urdu speaking persons were made rare species. One is therefore, forced to argue that it was Sindh, which embraced the Urdu speaking refugees, when they were shelterless and still struggling for their survival. They consume waters of the Indus and grains of Sindh.

Fallacious Analogy

Some Urdu speaking intellectuals and politicians compare the issue of repatriation of the Afghan refugees with the settlement of the Biharis. They complain that the Afghan refugees who are a security risk and financial burden on Pakistan, are harboured by the successive governments in the country, while the settlement of the Biharis is avoided on one excuse or the other. The government and no sensible person will disagree with them with repatriation and rehabilitation of Afghan refugees to their native place, *i.e.* Afghanistan. However, it may be reminded to those having sympathy with the Biharis that Pakistan is not a native place of the Biharis and they cannot be brought over here for settlement.

From their point of view, "Sindhis are bigots".[9] But the whole world is imbued with the deep imprints of Shah Latif's humanistic and universal message on their minds. Sindhis feel pity about the self-inflicted wounds of the Bihari's and wish that their sympathizers such as their co-linguists in Pakistan, Lord Ennals, the member of the British upper house of the parliament, the House of Lords, and the House of Saud, who have been sympathetic to the cause of Biharis, should have facilitated their rehabilitation either in England or the Muslim states of the Middle East with a higher per capita income than Sindh, in Pakistan. .

The Role of the Islami Jamhoori Ittehad (I.J.I). Government

After winning the general elections of October 1990 MQM joined the IJI (Islami Jamhoori Ittehad) Government of Mian Nawaz Sharif at the centre and Sindh Province. After assuming power9, the question of "repatriation of Biharis" was taken up with new vigour. The issue assumed new dimensions when the then Prime Minister Nawaz Sharif declared, as part of the deal for MQM's support at the centre and Sindh Province level, that the Biharis would be settled in Southern Punjab. The Siraiki speakers, who do not consider themselves as the Punjabis but a distinct nationality in their own right, reacted strongly against the government decision.

Commenting on Biharis issue, Punjabi intellectual, Ahmed Bashir, writes: "The worst part of the repatriation of the Biharis is that they will always live as Muhajirs in Pakistan and because of their cultural inhibitions, they will never identify themselves with the Siraikis, giving rise to new social contradictions. The support they are likely to get in their settlement, has never been available to Siraikis".[10] He further argues that the Biharis, after their settlement in the Siraiki belt, will sell their properties and residences as soon as they can, and move over to the urban centres of Sindh for resettlement.[11] Thus, the views of native Sindhis and Siraikis, who are going to be the worst affected by settlement of Biharis in their areas, are almost identical.

The Role of Peoples Party

Since the Pakistan Peoples Party (PPP) has principal support base in Sindh, it is considered to be pro-Sindhi on the national issues. After the October 1990 general elections, PPP was not even allowed to form the government in Sindh Province despite being the largest party in Sindh Assembly. Being pitched against the political vendetta of the Federal Government on the one hand and the IJI chief minister, Jam Sadiq Ali-MQM coalition in Sindh on the other, the PPP started opposing the repatriation of Biharis to Pakistan.

PPP leadership, particularly late Benazir Bhutto and her aling mother, mother, Nusrat Bhutto, who probably for political expediency, identified themselves to Sindh, knew very well that their power base for all practical purposes was rural Sindh and who had made tremendous sacrifices during the Movement for Restoration of Democracy (MRD) in 1983 against General Zia's dictatorship. They were fully aware of sensitivities of the native Sindhis that, Biharis will ultimately settle in the urban centres of Sindh, thereby reducing them into minority in their own province. Such an eventuality would shrink their power base in rural Sindh vis-à-vis other nationalist groups, who are almost unanimous on this issue and PPP coming closer to their view point on a number of issues directly affecting Sindhis including that of Biharis.

The Legal and Constitutional Aspect

If one looks at the Biharis issue from legal and constitutional point of view, they are not entitled to the Pakistani citizenship. During his rule, General Zia had issued an ordinance in 1978 through which a section 16A was inserted in the Pakistan Citizenship Act. This amendment deprived Pakistani Citizenship to all those who at any time before 16th December 1971 were domiciled in territories which constituted the then province of East Pakistan and who were residing in that area or outside Pakistan on that date.[12]

Thus, on the basis of above amendment made in the Pakistan Citizenship Act, Biharis are not entitled to Pakistani citizenship and their repatriation to Pakistan is not justified even on legal and constitutional grounds.

Therefore, in order to avoid further tensions and acrimony among various sections of population, particularly for the peace and harmony in Sindh, it will be advisable to settle these people in more prosperous Muslim states of the Middle East. Pakistan Government must take lead in this humanitarian issue, take up the matter of settlement of Biharis with Organization of Islamic Conference, Rabita Alam-e-Islami, and seek their help for their settlement in the Middle Eastern Muslim countries. This appears to be only viable and acceptable solution to the four decades old problem.

The Supreme Court of Bangladesh has granted citizenship to Biharis in 2005. Now they are treated as equal citizens of the state by the government of the day. Many of them have decided to settle down in Bangladesh once for all. They have learnt Bangla language and identify themselves with the soil. However, a few of them exhorted by the Pakistani politicians of Bihari origin still consider themselves as aliens in Bangladesh and wish to migrate to Pakistan and live with their kith and kin in Karachi. At the time of writing, (April 2010) Pakistan People's Party and MQM are coalition partners both at centre and provincial levels. There appears to be a tacit understanding between them over the Bihari issue. On its part, MQM, does not openly demand the settlement of Biharis in Pakistan. By doing so, the Sindhi populace does not markedly show any reaction to MQM's long term planning to bring all Biharis to Pakistan. As a quid pro quo, PPP connives to the trickling down of Biharis to Karachi via India by land and sea. Ironically, the portfolios of shipping and ports are always held by the ministers belonging to MQM. Such an arrangement facilitates the persistent arrival of Biharis from Bangladesh by sea also.

References

1. Statement of Altaf Hussain, the founding leader of the MQM on the issue of repatriation of the Biharis, in the *Daily Dawn*, (Karachi) December 12, 1988, and A.A. Usmani, "The Repatriation of Stranded Pakistanis", in the *Daily Muslim* (Islamabad), April 2, 1989.

2. For different shades of the Sindhi opinion on the Biharis issue for instance, see the statements of Dr. Hamida Khuro leader of the Sindh National Alliance, Manzoor Hussain Wasan, a PPP member of the Sindh Provincial Assembly and late Mohammad Khan Junejo, the President of Muslim League, respectively in the *DaiLy Dawn*,, April 9, 1989, The Daily *Dawn,* 11 April 1989, The *Weekly Guardian*, London, 21 August 1988. (Lord Ennals letter to the Editor).

3. For the British position in Palestine, E.H. Carr, *The International Relations between the two World Wars*: 1919-39, Macmillan, London, 1967, pp. 235-38.

4. Usmani, *op. cit*.

5. Latif Shervani is one of the main historians of the Pakistan Movement. He says nothing about the transfer of populations as envisaged in the 1940 Resolution. His *Pakistan Resolution to Pakistan*: 1940-1947(.Karachi: National Publication House, 1969).

6. Larry Collins & Dominique Lapierre, *The Freedom at Midnight*. (New Delhi: Vikas Publications, 1977) pp. 317-44.

7. *The Oxford Illustrated Dictionary*, 2nd edition, (London:, Clarendon Press, 1976), pp. 715.

8. M.B. Naqvi," Sindh's Simmering Caldron", *The Daily Dawn*, April 12, 1989.

9. Usmani *op. cit.*

10. Ahmed Bashir, "Repatriation of Biharis" *The Frontier Post: Sunday Magazine* , (Lahore), September 18, 1991, p. 9.

11. *Ibid.*

12. Makhdoom Ali Khan, "Repatriation: the legal aspect", *Daily Dawn*, November 21, 1991, p. 11.

(This article entitled "The Settlement of Biharis in Pakistan", was published in *Grassroots*, Journal of Pakistan Study Centre, Sindh University, Jamshoro, Sindh, Vol. Nos. XXI, XXII, 1992)

4

Muhajir Quami Movement (MQM): Aftermath of Partition

The objective of MQM, a party formed by Muhajirs, Urdu-speaking immigrants of Indian origin, who live mainly in Sindh and intend to divide it forcibly among themselves and the native Sindhis, put it on a collision course not only with the Sindhis but with the state of Pakistan. The fragmentation of the former federation of Yugoslavia suggests that any forcible change in the internal boundaries of a country is as dangerous to regional and world peace as the violent change of borders between independent states. The division of Sindh could be a prelude to the disintegration of Pakistan, which could set off chain reactions affecting south and south-west Asia. The stability of this region is indispensable to international security. In order to maintain regional stability, and international order in their own enlightened interests, the neighbouring states, such as India and Iran and other influential members of the international community, especially USA, UK and the EU, should help Pakistan in preserving its territorial integrity.

According to Sir Halford Mackinder, an influential early 20th century British political geographer, a pivotal state is a hot spot with a capacity to not only affect its own stability but the stability of its region and the international community as a whole'.[1] In order to redefine US strategy in the post-Cold War era, Professor Paul Kennedy and two of his students, in an article published in Foreign *Affairs,* in early 1996, reinterpreted the idea of 'pivotal states'. They consider Mexico, Brazil, Algeria, Egypt, South Africa, India, Pakistan and Indonesia to be the pivotal states. They argue that in the post-cold war era, these countries are not much threatened by external aggressors, but much more by forces within their own bounds, such as overpopulation, migration, environmental degradation, ethnic conflict, religious radicalism, and economic instability.[2]

Kennedy is a highly respected academic and many of the views expressed in his previous work, especially about the disintegration of the former Soviet Union, have become true.[3] His reference to Pakistan as an internally vulnerable state deserves serious attention. Like other pivotal states, Pakistan faces most of the problems mentioned by him. However, one of the most conspicuous internal vulnerabilities of Pakistan is the upsurge in ethnic tension in the province of Sindh, which has the potential of threatening not only the territorial integrity of Pakistan but also the stability of 'Southern Asia', a region which encompasses all of the Cold War Western classification of South Asia, West Asia and Central Asia'.[4]

The ethnic tension in Sindh, started immediately after the creation of the country in 1947. However, it has been aggravated since 1984 with the launching of the Muhajir now Mattahida Quami Movement (MQM), a political party which claims to represent the Muhajirs or Urdu speaking immigrants of Indian origin. One may argue why the MQM really poses a serious challenge to the security of Pakistan and to speculate about the likely consequences of MQM's activities upon neighbouring states and the wider world, with the attributed responsibilities of international community to help Pakistan in overcoming its difficulties in dealing with the MQM.

The Emergence of the MQM: An Overview

Pakistani's federating units of Bengal, Sindh, Balochistan, Punjab and North-West Frontier Province (NWFP), (now Khyber Pakhtunkhaw) were the historical homelands of their respective inhabitants (Bengalis, Sindhis, Balochs, Punjabis and Pashtuns). The partition of former 'British' India produced an unprecedented transfer of population from one successor state to another. People migrating to Sindh came mainly from Muslim minority areas especially of northern India such as the Madhya Pradesh, Uttar Pradesh (UP). Hyderabad Deccan, Delhi, and Gujarat, etc. These immigrants came to Sindh and settled principally in the big cities, such as Karachi, Hyderabad and Sukkur.

The cultural similarities of some newcomers with the native Sindhs and professional requirements of the new home state of Pakistan helped the Gujarati and Kutchi speaking immigrants, who were mainly businessmen and industrialists to settle and live peacefully with the Sindhis. The second category of people migrating to Sindh in 1947 onwards, were mainly Urdu speaking. They insisted on retaining their distinctive identity. They preferred to be addressed as *Muhajirs,* or immigrants. Quite a few of them were well educated, having held governmental jobs in pre-1947 India. These were the people, who formed the core of the Muslim League leadership in the Muslim minority provinces. Liaquat Ali Khan, the first Prime Minister of Pakistan, was their principal leader.

To the great resentment of the local Sindhis, Karachi, the capital of Sindh, was separated from it in 1948. Furthermore, Urdu, a language hitherto having no firm base in what had become Pakistan and spoken by only 4 per cent of the population of Pakistan, was made the national language.

Like Liaqat Ali Khan, many of the migrant leaders of the Muslim League had no constituencies in Pakistan. Thus, in order to create their own constituencies, they encouraged some further transfers of population from India to Sindh. Among many other issues, the transfer of population was a bone of contention between the local Sindhi and the immigrant leadership. From the very beginning of the Pakistan state, a tug of war thus started between the traditional local leaders and the new immigrant leadership.

In the early formative years, many of Pakistan's top bureaucrats were Urdu speaking, who exercised a high degree of influence over the country. This immigrant bureaucracy relied on the support of the military elite, which hailed mainly from Punjab. This civil-military bureaucratic nexus, brought Punjabis and Urdu speakers close to each other. In 1955, the bureaucracy-military nexus, by manipulating the political process of the country, dissolved the provincial assemblies of Sindh, Punjab, NWFP, and Balochistan at that time not really a province) in west Pakistan and imposed a one-unit system on them. Very next year, the same alliance, in effect deprived Bengalis of their overall numerical majority in the country by imposing parity on them. Thus, one can argue that from 1947 to 1955, Urdu speakers dominated the political scene of the country. From 1955 onwards, a Punjabi ascendancy came to the fore in Pakistan, in which Urdu speakers retained their disproportionate influence, but later on as the junior partners of the Punjabis.

In 1970, former provinces of West Pakistan were restored. Karachi once again became the capital of Sindh province. In 1971, after the separation of its eastern wing, a new configuration of forces emerged in Pakistan in which Punjabis became the largest ethnic group, followed by Sindhis, Pashtuns and Balochs and Urdu speakers, respectively. Moreover, as a result of the December 1970 elections, Pakistan's People's Party assumed power both in Sindh and Punjab. During this time, Punjabis in their own interests, forged links with Sindhis, instead of with the Urdu speakers.

Perceiving Sindhis as their main rival, most of the Urdu speakers were inclined to activate their working relationships with the Punjabis instead of Sindhis. Very few of them joined the People's Party led by Zulfiquar Ali Bhutto, an ethnic Sindhi. The majority of the Urdu speakers, supported either the Muslim League, or religious parties, especially Jamaiti Islami. At one place, when Sindhi Language Bill, aimed at reintroducing Sindhi as the official language of the province, was moved in the Sindh Provincial Assembly in June 1972, some Urdu speakers rioted. Many Sindhis, already outnumbered in the big cities, were forced to leave their homes. At this time, demands for creation of a Karachi province, were also raised by some Urdu speaking intellectuals.[5]

From 1972 to 1977 most of the Urdu speakers joined the ranks of the anti-Bhutto Nine Party Alliance, which resulted in the overthrow of his government and his subsequent execution by Zia-ul Haque in 1979. In 1983, as a reaction to Bhutto's execution and their persecution by the Zia regime, the Sindhis launched Movement for the Restoration of Democracy. Unlike other provinces of Pakistan, the MRD took a violent turn by confronting the security forces. The perception of Sindhis a docile people, was totally changed after their encounter with the security forces. Thereafter, the Sindhis were perceived *by* the Zia regime as a serious threat not only to it but to the power of Punjab, from where the army mainly hails. The regime made a long term plan for containing Sindhis assertiveness.

In 1984, Zia encouraged the Urdu speaking militants in forming the Muhajir Quomi Movement (MQM), under the leadership of Altaf Hussain. Karachi became its operational base.[6] Zia's purpose in encouraging the MQM, and providing it with training and firearms, was two-fold. First, it was seen to be a counterpoise to the Pakistan People's Party in the big cities of Sindh.[7] Second, it aimed to divide Sindh on ethnic lines.[8] In 1985 non-party elections, the MQM won overwhelming majorities in big cities of Sindh province. In 1991 the MQM split into two violent factions led by Altaf Hussain and Afaq Ahmed. This split was mainly due to the personality clash between two ambitious men, who aimed to outmanoeuvre each other in achieving their common goals. Since then both factions of the MQM, the Haqiqi and the Altaf Group, became forces to be reckoned with in the urban areas of Sindh.

The Major Demands of the MQM and the Reaction of other Communities

Unlike other parties of Pakistan, the constituency of MQM is almost entirely restricted to Karachi and other big cities of Sindh. Thus, it is an exclusivist party, principally of Urdu speaking immigrants and its demands are addressed accordingly. Its major demands are as follows:

Recognition of Muhajirs as a Nationality

MQM claimed that all those people, who migrated from India to Sindh, differ from the other ethnic groups of Pakistan. These people have undergone a common experience of migration and thus should be recognized as a distinctive nationality, Muhajirs.[9] On their part, the Sindhis argue :

The immigrants who came from different parts of united India, do not speak a common language. They neither have a common history nor do they have a common experience of migration. They came to Sindh for different motives. In addition, Sindh is not their ancestral homeland. Thus, Urdu-speakers cannot be recognised as an ethnic group let alone a nationality.

Moreover, in order to destabilise Pakistan, a particular section of Urdu speakers makes such a divisive demand.[10]

It is not only Sindhis but also Balochs who live in Karachi and the neighbouring province of Balochistan also rejected the MQM's demand for recognition of Urdu speakers as a nationality. Paradoxically, enough MQM's staunch supporters, such as Nawaz Sharif and late Ajmal Khatak, both Punjabi and Pushtun nationalists respectively, did not recognize this demand. They felt that the acceptance of such a demand and consequential partition of Sindh, would set a precedent for the division of Punjab between Punjabis and the Siraikis of central and southern Punjab. A similar division might take place in the Frontier Province between Pashtuns and the Hindko speaking Hazariwals. Thus, MQM's demand for recognition of the Urdu-speakers as a nationality was rejected by all political parties of Pakistan.

End of the Quota System

One of the major demands of MQM is abolition of the quota system in Sindh and the allocation of governmental jobs and admission to educational institutions on the basis of merit. The quota system was introduced in 1949 by Liaqat Ali Khan for candidates seeking entry into officer level ranks in the federal bureaucracy. Since then it has continued in one form or another.

After the separation of East Pakistan in 1971, the quota system was revamped. In 1973, on the basis of the 1971 census, each province of Pakistan was allocated governmental jobs according to its percentage of total population of the country. According to this scheme, in the federal service, allocations were made on the following basis: merit 10 per cent; Punjab 50 per cent; Sindh 19 per cent; Frontier 11.5 per cent; Balochistan 3.5 per cent; Northern Areas and Federally Administered Areas (FATA) 4 per cent; Azad Kashmir 2 per cent.[11]

Because of their huge socio-economic gaps the federal quota for Sindh was divided on an urban and rural basis. The rural and urban sectors of Sindh were allocated 11.4 and 7.6 per cent of the jobs respectively. A similar arrangement was made in the Sindh's provincial service structure. The quota system was supposed to be abolished when all areas of the country were stood at par with each other. It was to be reviewed after every 10 years.

It is also noteworthy that the quota system is not confined to Sindh and Pakistan alone. Balochistan, Punjab and the NWFP were also divided into zones, according to the level of their development.[12] In Malaysia, to bring the ethnic Malays up to the level of more advanced ethnic Chinese and other communities, the former have the special status of *Bhoomi Putra*, or the sons of soil.

From 1972 onwards, no significant change had taken place in removing the disparities between different areas of Pakistan. The socio-economic gap between rural and urban Sindh has not been bridged so far. According to independent observers, 65 per cent of rural Sindhis still live below the poverty line.[13] A survey about the allocation of governmental jobs conducted by the English language newspaper, *The Frontier Post,* reveals that, in contradiction to MQM claims, Punjab and urban Sindh are over represented in the federal services at the expense of rural Sindh, Balochistan and Federally Administered Areas. It suggests that instead of its 50 per cent allocation, Punjab has got 62.2 per cent. Instead of its prescribed quota of 7.6 per cent, the urban Sindh has acquired 9.75 per cent of the federal jobs. Conversely, rural Sindh has got only 6.32 per cent in contravention of its quota of 11.4 per cent.[14]

From a Sindhi perspective, in addition to the federal jobs, employment in the private sector goes mainly to Karachites because Karachi is the financial hub of the country. Much of the industry of the country, banking headquarters, autonomous and semi-autonomous bodies and multinational corporations, are located there. In contrast to Karachi, the rural areas of Sindh still suffer from abject poverty. The quota system gives a chance to the children of rural areas to get some of the governmental jobs. From the viewpoint of rural Sindh, if the quota system were abolished, Sindhis would be further underrepresented in the civil service structure of Pakistan. It might be dangerous for national cohesion. Thus in this situation, neither Zia in 1983, nor Nawaz Sharif in 1993, abolished the quota system. Its continuation has become one of the principal reasons for the discontent of MQM with different governments of Pakistan.

Demand for 60 per cent Jobs

MQM claims to represent 22 million constituents, thus forming 60 per cent of the total population of Sindh. It is maintained that they should be given 60 per cent of the provincial jobs accordingly. The Sindhis for their part argue that Urdu speakers hardly comprise more than 5-6 million out of about 22.6 million population of Sindh, and their demand for a 60 per cent share in the provincial jobs is untenable.[15] In the absence of contemporary census in Pakistan, there are no reliable up-to-date figures for any political party to support MQM in its bid for 60 per cent of the jobs in Sindh.

The Repatriation of Stranded Pakistanis

MQM persistently insists that the Biharis living in Bangladesh should be repatriated to Pakistan. Sindhi opinion makers, considering Pakistan a territorial state, argue:

From 1947 onwards Biharis went to East Pakistan from India instead of to any constituent units of Pakistan; thus they are not entitled to repatriation to Pakistan. Moreover, if the Biharis were brought from Bangladesh they would settle in

Sindh, where their relatives already live. Any further settlement of Biharis would not only upset the demographic balance against the Sindhis but would let loose a reign of terror on Sindhis and other communities in Karachi.[16]

General Zia and Nawaz Sharif were in favour of the settlement of a limited number of Biharis in Pakistan, but not the transfer of the entire Bihari population from Bangladesh to Pakistan. The issue of 'repatriation of stranded Pakistanis' still receives a cold shoulder from most of Pakistan's politicians in a wider interest of the country.

The Creation of a Muhajir Province

The most contentious demand of both factions of MQM is the division of Sindh and the corresponding creation of a Muhajir province. Sometimes Altaf, the leader of the main faction of the MQM, goes even further and implicitly demands the creation of an independent Muhajir state, carved out of the boundaries of Pakistan.[17]

The issue of the boundaries of a proposed Muhajir Suba or of a Muhajir independent state, Muhajirdesh, is deliberately kept vague. In some maps, captured by the army in June 1992, Karachi is mentioned as Muhajir Suba or Jinnahpur. In other maps, Karachi, Thatta, Badin, Mirpur Khas, Tharparkar, parts of Nawab Shah, Sangher and Sukkur districts are mentioned as the parts of the state of Muhajirstan.[18] The MQM-Haqiqi link includes the Moro talko in central Sindh and excludes Sukkur, in upper Sindh, within the boundaries of a proposed Muhajir Suba.[19] Each of these districts of Sindh, earmarked by the Altaf Group as parts of a Muhajir Suba, share land or sea borders with the Indian states of Rajasthan, Gujarat and the Arabian Sea.

To popularize the demands of Muhajir Suba within Pakistan or for a Muhajir state outside Pakistan both factions of MQM use the label 'Southern Sindh'. They claim that in this area, Urdu-speakers are in a majority, and that Sindh should be divided accordingly.

Most Sindhis react furiously to the demand of the division of their homeland. They argue that there is no physical or demographic demarcation line dividing Sindh into northern or southern zones. Many Sindhis insist that if they have to choose between the division of Sindh and the disintegration of Pakistan, they would prefer the latter.[20] None of the all-Pakistani politicians overtly support this preference. As stated earlier, because of the multiethnic characteristics of each and all of the provinces of Pakistan, the division of Sindh would set a dire precedent for the division of other provinces as well.

In 1997, Mohajir Quami Movement (MQM) was renamed Muttahida Quami Movement. At the February 1997 elections to the National Assembly and provincial assemblies, MQM retained its firm hold in Pakistan, winning 12 seats in National Assembly. But its constituency remained confined mainly to the Urdu speakers in pockets of Karachi and Hyderabad.

Neither gradually integrating themselves into the host Sindhi community, nor remaining a minority in Sindh, is acceptable to those Urdu speakers who associate themselves with the exclusivist politics of MQM. It is noteworthy that in pre-independence days, the Muslims in Hindu majority areas were a privileged minority. The MacDonald Communal Award of 1932 accorded special treatment to them. Instead of their approximate ratio of 20 per cent, 40 per cent of jobs and cabinet posts were given to the Muslims in these areas. Despite this privileged position, these Muslims felt themselves to be a discontented minority and strove for a separate state.[21] MQM leadership seemingly retains much of the same mentality of being a privileged minority at the expense of the majority.

Unlike other political parties of Pakistan, both the factions of MQM aim to achieve their political objectives by using violent methods against their adversaries. Because of its violent nature, prestigious research institute, the International Institute for Strategic Studies (IISS), London, has characterized MQM as a neo-fascist political party.[22]

MQM as a Security threat to Pakistan

In 1988, MQM formed a coalition with Benazir Bhutto's People's Party. It broke on the issues of the repatriation of Biharis and the end of the quota system. The MQM then helped President Ishaq and the Urdu-speaking army chief, General Baig, to overthrow Benazir Bhutto's first government in 1990. It then forged an alliance with Nawaz Sharif's Islami Jamhuri Itahad (IJI), which also disappointed it on the same issues.

In 1991, MQM turned against its own patron, the army, by acts of kidnapping, torture (a serving major, Kalim) and killing military personnel. Thereafter, the target of MQM was not any particular party but the state of Pakistan itself. Altaf Hussain started challenging the Two Nations Theory, the rationale for the creation of Pakistan in 1947.[23] The change in the tone of the MQM coincided with the rising graph of its militancy. In 1992, Pakistan army considering the MQM as a security risk, decided to flush out its 'anti-state cadre'. The then Prime Minister of Pakistan, Nawaz Sharif, ironically an intermittent ally of the MQM, alleged that MQM was infiltrated by terrorists.[24] He approved of army action against the MQM. Its leader, Altaf Hussain, fled to London.

Karachi-Kashmir linkages

Pakistan tends with India to interfere in other's internal affairs. Its common culture enables it to do so with considerable ease. The older rank and file of the present day MQM originally migrated from India. They speak Urdu, which is spoken in India.

Urdu speakers in Pakistan are thus often members of divided families living in India. Their older generation still looks at India with nostalgia and India is a cultural model for many of the younger generation of Muhajirs.[25] Thus, speaking in psychological terms and given the MQM's prevailing frustration with Pakistan, India, its adversary for five decades, thus looked as a 'natural ally' of MQM.

MQM's mounting militancy in Pakistan coincided with increased infiltration and insurgency in Kashmir, which started in 1989 and gained momentum in the early 1990s. Mani Shanker Ayier, who spent many years in Karachi as the Indian consul-general, argues:

> The possibilities of secession in Pakistan have decreased significantly. Because of the Soviet intervention in Afghanistan, Pashtuns are more interested in that country. Wali Khan is alone and he is surrounded by pro-establishment Pushtuns in the NWFP. Balochs have either joined the Pakistani establishment or live in a self-imposed exile. Sindhis are supporting either PPP or other federalist parties. Only a few of them still cherish the fantasy of Sindhudesh. And their influence in Sindh is marginal. In these circumstances MQM is now the unrivalled power centre of Karachi politics. Though the MQM is divided against itself, it is united against all non-Muhajirs. Thus, MQM is a force to be reckoned with.[27]

The forerunners of the MQM, such as the Jamati Islami or All Pakistan Muhajir Students Organization, had resorted to arson, stabbing and acid throwing against their enemies. Hereafter, 'in order to gain control over Karachi, MQM use sophisticated small arms against different communities and the law enforcement agencies.[28]

The clashes between MQM activists and the security forces resulted in casualties on both sides.

Over the years, Pakistan has been insisting that Kashmir should join Pakistan. Any other policy option has been rejected by Pakistan. However, in a statement in the United States, Pakistan's former Foreign Minister, Sardar Asif Ahmed Ali, in January 1996, implicitly endorsed the idea of an independent Kashmir, if the Kashmiris wished it.[30]

If MQM succeeded in the creation of an Urdu province within Pakistan, it would be at war with other communities living in Karachi, in particular and throughout Pakistan in general. Being a pariah province in Pakistan, this area might find some solace only from India where Urdu/Hindi has a natural habitat. In this scenario, the proposed Urdu province might prefer to be associated with India instead of Pakistan. Thus an Urdu Suba within Pakistan could be conceived of as a stepping stone towards the creation of an Urdu state carved out of the boundaries of Pakistan. As mentioned earlier, the boundaries of the proposed province or state of Muhajirstan abut India. From Karachi, Bombay is just two hours sea journey by fast boats.[32]

Karachi and the great game in Central Asia

Karachi is situated at a sensitive strategic location. It is a halfway house between Bombay and the Iranian port of Chah Bahar. In the post-Cold War era, Iran for a host of reasons had moved closer to India than to its Muslim neighbour, Pakistan. Iran supported the ousted government of President Rabbani in Afghanistan against the Pakistani backed Pashtun Taliban religious militants—which has proved to be backing for a losing cause. One of the reasons for such a support to the then President Rabbani was to help him open routes to Central Asia. Indians have made road between the Iranian port of Chahbahar to Kabul.

By comparison with these trans-Iranian routes, Karachi is closer to both India and Central Asia. By Kandahar-Chaman-

Quetta or Jalalabad-Peshawar routes Karachi is connected with Afghanistan and correspondingly with Central Asia. Without a settlement of the Kashmir dispute, Pakistan may not give transit facilities to India for Central Asia. However, if Karachi becomes the heart of an independent state, it would in effect be a de facto province of India. It would then simply help India to use its port and railway terminus for gaining access to Central Asia.

One of the characteristics of international politics is that states tend to be expansionist by nature.[33] The boundaries of the Persian Empire once stretched up to the Hub River, near Karachi.[34] After the creation of Bangladesh in 1971 the Shah of Iran said that in the case of further disintegration of Pakistan the River Indus will form Iran's border with India.[35] If Karachi fell to India then Iran would like to move its borders up to the Hub by occupying the Pakistani province of Balochistan.

The Urdu language is quite similar to Persian. Iranian diplomats based at Karachi, like their other Muslim counterparts, maintain cordial relations with the MQM leadership. At one stage an Iranian diplomat offered his mediation between the Bhutto government and MQM. Moreover, MQM has many Shias activists and legislators in its ranks which makes it more acceptable to the Iranians.

MQM and the stability of Southern Asia

Altaf Hussain conceivably means an active intervention by India on the side of the MQM against Pakistan.[36]

Being its only developed port, Karachi is a much more sensitive area to Pakistan than the whole of Kashmir. Any provocation by Pakistani authorities could plunge into war with India: Pakistan has weak command and control structures. The principal purpose of both India and Pakistan going nuclear is to avert the possibility of one's interference in the internal affairs of others. In 1990, 1999, and 2001 India and Pakistan were at the brink of a nuclear war which was averted mainly by US diplomacy.

The irony of the present situation is that the dropping of an Indian bomb over any major city of Pakistan would release almost the same amount of radiation to India itself as that inflicted on Pakistan. Any Pakistani bomb dropped over Mumbai could have similar fatal results for Pakistan in general and Sindh in particular.

Even short of doomsday scenarios, division of Sindh and the corresponding disintegration of Pakistan might be dangerous. The creation of a Muhajir state would increase the incentives for dissatisfied communities within Pakistan to have their own mini states. If Pakistan disintegrates, the secessionist movements in Sindh Balochistan, and irredentist tendencies in Punjab and NWFP might gain momentum. It would be difficult for Islamabad to quell them.

At present, Pakistan is a state between India and Iran. If Pakistan disintegrates India would have to deal with four countries instead of one united Pakistan. They would be each other's nearly contiguous rivals in the Persian Gulf and the Arabian Sea and in Central Asia. The disintegration of Pakistan would lead to acute tensions in South and South West Asia. Pakistan is situated in the backyard of Iran. Its disintegration could affect the territorial integrity of Iran which itself is a multi-ethnic state. The minorities in Iran, such as Balochs, Azeris, Turkeman and the Khozisitani Arabs, might be encouraged by Iran's enemies into breaking away from it in the event of a convulsion in its neighbourhood. Thus, the division of Sindh and the resultant creation of a Muhajir state at the expense of Pakistan, would open a Pandora's box in other Islamic countries.

MQM and extra-regional powers

The Western powers, especially the USA and the UK, have a variety of commercial, economic, political and strategic interests in Pakistan and around it, which could be significantly affected by the creation of a Muhajir Suba and the resultant greater instability in Western Asia. There is an impression amongst some Sindhi intellectuals that MQM has blessings of the Western powers in its designs to divide Sindh and weaken Pakistan[37] From their perspective, such a scheme of things would allow West to impose their hegemony in this region. These intellectuals further point to the meetings of Western diplomats with MQM leaders, the refusal of UK to extradite Altaf Hussain and the pressure of these powers on Pakistan government to come to terms with MQM. All this bears testimony to the assumption that these powers endorse MQM's plan to create a free-port or even a mini-state like Hong Kong, where Western money could be invested and garner huge profits or so, it is believed.

Such Sindhi apprehensions about Western support for MQM appear to be unrealistic. Although Britain could not extradite the MQM leader Altaf Hussain, as requested by the government of Pakistan, because of the lack of a extradition treaty between the two countries; British and American diplomats denied that any support was being given to the MQM in its bid for the division of Sindh and creation of a Muhajir state. Former Consul-General in Karachi, Mary Kennedy, made it clear that United States was not interested in the separation of Karachi from rest of Sindh.[38] Great Britain retained an almost identical stance on this Karachi issue. The Anglo-American position on this issue appears to be plausible on a number of grounds.

First, although a port-city, Karachi is dependent for its supply of fresh water, electricity and much else, from its hinterland of Sindh. Thus, it cannot be physically insulated from it.

Secondly, disturbances in Karachi and its surroundings will affect the foreign investment, Especially in the private sector. In 1995 two American diplomats were killed by one of the factions of MQM. Being the premier port-city of Pakistan, Karachi is the major hub of industrialization in Pakistan. Almost all of the multinational corporations operating in Pakistan have their main offices in Karachi. Thus, in order to promote the process of privatization and protect employees of multinationals, other investors and their diplomats, Western powers would like to see the return of normalcy in Karachi.

Thirdly, disintegration of Pakistan could exacerbate instability in the Gulf and Central Asia. Pakistan's disintegration would very likely strengthen the forces of Islamic extremism and their main target would be pro-West rulers of the Gulf region. Among other things, instability in Gulf would affect the oil price in the world market, which would hit the industrialized world.

Fourthly, in the post-Cold War era, because of its oil, minerals, nuclear weapons, newly independent ex-Soviet states and strategic location in the Eurasian landmass, Central Asia has acquired an enormous importance for USA.[39] Along with other joint ventures, a Saudi-American oil consortium signed an agreement with Turkmenistan in 1995, to build a pipeline to transmit gas and oil to Karachi (through Afghanistan and Iran). If Pakistan disintegrates western interests in Central Asia would also be drastically affected. The stability of these Central Asian republics is inseparable from the conditions prevailing in Afghanistan and vice versa. Afghanistan, which for most of the 1990s has been, practically speaking, a fiefdom controlled by warlords, now has semblance of an imperfect democratic state. Stability and perhaps even the existence of

Pakistan is dependent on the maintenance of internal peace and inviolability of borders of Sindh. Thus, Sindh holds a key position in geo-strategic map of Southern Asia. This geo-strategic significance of Sindh was realized by Britain at the time of its conquest in 1843. Sir Charles Napier, the British General who conquered Sindh, said the control of Hirat, a far distant Oxus and Samarkand, lies in Karachi, Hyderabad and Shikarpur.[40] Thus, Western powers, especially Britain and America, in their regional and global interests did not support any designs of MQM, which might have unleashed convulsion in and around Pakistan.

The Collision Course II

The objectives of MQM, and violent manner in which it attempted to achieve them, put it on a collision course not only with Sindhis but with the state of Pakistan. This unfortunate situation posed threats not only to Pakistan itself but to the stability of Southern Asia. Pakistan, a weak state, lacking much internal cohesion, is susceptible to disintegration. Its vulnerabilities would increase if extra-regional powers including America and Great Britain, lend any moral or material support to MQM, which certainly harboured secessionist tendencies. Disintegration of Pakistan most probably would set in motion a chain reaction and convulse all the southern Asian states. Western powers which have a wide range of interests in the region, would not gain, but would most likely lose from this convulsion.

In the post-Cold War era, ethnic conflicts within ostensibly independent states, and their spill-over beyond the international borders, pose serious threats to international security. In the light of recent Yugoslavian experience, members of the international community have realized that forcible change of frontiers within the states, can be as dangerous as between states.[41] MQM tried to change the frontiers of Sindh by use of force and this policy is bound to heighten national, regional and international insecurity.

Members of the international community would be wise to help Pakistan in combating forcible and dangerous change of intra-provincial borders. In order to achieve this objective, MQM needs to be declared and treated as a neo-fascist and terrorist organization. The declaration of Sharm-el-Sheikh (Egypt) Summit Meeting for condemnation of terrorism, held in March 1996, should be put into practice. In this conference the then British Prime Minister, John Major, suggested that 'the doors should be shown to people who abuse the hospitality and protection of countries offering them asylum'.[42] By putting its words into action, the British government would not allow MQM to misuse British hospitality in order to wage war within a friendly state. Like other terrorist organizations, MQM's overseas bank accounts should be frozen.

In the final analysis, in late 1990s, Pakistan was a land, distant from the West. Iran situated at the crossroads of South Asia, South-West Asia and Central Asia, has a host of interests. Any serious threats posed either by MQM terrorists, religious fanatics or by adventurous military elements, might explode into a wider instability affecting Pakistan. Paul Kennedy has warned USA about such an eventuality and international community should take his words seriously.

Before the Musharaff era (1999-2008), Karachi was divided into five districts. Just to make the Urdu speaking population as a majority in the whole city, five districts were abolished which created a great deal of unease for Sindhis because their inhabitations and votes were divided into different zones. Conversely, the district of Hyderabad was divided into four districts, so that Urdu speakers should hold reigns of power in the city. This move was also resisted by Sindhs, who time and again demanded the restoration of old status of Karachi and

Hyderabad Districts. PPP, which claims to be the principal party of Sindhis was under constant pressure from its constituents to restore the pre-Musharraf administrative structure of Sindh in general and Hyderabad and Karachi in particular. And it announced to restore the old Hyderabad district on 9th May 2010. Despite being a coalition partner of the PPP government, MQM has vehemently resisted PPP ' s policy of restoration of Hyderabad district. MQM leadership from Karachi and London is threatening of the dire results in case of remarcation of Hyderabad and Karachi district.[43]. Sindhis on the other hand, are adamant to restore the pre-Musharraff, order. Situation is seemingly lurching to the ethnic war in Sindh, which is bound to destabilize Pakistan and South Asia. Thus, arguably MQM acts as a destabilising force in Pakistan.

References

1. Cited in Robert S. Chase, Emily B. Hill and Paul Kennedy, "Pivotal states and US strategy", *Foreign Affairs,* Vol. 75, No. 1, 1996, pp. 33-51.

2. Paul Kennedy, 'Pivotal states and US strategy', p. 37.

3. Paul M. Kennedy, *The Rise and Fall of the Great Powers: Economic Changes and Military Conflict,* Fontana, London, 1988, pp. 631-664.

4. C. U. Bhasker, 'Pakistan in New Post-Cold War Strategic Context', *Strategic Analysis, (New Delhi:* January 1996), p. 1304.

5. *Daily Jang,* in Urdu, Karachi edition, 4 June, 1972.

6. Ayesha Jalal, *Democracy and Authoritarianism in South Asia,* Cambridge University Press, Cambridge, 1995, pp.107-108.

7. Salamat Ali, 'Soldiers and Spooks', *Far Eastern Economic Review (Hong Kong),* 10 November 1988), p. 36.

8. *Daily Hilali Pakistan,* Sindhi (Karachi), 27 September, 1992.

9. Khalid Akhtar (ed.) *Altaf Hussain Ki Kahani Unki Zibani* (autobiography of Altaf Hussain), in Urdu, Jang Press, Karachi, fourth edition, 1991, p. 12.

10. Ghazanfar Hussain Hidayatullah, 'The Mohajir Quami Movement and Sindh', *The Daily News International,* Karachi edition, 26 August, 1995.

11. Charles H. Kennedy, 'Politics of Ethnic Preference in Pakistan', *Asian Survey,* (Berkeley) Vol. XXIV, No. 6, 1984, p. 692.

12. *Ibid.*, p. 693.

13. C. G. P. Rikisits, 'Centre-Provincial Relations in Pakistan Under President Zia: Government's and Opposition's Approaches', *Pacific Affairs (Vancour)*, Vol. 61, No. 1, Spring 1988, p. 81.

14. 'Punjab and urban-Sindh enjoy major chunk in civil services', *Daily Frontier Post,* Peshawer, 1 February, 1996.

15. Hidayatullah, 'The MQM and Sindh'. According to the 1992 UN estimates. Pakistan's total population is about 119 107 000. *Whitaker's Almanack 1996,* p. 980. In the 1972 census, Urdu speakers comprised 7.6 per cent of the total population of Pakistan. Two-thirds of them live in the urban centres of Sindh and about one-third is scattered all over the country. Feroze Ahmed, 'Ethnic politics is a dead end street-II', *Daily Dawn.* By these calculations the Urdu speakers just comprise about 5-6 million population of Sindh, which confirms Hidayattulah's estimates about them.

16. Mukhdoom Khalique Zaman, in an interview with monthly *Herald,* Karachi, January 1990, p. 56.

17. Surbramanyam K, 'Crisis in Karachi', p. 13 18.and Hanif "Karachi: the City of Death", p. 42. *Front Line (Chennai)*, 12 January 1996.

18. *Daily Jang,* London edition, 22 July, 1992.

19. *Daily Dawn,* 17 July, 1996.

20. Statement of Mumtaz Ali Bhutto, the President of Sindh National Alliance, *Daily Barsat,* Sindhi, (Karachi), 17 July, 1996.

21. Ayesha Jalal, *Jinnah: The Sole Spokesman, the Muslim League, and the Demand for Pakistan,* Cambridge University Press, Cambridge, 1985, pp. 14-18.

22. IISS, London, *Strategic Survey 1994*-95, p. 195.

23. *Frontline op.cit*

24. *Daily Jang,* London edition, 2 July, 1992.

25. The poem of Rais Amrohi, 'O Hind jani wali mera salem le ja': 'Oh you who go to India, carry to them our greetings' (translation), in Mani Shanker Aiyer's *Pakistan Papers,* UBS Publishers and Distributors, Delhi, 1994, pp. XI-XX.

26. H.S. Sondhi, 'India's internal Troubles and Foreign Factor', *Indian Defence Review,* (Delhi), Vol. 8, No. 2, April 1993, p. 83.

27. Aiyer, *Pakistan Papers,* pp. 73-74.

28. Chris Smith, *The Diffusion of Small and Light Arms in Pakistan and Northern India,* Defence Studies, London, 20, 1993, pp. 15-16.

29. *Daily Barsat,* 27 March, 1994.

30. *Daily Jang,* London edition, 25 February 1996, and *Asian Age,* 21 March, 1996.

31. Mehtab Ali Shah, 'The Kashmir Dispute: a View From the Four Provinces of Pakistan', *Contemporary South Asia,* Vol. 4, No. 1, 1995, pp. 110-111.

32. 'Seize routes to coastal area: MQM (A) asks its activists', *Daily Frontier Post,* 18 February, 1994.

33. Martin Wright, *Power Politics*, Leicester University Press, 1978, p. 144.

34. Alexander F. Baillie, *Kurrachee: Past: Present: Future,* Thacker Spink, (Bombay), 1890, p. 4.

35. Selig Harrison, *In Afghanistan's Shadow: Baluch Nationalism and the Soviet Temptations,* Carnegie Endowment for International Peace, (New York, 1981), pp. 97-99.

36. *Daily Jang,* London edition, 9 February, 1996.

37. Sobho Gianchandani, a communist leader and many other Sindhi intellectuals expressed these views in a gathering, *Daily Barsat,* 27 July, 1996.

38. *Daily Dawn,* 12 October 1996.

39. Charles Underland and Nicholas Plat, *The Central Asian Republic: Fragments of Empire,* The Asian Society, (New York), 1994, p. 117, cited in U. Bhaksar, 'Pakistan in the Cold War Context', p. 1306.

40. Priscilla Napier, *I Have Sind, Charles Napier in India: 1841-1844,* Michael Russell, (Wilton, 1990), pp. 60-61.

41. Adam Roberts, 'The United Nations and international security', in Michael E. Brown (ed.), *Ethnic Conflict and International Security,* Princeton University Press, (New Jersey), 1993, p. 215.

42. Derek Brown and Emad Merkay, 'Summit lets Iran Off hook', *The Guardian,* 14 March, 1996.

43. Staff reporter, "M.Ps File Resignation With Altaf Over Hyderabad: MQM Flashes Coalition Card, Asks Zardari to Intervene", *Daily Times* (Karachi) 10th May 2010.

(This article, entitled, The Emergence of the Muhajir Quomi Movement (MQM) in Pakistan and Its Implications for Regional Security", was published in *The Round Table,* (Oxfordshire : Carfax Publishing Ltd, 1998) Number; 348, October 1998).

5

Highest Production-Centre Karachi a haven for the Political Militia

Since 1984, Karachi has been passing through different phases of violence, ranging from relatively minor issues such as the theft of push bicycles, to arson, the destruction of property and on to murder. It is estimated that during the 1990s at least 1,000 persons were killed in the city every year[1]*. Murder, extortion (bhatta) and other crimes in the city, have mainly political purposes. The levels of criminality are so high that the city is regarded as one of the most violent in the world*[2]*. The situation shortly changed after the imposition of Governor's rule in the Sindh Province in 1998 and military take-over of Pakistan by General Pervaiz Musharraf in 1999. This chapter investigates the nexus between crime and politics in the city and the principal causes if this phenomenon. In addition, it seeks to examine the remedies that could be taken to mitigate the situation. This study principally covers a period if ten years*

(1990-2000), but occasionally, it briefly goes back even on to 1947, when Pakistan came into being.

Karachi, the capital of the southern province of Sindh of Pakistan, is almost 200 years old. It is one of the five commissionerates of Sindh province. The city itself is administratively divided into five districts: district west, district centre, district south, district east and the district Malir. District centres west and south touch the province of Balochistan and Arabian Sea. Districts east and Malir abut Thatta district of the interior of Sindh and sea. In geophysical terms, Karachi on the whole is a part of the hinterland of Sindh province.

Located adjacent to the Arabian Sea, the city has two seaports, Karachi port and Qasim port. In fact, these are the only fully developed ports of the country, which connect Pakistan to the major sea-lanes of the world. Similarly, Karachi airport also connects Pakistan with major air routes of the world linking Far East with Middle East and Europe. Thus, Karachi occupies an important position in the strategic and commercial life of Pakistan in general and Sindh province in particular. Speaking in geopolitical terms, one can suggest that, he who controls Karachi, will dominate the whole of Pakistan, if not far beyond it.[3]

The port city of Karachi is the principal industrial centre of the country as well. The biggest industrial unit of the country, Pakistan Steel Mill, which employs a strong workforce of about 25,000 persons is based in the suburbs of the city. On the whole, 75% of the industry of Pakistan is based either in Karachi itself or its satellite townships of Hub Choki and Nooriabad. This industrial base makes Karachi the biggest commercial city of Pakistan. Karachi has the highest number of branches of different national and international banks[4] and is the headquarters of the international multinational corporations in Pakistan[5]. It has biggest stock exchange of the country. With two seaports and one highly developed airport of the country within its boundaries, Karachi is a transit point to oil rich Gulf region and other parts of the world. Being the industrial, commercial and financial hub of the country and provincial capital of Sindh, Karachi plays a dominant role in economic and political life of the country. It would be appropriate to say that when Karachi sneezes, the whole country catches a cold. Peace and tranquility in Karachi plays a vital role in the stability of the country but over the last 20 years or more, there has been little peace or tranquility our there. Karachi has become a centre of violence and criminality.

Major Causes of Criminalisation of Politics in Karachi

A number of interconnected reasons that have led to the process of criminalisation of politics in Karachi, could be identified. The first of these is what may be called the "feudalization" of politics. About 75% of the population of Pakistan lives in the rural areas, where naturally, enough agriculture is the main source of income. The feudals (prominent *zamindars),* keep private armies both to intimidate their peasants and to fight against other *zamindars.* In the process, they use enormous pressure on the electorates to vote for a political party, with the *zamindar's* support from there could secure a seat in parliament. The ruffians they use support, get full protection of the *zamindars* and usually they are not apprehended or if apprehended, not punished by the law.

Ironically, the situation of the urban areas like Karachi is not different, although the influence of the *zamindars* in the city itself is minimal. Analyzing the criminalization of politics in Karachi, Yusuf Haroon, an octogenarian businessman and twice chief minister of Sindh in the past, explained this phenomenon by pointing out that in a metropolitan and industrial city like Karachi, industrialist are competing with other industrialists of different or the same ethnic group.

Elaborating his point of view further, Yusuf Haroon argued there might be a group of businessmen who try to outbid their opponents.[6] Moreover, as a port city, Karachi is the transit point for the transfer of drugs to other parts of the world. Thus, in this infighting, smugglers and drug pushers are key elements. The criminal elements used the range from *softies* (unemployed and inexperienced youth) to professional *dadagirs* or *ghoondas* (musclemen) and *qabzagirs* (trespassers). The white collar or educated bosses of Karachi's criminal syndicates, like Italian mafia leaders or American syndicate criminal leaders, have connections up to the top echelons of the power structure.[7] In discussing the factors in the emergence and development of politically motivated crime in the city, Ghazanfar Hussain Hidayatullah, a Karachi based intellectual highlighted the role of a builder mafia, who are engaged in a ruthless competition to grab state-owned land.[8]

When Pakistan came into being in 1947, it had a Westminster style model of parliamentary democracy and a federal form of government. However, the overbearing influence of the Punjabi military and bureaucracy *vis-a-vis* the non-Punjabi provinces in the country, led to successive periods of martial law, 1958-68, 1968-71 and 1977-88, and the military takeover 1999-2008.

When civilian rule is restored between periods of military rule, the prime ministers, uncertain of their own future, recommend the appointments of high ranking civil and military officials to the president, not so much on merit as on the assumption that such an officer or official would remain loyal to them or that a General would not stage the *coup*. Thus, Zulfiquar Ali Bhutto made this mistake when appointing General Zia as the head of the army in 1977. During his second stint in the office, Nawaz Sharif initially extended the tenure of General Pervaiz Musharraf, on the assumption that being

Urdu speaking, he would be unassertive. But the army proved Nawaz Sharif wrong by overthrowing him. Benazir Bhutto was twice overthrown, indirectly by armed forces. Armed forces and the intelligence services are allegedly implicated in her murder in 2007.[9] Thus, one can argue that in the case of Pakistan, recurrent military rule in the country and behind the scenes influence of the armed forces, combine to create an atmosphere of political uncertainty. This state of affairs leads to favouritism and cronyism, which take precedence over the law and procedure and these processes seep down to the lowest level. In these circumstances, politics becomes an activity, where he who is in power or supports the ruling party, plunders the public resources or violates the law for personal benefits, at the expense of society as a whole.

Influx of Population

As the industrial and financial hub of the country, Karachi attracts a large number of migrants from other parts of the country and from abroad. This influx of migrants has changed the ethnic and political culture of the city and is one of the major reasons behind the crime and violence for which Karachi is notorious. A mere fishing village of about 14,000 souls in 1839[10], it has become a mega city of about 15 million within the passage of about 260 years. The *Katchi Abadis* (irregular and unauthorized construction) and slums, harbour about half population of the city.[11] These slums are the main dunes of the jobless persons, many of whom turn out to be criminals. This rapid expansion of population in Karachi, is a reflection of worldwide trend of urbanization of the population in developing countries. The policies of successive governments of Pakistan seeking to lure people for settlement in Karachi, have also contributed markedly towards the expansion of the population of the city. This issue of the politicization of demographic change needs careful analysis, because it is directly related to the process of the criminalisation of politics.[12]

With the conquest of Sindh by the British in 1843, Karachi was the capital of the Commissionerate of Sindh.[13] In 1936, Sindh became a separate province of British-India with Karachi as its capital. In 1947, Pakistan came into being and Karachi became the concurrent capital of Sindh province and of Pakistan. The first prime minister of the country, Liaqat Ali Khan, in order to create his own constituency in Pakistan and to change the Sindhi cultural character of the city, persuaded ailing Mohammed Ali Jinnah, Governor-General of Pakistan, to separate Karachi from rest of Sindh and to make it a federal capital. Such a move precipitated the exodus of Sindhi Hindus to India and encouraged the settlement of migrants from the Urdu/Hindi speaking areas of northern India to Karachi.[14] Before 1947, Karachi was a Sindhi city with 90% of the population being Sindhis. At the time of the 1951 census, out of about 1.37 million inhabitants, as many as 72% were of Indian origin[15]. Separation of Karachi from the rest of Sindh, was arguably, a calculated act of political, ethnic and social engineering under which, a particular community was made happy at the expense of the native Sindhis.

In 1955, the provinces of western wing of Pakistan, Sindh, Balochistan, Punjab and North Western Frontier Province (NWFP) were merged into one administrative unit called West Pakistan. Thereby, successive prime ministers and governors-general of Pakistan, such as Ghulam Mohammed and Choudhry Mohammed Ali, who happened to be Punjabis, encouraged the migration of Punjabis and Pashtuns to Karachi. In 1961, General Ayub Khan shifted the federal capital of the country from Karachi to Islamabad, but his son, Gouher Ayub persistently encouraged the migration from the upcountry areas to Karachi. Because of Punjab's domination over the politics of Pakistan, this trend still continues through the military and the bureaucracy. According to some estimates more than three million inhabitants of the city are Pashtuns and Punjabis.[16] The

Punjabi migrant workers settle down mainly in the districts of east and Malir. They find jobs in industry, private security services and the local police force, which is dominated by them. The unemployed among them resort to crime, including robbery and car snatching and secure the patronage of the police.[17] A robbery has illustrated the linkages between migration, crime and politics in Karachi. Stolen car belonging to a Karachi based member of the National Assembly, Hassan Masna of the Mohajir Qaumi Markaz (MQM) was recovered from the possession of the nephew of a former chief minister of Punjab, belonging to the Muslim League.[18]

In 1970, one unit system was dismembered, and Karachi became once again the provincial capital of Sindh. Considering Karachi as their ancestral home, the Sindhis from the interior of Sindh began settling in Karachi, once again, Especially in the suburbs of the Malir district, which has had its own Sindhi and Baloch settlements for centuries. Learning a lesson from criminals of other ethnic groups, some Sindhi criminals were soon connected with the *waderas* and police involved in robberies and car snatching.

The dismemberment of Pakistan in 1971 and the creation of Bangladesh, resulted in the exchange of population between the two countries. About 100,000 Bangladeshis went to their new state and about 200,000 Biharis came to Karachi from Bangladesh and they are still gradually but continuously trickling into Karachi.[19] Since Biharis speak Urdu, they mix with the Urdu-speaking population of the city and cannot be easily detected by any investigation agency. As stated earlier, being a transit point to the Gulf, Karachi attracted many Burmese, Biharis, Bangladeshis, Somalis, Vietnamese, Filipino and Sri Lankan guest workers.[20] Afzal Shigri, a former inspector general of police, in a press conference in January 1995, revealed that there were more than two million illegal immigrants in the city, who also contribute to the deteriorating law and order situation in the country[21]. Indeed, Sindhi sources believe that the number of illegal immigrants is much higher, as much as three million.[22] Because of their ethnic background, the illegal immigrants from India and Bangladesh find allies in the ethnic party MQM. These illegal immigrants get involved in crimes or terrorism.

As a result of the interminable conflict in Afghanistan, which started in 1979, Afghan refugees also started pouring into Karachi, where they mingled with the Pashtun population of the city. According to some estimates the number of Afghan refugees in the city may be more than half a million. Population of the locality of Suhbrab Goth, in the north of Karachi, is principally composed of Pashtun and Afghan refugees. It is also reportedly a stronghold of drug traffickers, gun dealers and Islamic fundamentalists.[23] The induction of illegal weapons in Karachi and upsurge of sectarian violence, are closely linked to the Afghan war. The ethnic Pashtun parties, like the Jamait Islami, the Jameeti Ulama Islam and Awami National Party, Karachi wing, maintain connections with the Afghan refugees, including the criminal elements living in Karachi.[24] After the Islamic Revolution of Iran in 1979, many Iranian dissidents, especially of *Bolach* ethnic origin, flew to Karachi and settled down in the *Baloch* localities such as Liyari, and Hub Choki, adjoining Balochistan. These illegal immigrants of Iranian origin join the gangs of drug dealers and car lifters and are part of the criminal elements in the city.[25] Most of the cars snatched in Karachi are openly sold in Khuzdar town in Balochistan.[26] Many of these vehicles are in the use of local influentials, the Sardars.[27] According to a report, at least 2,000 vehicles, stolen or snatched in Karachi, go to the Taliban controlled Afghanistan and after overhauling are resold in the Pakistani provinces of Balochistan and the NWFP[28]. Thus, the uncontrolled inflow of people towards the metropolis, contributes enormously towards the criminalisation of politics of Karachi. Since much of this crime is undetected or if detected goes under the patronage of politicians and corrupt officials, it contributes to the deterioration of the law and order situation and to bad governance as well.

The Politics of Ethnicity

The remarkably persistent huge inflow of people from Sindh and abroad to Karachi, has given rise to the politics of ethnicity, which is one of the main reasons of the criminalisation of politics of the town. There are three claimants of the city and their rivalry has charged atmosphere of the city. First, Sindhi and Balochs, who claim that Karachi, is their ancestral city. It is the capital of Sindh and they feel it should remain part of Sindh. They are vehemently opposed to the idea of separation of Karachi from Sindh in any form.[29] The number of these Sindhis and Balochs, living in Karachi and its suburbs will be about three million. After the 1997 elections, they have only one seat out of the 12 seats of the National Assembly reserved for the different constituencies of Karachi. Similarly, the Sindhi-Baloch population has only three seats out of 27 of Karachi in provincial assembly of 110 seats[30]. Their main allies are Sindhis of the interior and Baloch politicians in Sindh, Balochistan provincial and the national assemblies. One of the reasons for reduction of Sindhi-Baloch representation in the constituencies of provincial and national assemblies of Karachi, is the policy of gerrymandering, pursued especially under the successive Nawaz Sharif governments. For instance, the Sindhis of Malir district do not have a seat in the provincial and national assemblies, because parts of Malir are connected with the districts east and centre, which are dominated by the Urdu-speaking community, which usually votes for the MQM. This policy of gerrymandering of constituencies is one of the major reasons for the resentment of Sindhis and Balochs in Karachi against the establishment.

The second sets of contenders for the control of Karachi are the Pashtuns and Punjabis, who form more than one-third of the population of the city. Pashtuns are usually labourers, taxi drivers, and security servicemen. They co-ordinate their policies with the Punjabis in Karachi, in the running of the state as they usually used to do for three decades (1960s-90s). Since Punjabis on the whole, dominate Pakistan, they control service structure of Karachi, police, labour force, industry and even the chamber of commerce, usually a domain of the Kutchi-Gujarati Memons. In 1997 election Punjabis won two seats in the National Assembly from Karachi and five seats in the provincial assembly. In order to consolidate their position, Punjabis and other people from the upcountry, seem intent on making Karachi a federal enclave or a federally ruled area.

The third and most serious contender for the control of the city, is Urdu-speaking migrants from India who call themselves, the *Muhajir* or refugees. The Urdu speakers principally live in the districts of centre, west, south and east, highly organized and politically conscious. Muhajir Qaumi Movement, won most of the seats of the provincial and National Assembly from Karachi. During 1997 elections, MQM won 21 out of 27 seats (reserved for Karachi) of the provincial assembly[31]. Similarly of 12 seats that Karachi has in the National Assembly, MQM won as many as nine.

The genesis of the MQM and its implications for Karachi, Sindh province and the country as a whole, is an essential part of the politics of ethnicity and of political violence. Urdu speakers, settled down in Karachi, consider Karachi as their own city.[32] They have developed an identity of their own, "Karachite", which they do not wish to share with any other group, even with the natives of Karachi, Sindhis and Balochs who consider them outsiders and resent their presence. While abhorring Sindhis, Balochs and the people of the upcountry, most of the Urdu speakers of Karachi, find affinity with their fellow Urdu speakers, living in the other urban centres of Sindh, such as Hyderabad and Sukkur. They wish to have their own administrative niche in Pakistan, stretching from Karachi, through Hyderabad and Mirpurkhas to Sukkur in the upper Sindh. In order to achieve this goal, they regard their dominance of Karachi, as the first stage of their quest for a separate province. The quest for separation of Karachi from the rest of Sindh and ultimately from Pakistan, has put them on a collision course with the Sindhis and rest of the people of Pakistan.[33]

The Sindhis feel that Karachi is part and parcel of Sindh and its separation is unthinkable for them. The Punjabis and other communities living in Karachi have two apprehensions about the creation of a Karachi province. First, after the creation of this province, the Urdu speakers will dominate the city to a greater extent than they do now. Secondly, the division of Sindh, will set a precedence for the divisions of other provinces, such as NWFP into a Pashtun and Hazara province; Balochistan into a Baloch and Pashtun province and Punjab, into a Punjabi and Siraiki province.[34] Thus, apart from these Urdu speakers, who subscribe to separatism, nobody else supports the policy of division of Sindh. The policy of a separate status of Karachi isolates its advocates from the rest of Pakistan. The resulting tensions contribute greatly to the criminalisation of politics of the city.

As we have seen, city of Karachi was separated from the rest of Sindh in 1948. In 1972, when Karachi was made the capital of Sindh once again, government of ZA Bhutto, reintroduced Sindhi as the official language of the province. Considering such a move as a threat to their privileged position, majority of the Urdu speakers campaigned against it and resorted to several episodes of violence. There was a great loss of life in Karachi, Hyderabad and Sukkur, where Sindhis were a minority.

General Zia found in Urdu speakers allied against Sindhis. With his active support, an ethnic party, Muhajir Qaumi Movement (MQM) under the leadership of Altaf Hussain, was formed in 1984. Formation of MQM coincided with the war in Afghanistan. A huge amount of arms was brought to Karachi by Afghan smugglers. MQM generally demanded a better life for its constituents: the abolition of quota system on jobs, improving civil amenities in Karachi repatriating Biharis from Bangladesh and settling them down in Sindh. However, its long-term objective, appeared to be the creation of a separate province for Urdu speaking community, carved out of the province of Sindh.[35]

Built on a highly planned structure, MQM reportedly has two wings, one political, which divides the city into sectors and maintains offices in each of them and contests elections, which they did successfully in 1985, 1988, 1991, 1993, and 1997. Another part of MQM: the establishment is, its invisible military wing, which co-ordinates its activities with the political wing in keeping with the grip of the party on its constituencies.[36]

The military wing of MQM, commonly known as Black Cats is modeled on defunct Liberation Tigers of Tamil Eelam (LTTE) of Sri Lanka, which has been recently defeated by the Sri Lankan army. It has two objectives: first, to fight against law enforcement agencies of the country for the purpose of creating an Urdu speaking province, a stepping stone to an independent state and secondly, to intimidate Urdu speaking population to vote for MQM at elections.[37] Its military wing, disguised as *Khidmat* (welfare) Committee collects donations from expatriate Urdu-speakers, receives extortion money *(bhatta)* from shopkeepers, mill owners and businessmen.[38] It forcibly shuts down the businesses if a call of strike is given by the party bosses on a particular day, removes the dissidents within MQM itself and neutralizes any alternative leadership emerging within the Urdu speaking community.[39] This military wing is reportedly composed of hard core criminals,[40] who initially got involved in crimes ranging from petty thefts to large-scale robberies, car snatching and personal and sectarian violence, among others. Naturally they were regarded as terrorists.[41] The military wing is divided into sectors and specified areas are controlled by an individual known as the sector-in-charge, who is responsible to the local members of the provincial and national assemblies. These members receive instructions from MQM headquarters, 90 Azizabad, which itself is hooked up with MQM secretariat in London by modern communication technology.

In the early stage of MQM, its activists reportedly received training from Pakistan's intelligence services; from Sindhi nationalists and the Afghan Mujahideen. In late 1980s, death of Zia, coincided with the *intafada* (uprising) in the Indian administered Kashmir. General Zia created MQM in 1984, to intimidate Sindhis living in urban centres of the province. In 1986, MQM, confronted Pashtuns in Karachi and Hyderabad. Within a short period of five years, it became so powerful that it started challenging the ruling political parties of the country and law enforcement agencies. In 1985, MQM won local elections in Karachi. In general 1988 elections, it became the third largest party of the country. Any political party forming government in Sindh became dependent on the support of MQM. By resorting to strike calls *(hartals),* roadblocks and assembly boycotts, they were able to compel other political parties to accept its demands or lose power. In 1986, MQM created problems for the government of late Mohammed Khan Junejo at the center, by staging riots against Pashtun population of the city. From 1988-90, MQM while remaining the coalition partner of the Pakistan People's Party (PPP) in Sindh, created problems for the PPP and precipitated its dismissal by the President in 1991. From 1991 to 1993, MQM became a coalition partner of Islamic Jamhuri Itahad (IJI) of Mian Nawaz Sharif, but continued with the policy of intimidation of such intensity that in 1992, Nawaz Sharif was forced to call the army for restoration of peace in the city.

In order to break the power base and militancy of MQM, Nawaz Sharif and his ally Jam Sadiq Ali, then Chief Minister of Sindh, encouraged the formation, according to a senior police officer, of a splinter group within MQM, the *Haqiqi,* or the real (MQM-H) in 1991. Since the formation of the MQM-H, a war started in the city between the two bloodthirsty factions of the MQM over its control a struggle that seems to be unabated.[44] In this war, at least 1,000 persons members of both factions of MQM-law enforcers were being killed every year.45 The city was divided into "no go areas". The activists of the MQM Altaf Group (MQM-A) were not in a position to visit the Landhi-Korangi areas dominated by the MQM-H. Conversely, many localities such as Liaqatabad, Lines area, Golimar among others, were "no go areas" not only for the MQM-H activists, but for the local police as well.

In 1993, after winning the provincial and National Assembly elections, PPP formed government at province and centre. The MQM-A boycotted the provincial assembly elections. It unleashed a campaign of terror in the city and made it ungovernable, with a loss of millions of rupees in every strike call. Eventually, PPP government withdrew army from the city in 1995, as a gesture of goodwill to the citizens of Karachi, but continued to deploy paramilitary force, the Rangers. A full-blown mini insurgency broke out between the government and MQM-A, in which 96 activists of Altaf Group, 101 members of Haqiqi and 199 members of law enforcement agencies were killed.[46] In 1996, President Farooq Laghari dismissed the PPP government. One of the charges leveled against the dismissed government was committing extra-judicial killings.[47]

After his victory in 1997 February elections, Nawaz Sharif formed a government at the centre. In an attempt to outbid the

PPP in Sindh, he formed a coalition government in Sindh with the MQM. His government released 2000 terrorists arrested by the previous government and made a cash grant of about Rs. 100 million as compensation to those families whose members died in action against the law enforcement agencies[48]. According to unofficial sources, the amount paid by Nawaz Sharif, was much higher than the official figure.[49] MQM ministers, such as Shoab Bukhari and Farooq Sattar, who were implicated in a number of cases by the PPP Government, were released by the Nawaz Sharif government and given important portfolios.[50]

Frequent calls to the MQM headquarters, 90, in Karachi by the government or at the MQM international secretariat, London, did not cut much ice with the MQM, which persisted with its policy of terrorism against its opponents. The infighting between the two factions of the MQM also took its toll. In 1997, it is estimated that around 396 were killed in politically orientated murders.[51] This tally included the Chairman of the Karachi Electric Supply Corporation (KESC), Shahid Hamid Malik, who in order to reduce the deficit of the corporation, wished to sack ghost workers who were allegedly the activists of the MQM.[52] Four employees of an American Multinational Corporation, The Union Texas Petroleum, also allegedly became the victims of the MQM hit men, during the same year[53].The MQM-A was repeatedly pressing the Nawaz Sharif Government either to wipe out the other faction of the MQM or allow it to do so.[54] This demand was not acceptable to Sharif, who did not wish to give a monopoly of control over the Urdu speaking community to the MQM-A. It must be remembered that while MQM-A, a creation of Nawaz Sharif's mentor, General Zia, was his political ally, whereas, the MQM-H, was a creation of Nawaz Sharif himself and the establishment of Islamabad. It appears that out of expediency, Nawaz Sharif was playing one faction against the other, as a result of which, law and order situation in the city deteriorated even further.

In order to put more pressure on Nawaz Sharif government, MQM left the coalition government from August to October 1998, but did not join PPP. During this period of uncertainty, only three days after rejoining the Muslim League on 28 October 1998, MQM-A activists allegedly assassinated Hakim Said, the former governor of Sindh province. He was an apolitical person, who enjoyed a great deal of respect among members of the Urdu speaking community and desired to keep a distance from the two warring factions of MQM. Because of this high profile murder and other 957 murders in the city carried out in 1998,[55] the city became virtually ungovernable.

Once again Nawaz Sharif put the blame on MQM-A for lawlessness. He dismissed the then Sindh government of Liaqat Jatoi and imposed governor's rule over the province, without dissolution of the provincial assembly. MQM parliamentarians were once again arrested over murder and extortion charges. Military courts were established in the city to try terrorists and other persons who committed heinous crimes like rape. Four persons were tried and hung by these courts. After dissolution of the Muslim League Government, the town witnessed a lull in crime. Up to the end of February 1999, not a single case of terrorism was reported to the police. Car snatching also declined by 30%. Cases of *bhatta* were also unreported.[56]

In October 1999, government of Nawaz Sharif was dismissed by army chief of staff, General Pervaiz Musharraf. He followed a carrot and stick policy towards the MQM. On the one hand, one of the main leaders of the MQM, Farooq Sattar was arrested on charges of corruption. His arrest forced many in MQM rank and file to curtail if not stop their activities. On the other hand, a programme on devolution of power was introduced in the country, under which, district governments would be created at the expense of the provincial government. A version of this programme of devolution of power was specially evolved for Karachi, which envisages the creation of a divisional government and dissolution of five districts. It expected this divisional government would lead to creation of a city government.[57] This scheme seem and to be in tune with the MQM's long standing demand of separating Karachi from the rest of the Sindh province. In addition, seven out of 13 ministers in the cabinet of General Musharraf, were Urdu speakers. So was the then chief justice of Pakistan, Justice Irshad Hassan Khan. In other words, Urdu speakers had greater share in power than their actual percentage in the country. This offering of a carrot policy pacified MQM and as a result, its cadre was not actively involved in crime. People associated with criminal activity came from other parts of the state. However, one could argue that there was a connection between crime and politics. Whenever action was taken against MQM, or significant concessions were offered to it, the crime rate droped in the city.

Crimes Committed in Karachi

Karachi, is one of the most violent cities of South Asia. Most of the crimes committed here have political patronage. Politically motivated murders and gang warfare and car snatching have been discussed already. A few more categories of crime will be reviewed here. These include *bhatta* or extortion, kidnapping for ransom, land grabbing and corruption of various sorts.

(*a*) *Bhatta or Extortion*

Bhatta is a practice, by which musclemen, belonging to different political parties, compel shopkeepers, owners of industry, builders, vendors, even taxi drivers, or for that matter even householders to contribute a certain amount of money on a regular basis to their organization. Those who refuse to pay are threatened with death; indeed, often they are actually killed or their property is destroyed, as it happened for instance on 15 August 1998, in the industrial area, Korangi's Taj market.[58]

Although a *ghoonda (musckman)* tax was collected by thugs in the bazaars of Karachi previously, *bhatta* collection started in Karachi after the emergence of the MQM in 1984. It was prevalent throughout the province.

Political parties collected *bhatta* in their respective constituencies. This money was collected through intimidation for the purpose of supporting arrested activists, hiring best lawyers for them, supporting their families or for running offices, and for buying weapons. In MQM-H, dominated areas, like Landhi and Korangi, the Haqiqis had to share this money allegedly with the rangers[59]. Thus their charges were higher than in the MQM-A constituencies. For this reason the MQM-A, was considered the lesser evil there. The areas falling within the jurisdiction of the MQM-A, such as Tariq road, Saddar, I.I Chundriger Road, and Burns Road are, commercial centres of Karachi, and the collection of *bhatta* there is much higher than any other part of the country, let alone of Karachi. In the poverty stricken locality of Liyari, the activists of the Shahid Bhutto faction of the PPP, allegedly receive *bhatta* from the shopkeepers and drug pushers. While the Bombay Metropolitan police has collected some figures about similar extortion money in the city,[60] such data on *bhatta* collection are not available in Karachi. However, according to the late Ashtiaq Azhar, an MQM dissident, as much as six billion rupees was collected by the MQM-A activists, for remittance to Altaf Hussain in London.[61] *Bhatta* collection discouraged investment in the city and makes life unsafe for persons ranging from big and small businessmen down to even grocery shop owners.

It is not only party activists but also members of the law enforcement agencies who collect *bhatta,* or receive a share from the gangsters. A police officer told this researcher that the poorly paid policeman cannot sustain his family in an expensive city like Karachi on his salary alone and therefore had to supplement his income by taking a few rupees from bus drivers who overload their buses, taxi drivers who overcharge their passengers, or from vendors.[62]

In Police Department in Karachi, the most sought after job is that of the Deputy Inspector General, Police Traffic (DIG). A DIG traffic is usually a millionaire. Karachi has the highest number of vehicles of all kinds in Pakistan.[63] Most of these vehicles can be charged for one offence or the other. In minor cases such as the non-renewal of licenses, or improper driving, offenders would like to grease the palm of traffic sergeant instead of facing a court trial. There is also a hierarchy of police officers who make a substantial income from collecting *bhatta* of this sort. These police officers are well connected with the politicians and nobody dares touch them during the term of office of the party which supports them.[64]

(*b*) *Kidnapping for Ransom*

With Karachi as the hub of commercial activity of the country, as much as 60% of the wealth of the country, circulates among the Karachites. In order to make easy money, politically connected criminals, kidnap or threaten to kidnap businessmen or their children for huge amounts of money. Often enough, children are kidnapped on their way to or from schools. According to a report published by the Citizen-Police Liaison Committee (CPLC), it had handled 219 reports of kidnapping from 1990 to 1998. While 68 groups of kidnappers consisting of over 300 criminals were rounded up, many of them are still at large. In March 1999, son of the owner of the Bhoja Airline was kidnapped and killed though their parents were willing to pay a ransom of Rs. 5 million.

Kidnapping is closely connected with politics. Whenever new elections are held, the number of kidnapping cases increases, because money is needed for launching election campaigns. In 1990, after the dismissal of PPP government, and in preparation of the new elections, 65 cases of kidnapping for ransom were reported in just two months.[65] Where the ransom money is not forthcoming, the victim is killed. Ashique Ali H. Hussain, is a case in point. He was kidnapped during the period of Muslim League-MQM government in 1992, and was never seen alive thereafter. During the same period, kidnapping for ransom became so common for the politically connected underworld in Karachi that the criminals in the interior of Sindh also adopted it. In this period, four Chinese were kidnapped in the Dadu district and they were released after payment of Rs. 3.5 million to dacoits through their patron, a friend of Jam Sadiq Ali, the then Chief Minister of Sindh.

(c) *Land Grabbing*

Because of rapid urbanisation, and proximity to the sea, land is a much sought after commodity in the city of Karachi. Till 1999, Chief Minister of Sindh had discretionary powers of allotting government land to anybody at any price, generally to cronies for buying their loyalty. Much land is also grabbed by so-called *qabzagirs* (occupants). They occupy the land, and then get it allotted to them by the government of the day, and thereafter land is sold to builders who, in fact, are partners of the *Qabzagirs*. These builders construct flats and small bungalows in the housing schemes for sale to the public.

Land grabbing has been taking place unabated and beneficiaries included men like Gouher Ayub Khan, son of Field Marshal Ayub Khan, who got land allotted to him in the district south in the 1960s. Similarly, Jam Sadiq Ali, as a revenue minister in the Bhutto era (1972-77) disposed of much of the land in the city in the form of plots, sold at a much lower price than the market would have dictated. He broke his own record once again, when he became the Chief Minister of Sindh under the first government of Nawaz Sharif (1990-92). Large tracts of land were allotted at a throwaway price to Muslim Leaguers or those who switched allegiance from the PPP to the Muslim League, in districts east and Malir.[66] Abdullah Shah, as the

Chief Minister of Sindh, and leader of Sindh PPP (1993-96) did the same.[66] Abu Bakar Sheikhani and Alim Adil Sheikh, two Muslim League leaders, pursued the same policy during the second term of the Nawaz Sharif government.[67]

Karachi Development Authority (KDA) also misuses its power and appropriates even private land. Whenever MQM becomes a coalition partner of any government, it insists on holding the folio of the local bodies, which gives its influence over the KDA. Amenity plots are converted into commercial plots and sold cheap to MQM financiers. Under the influence of MQM, slums of illegal immigrants and old Sindhi-Baloch villages are demolished and land is sold to pro-MQM builders. In 1994, 24 acres of government land occupied by the illegal Bengali immigrants in Bengali Para were appropriated and their settlements were demolished. Subsequently, Senator Zahid Akhtar (MQM) whose father owns an organization called the Construction Company bought the land for Messrs Rukunuddin Ahmed.[68]

The irony is that, much of residential areas approved by the KDA, are actually centuries old Sindh-Baloch villages. Karachi of the post-partition era is built on 1,200 Sindhi and Baloch *goth* (villages).[69] Although the inhabitants of these villages have genuine documents of ownership,[70] their validity is denied by the KDA. While taxes are collected from these Sindhi and Baloch villages, their land holdings are neither regularized, nor leased to the villagers by the KDA. On the contrary, they are declared encroachments and demolished without compensation. Localities such as Liaqatabad, originally, Lalookhet, Gulshani Iqbal, Defence and now Gulistan-i-Johar used to be Sindhi villages and land belonged to villagers, not the state. However, this land was confiscated from Sindhi owners who were forcibly ejected from their ancestral homes. This land grabbing policy of the KDA continues unabated. As late as February 1999, four Sindhi-Baloch *goths* were demolished in district west[71] and one big locality, Suhrab Gizri *goth,* was demolished in district east.[72] In addition to the private and public land grabbing agencies, armed forces also take control of land in the city of Karachi by declaring it state property procured in the name of national defence. The Sindhi and Baloch settlements are demolished and the plots in these areas are sold to ex-servicemen at a concessionary price and these buyers sell them at a much higher price to any bidder. Askari apartments owned by the army and the Bahria colony, built by the navy, are cases in point. The Civil Aviation Authority does the same around the airport area. Thus in one way or another, several departments and builders are involved in land grabbing.

It is also worth mentioning that holdings of illegal immigrants, such as the Orangi Pilot Project of Hamid Akhtar Khan, are regularized and patronized by Pakistani and International governmental and non-governmental organizations, while little or no attention is being paid to the plight of the Sindhi villagers, whose holdings are demolished by KDA or private builders.

Land grabbing has been a new turf war between MQM, ANP, PPP and Sindhi Taraqi Pasand Party in different parts of the city. In January 2010, Baloch populace and MQM fought pitched battles over the control of piece, Ghattar Baghachi in lyari, MQM and armed men in Suhrab Goth, PPP and MQM muscleman in Gulsitan Joher in central Karachi, with heavy loss of life.[73] At the time of writing, in a mafia gang warfare over the occupation of state land, two land grabbers and three of their accomplices were killed in north Karachi.[74] This deadly practice will continue till rule of law is enforced in the city and wiped out mafias.

(*d*) *Financial Sleaze*

Karachi is banking centre of the country. Bank frauds committed in Karachi set the trend for whole country, which not only tarnishes Pakistan's image abroad but also becomes one of the main reasons of its economic difficulties. The Bank of Credit and Commerce International (BCCI), owned by Agha Hassan Abidi, a Karachi based tycoon who had made his fortune in Dubai, originated in Karachi and operated all over the world. The BCCI was used by international drug and arms dealers and money launderers. It is alleged that even General Zia laundered money through this bank.[75] The BCCI, was also the benefactor of the MQM. It collapsed in 1991, depriving thousands of account holders of their savings throughout the world.

In 1990 a new provincial bank, called the Mehran Bank under the chairmanship of Yunus Habib was established in the city. He was forced to lend money to the anti-Benazir group of politicians and the intelligence agencies to defeat her in the elections. The then army chief, General Aslam Beg, reportedly received Rs. 140 million from Yunus Habib.[76] The money was not recovered and because of bad loans, the bank ultimately collapsed in 1993 and Yunus Habib received a jail sentence.[77]

During his first tenure of office, Mian Nawaz Sharif, introduced "Blue Cab Scheme". Muslim League supporters were given loans by different banks to buy South Korean manufactured cars. These banks did not recover the loans because defaulters were well connected. Ultimately the sponsor of the Blue Cab Scheme, especially the United Bank Limited, suffered heavy losses.

Late Benazir Bhutto and her widower, now President, Asif Zardari, were also accused of money laundering and receiving kickbacks to the tune of three billion dollars.[78] Similarly, Nawaz Sharif is being blamed of receiving donations from Ayub Afridi, a notorious drug smuggler. Nawaz Sharif is also accused of tax evasion. His Chief of the *Ehtasab* Accountability Bureau, Senator Saif Rahman was also a defaulter.[79]

This high level corruption which started in Karachi, has become part of the national culture of Pakistan and it is plundering the wealth of the country. Transparency International, an agency monitoring the financial deals of politicians, investigating the behaviour of 72 states in 1996, declared Pakistan, the second most corrupt state. After two years, Pakistan was bypassed by nine other states and in 1998; the same agency declared Pakistan as the 11th most corrupt state in the world.[80]. When an international conference on elimination of corruption was held in Washington in 1999, Pakistan did not participate to avoid facing criticisms of its record of corruption.[81] In 2009, out of 180 countries, Pakistan was declared as139 corrupt country by the Transparency International.[82] In this report, police, power generation department, health and education were declared the mot corrupt departments in the country. The heads of these departments undoubtedly, enjoy the patronage of the politicians in power. In case of Karachi, they belong to the PPP, MQM and the ANP.

Impact of Criminalisation of Politics on the City, Province and Pakistan

Criminalization of politics in Karachi has wide, social, psychological, economic and political implications for city itself, the province of Sindh, whose capital Karachi is, and for Pakistan as a whole. Some of them are as follows :

(a) *Psychological Implications*

The social life of the city has been greatly disturbed by frequent killings, gang warfare, arbitrary arrests, strikes and a general atmosphere of lawlessness. The tough measures adopted by second government of Benazir Bhutto (1993-96) succeeded for a while. However, after its dismissal, the city lurched once again into anarchy. Arguably, imposition of Governor's/military rule in Sindh and Pakistan (November 1988) brought a semblance of normality to the city. Nevertheless, people still felt themselves unsafe in the city. While the number of crimes were reduced, situation was not been brought under control.

According to one survey, published in February 1999, 35% of the people of Karachi suffer from mental stresses, stemming from the state of uncertainty and frustration prevailing in the city.[83] A good number of citizens of all agers of the city, linguistic groups and classes, have turned into drug addicts. It is estimated that there are five million drug addicts in Pakistan and one-third of this number live in Karachi.[84]Another survey conducted by GA Asghar Institute of Psychiatry and Behavioural Sciences, shows that Karachi has the highest suicide rate for metropolitan cities of Pakistan.[85]The well known journal *Herald* examining suicides in the major cities of Pakistan, reported the rates as follows: Karachi: 27.82%; Lahore: 18.95%. Rawalpindi-Islamabad: 6.78%. Suicides were not confined to any particular class or an ethnic group[86] but was common to all. This prevalent phenomenon of uncertainty of life and property, has shaken faith of people in the state and a deep state society cleavage has developed in the city. Analysts suggest the separation of Karachi from Sindh and making it a new province or making it a federal area as an answer to these problems. But it is doubtful whether this would be viable or bring normality to the city[87]. The more this state society cleavage widens in Karachi, the more it will affect the stability of Pakistan itself.

(*b*) *Economic Implications*

As much as half of the wealth in Pakistan is produced in Karachi and its surroundings. The strike calls given by the political parties in general and MQM in particular, paralyze the economy of the country. Each strike call costs Pakistan dearly in economic terms. A Punjabi industrialist based in Karachi estimates the loss at Rs five billion.[88] Quoting S.F. Muneer, former President of Pakistani Federation of Commerce and Industry, the renowned economic analyst, Farhan Bukhari, estimated in early nineties about one-third of 10,000 small and big industrial units of Karachi had been shut down, largely because of the violent situation of Karachi.[89] The situation improved slightly after the imposition of the Governor's rule in Sindh. Even then, there was a partial shut down in the city despite a heavy deployment of the Rangers, after the alleged extra-judicial killing of a pro-MQM activist by the police.[90] Yusuf Haroon, a former governor of the Sindh province felt that the terrorists were buying time and they would restart war activities at any time, despite prolongation of the governor's rule.[91] These views were also shared by the Citizen Police Liaison Committee chief Jameel Yusuf.[92] Because of killings, extortion, and frequent strikes, burgeoning Punjabi industrialist class shifted its units from Karachi and Nooriabad industrial areas to the Central Punjab. The murder of four employees of an American multinational, allegedly by MQM activists in 1995, discouraged new foreign investment in Karachi. Disinvestment and lack of vibrant commercial activity have created more unemployment in the city.

Sindh province on the whole produces about 75% of the wealth of Pakistan. Because of lawlessness in provincial capital Karachi, Sindh government spends increasing amounts of money every year on the maintenance of law and order in the city. Thus, Choudhry Shujaat Hussain, then interior minister of Pakistan, discussing the Karachi situation in then National Assembly, stated that for an eight year period, 1990-98 no less than, 21,719 Rangers were deployed in the city at a cost of Rs. 7 billion[93]. Because of this huge amount spent on law and order, and the ransom of Rs. 100 million,[94] paid by the Muslim League to MQM, Sindh Government is facing a deficit of over Rs 8 billion[95], a deficit which is not being met by the Central Government. Development work in Sindh province virtually came to a standstill. Sindh was thus reduced to a state of bankruptcy.

Pakistan as a state, faces a huge deficit in payment of its internal as well as external loans. According to the Secretary of Commerce, Ishtiaq Hassan Khan, Pakistan's external debt exceeded US $ 15.4 billion.[96] One reason for this huge deficit, according to Akber Zaidi, a leading economist, was the decline of its exports in the 1990s, due to strikes and the shut down in Karachi.[97] Each strike costs Pakistan the loss of about Rs. 5 billion (about US $ 1 billion).[98] Pakistan's difficulties were compounded by the decision of Nawaz Sharif government going nuclear in May 1998, which resulted in the imposition of economic sanctions by the US. Ironically, MQM, the then political ally of Nawaz Sharif's Muslim League, supported his decision, little realizing its economic cost and the impact on Karachi itself. The country has became an economically defaulter state. Lending agencies, such as World Bank and International Monetary Fund (IMF) are reluctant even to ease it out. Volatile situation in Karachi plays a key role on Pakistan's economic instability and the reduction of the country to the level of a failed state,[99] whose existence is tolerated for fear of avoiding any wider convulsion.

Policy Initiatives for Containing the Situation

Criminalization of politics in Karachi has a devastating effect on the governance and development of the city, the province and on the image of the country as a whole. If it is not contained, it could lead to the collapse of the state. In order to avoid that eventuality, a number of interconnected, administrative economic and political initiatives are required. Some of them are as follows:

(a) The Creation of More Jobs in the Upcountry

Karachi, as the principal commercial and industrial hub of the country, attracts many migrant workers from the upcountry. In case of non-availability of jobs, they resort to crime. Because of this state of affairs, many industrial units have shifted to the upcountry. There is a need of having more industrial units in the upcountry. There will be two benefits of this policy — it will provide jobs to the local people there, while jobs in Karachi would be left to the people of Karachi and areas adjacent to it. Secondly, more jobs will be created in the upcountry, especially in Pothohar (Rawalpindi), Kohat, Mardan and other traditional places of military recruitment. It would also make recruitment in the armed forces a less attractive. Sindhi and Baloch youth have no marked interest in joining the defence forces and it is unlikely that they would replace the Punjabi or Pashtun recruits. One other point in this regard is that, creation of more jobs in the upcountry will be beneficial for granting provincial autonomy to smaller provinces in the long term.

(b) *Registration of Aliens*

Illegal immigrants from a host of countries, make up a sizeable portion of population of the city. Their number may exceed two million.[100] Immigrants from India, and Bangladesh (both Biharis and Bangladeshis) compete with locals for jobs. They themselves face hardships, including blackmail and are forced to become the cannon fodder of the MQM or pay extortion money to the police.[101] At the instance of Ministry of Interior and CPLC, the Central Government formed the Alien Registration Authority (ARA) for registration of aliens. But it is not fully functional, because of the lack of co-operation of local politicians who use illegal immigrants as their bogus voters or cheap labourers. If the aliens were registered effectively, not only would drug and arms smuggling and other sorts of crimes, be controlled, it would improve the job prospects to local Sindhis and Balochs.

(c) *Revamping of the Police Force*

The maintenance of law and order by a competent and honest police force is the main hallmark of good governance.

Total strength of the police force is 37,167 in 96 police stations (*Thannas*).[102] They have to deal with crime in Karachi, a city of about 14 million. The policemen, mostly from the upcountry and the interior of Sindh, posted in Karachi, do not have adequate residential quarters. An individual policeman gets a salary of less than Rs. 6,000 per month and works eight hours a day in a very dangerous and tense situation. A Station House Officer (SHO) gets a salary of Rs. 12,000. In comparison, a sector-in-charge of MQM, who collects *bhatta,* (extortion money) gets the regular salary of Rs. 6,000 plus 10% of the *bhatta* from his organization. In case of being murdered in a police encounter, the family of a sector-in-charge is fully compensated by the MQM and its ally of the time. The activists of the other political parties do the same in their areas of influence. If a policeman dies he receives the compensation of just Rs 10,000: Half of this amount is spent on his funeral and transfer his body to his ancestral home, either in the upcountry or in the interior of Sindh.[103] Naturally, either the police force is demoralized or it resorts to *bhatta* collection. In both cases, it cannot cope with crime in the city. Thus there is a need of providing good accommodation to the policemen and giving them a special allowance for serving in Karachi. There is also a need for providing more vehicles and sophisticated weapons for combating crime, especially terrorism.

Police officers in Karachi are appointed on a political basis, which makes them less professional, and more politicized. They either work for the party that brings them to the city or protect the criminals of a particular ethnic background to which they themselves belong to. In 1990, Arfan Murwat, the son-in-law of the then President of Pakistan, Ghulam Ishaq Khan was appointed Deputy-Inspector General of Police of Karachi. Arfan Murwat allegedly brought all sorts of criminals from the NWFP and inducted them into the police service. The result was a higher rate of robberies and car theft/snatching during the time he held office. In 1992-93, on the recommendation of the MQM, Jam Sadiq Ali, then Chief Minister of Sindh, appointed Aftab Nabi Khan as DIG of Karachi. The soft-spoken Aftab Nabi Khan, allegedly maintained links with MQM. In 1993-96, the PPP government inducted Shoaib Suddle and Wajid Durrani, into the Karachi Police as DIG and Senior Superintendent of Police (SSP) South, respectively. Both these officers maintained a close relationship with Asif Ali Zardari, the spouse of Benazir Bhutto.[104] The three of them were implicated in the murder of Mir Murtaza Bhutto, the estranged brother of Benazir Bhutto. In 1997, once again on the recommendation of MQM, Aftab Nabi Khan, whose elder brother, Islam Nabi Khan, a Federal Minister in the cabinet of Nawaz Sharif, was promoted and appointed Inspector General of Sindh. He reportedly leaked sensitive information to the MQM.102 During his tenure of office, top enemies of MQM-A, such as Shahid Hameed and Hakim Saeed, were killed. In his second term of office, Mian Nawaz Sharif gave the command of civil and polices authority to Punjabis by appointing a close associate, Maqbool Rana as Inspector General Police of the province. After the removal of Nawaz Sharif, Aftab Nabi was back in the saddle. There was tranquility in the city conceivably, because MQM apparently has a secret understanding with the government. Thus there is a need of appointing apolitical police officers to beat the crime.

Police force of Karachi is mainly composed of non-locals, people from the upcountry. These *policewallas* (policeman) are accused of making money in the city by patronizing the criminals of their own ethnic background. There is a need of a local police force raised from the youth belonging to the city, its surrounding areas and the Sindh province. In comparison to the policemen from the upcountry, these local policemen are more likely to receive the co-operation of the local population than outsiders, which will be helpful in beating crime in the city. A visiting team of Colombian experts who were invited to Pakistan, under the sponsorship of the United Nations Development Programme (UNDP) has made a similar recommendation on urban terrorism.[105]

Citizen Police Liaison Committee, an independent organization, is doing a good job in registering and combating crime in the city. It has recommended the formation of the Metropolitan Police on the model of the Tokyo police, a non-political body, headed by a Police Commissioner with magisterial power. The idea appears to be fine on paper but might not be workable on two ground realities: first, Tokyo has one of the highest literacy rates among the metropolitan cities of the world, while the situation in Karachi is the reverse of this. Secondly and more pressingly, Tokyo is an ethnically homogeneous city, whereas Karachi is an ethnically heterogeneous city. In the case of Karachi, there is a close connection between ethnicity, politics, and crime, while there is no such thing in Japan. The creation of a special police force for Karachi separated from the Sindh police, is treated with suspicion by native Sindhis who see it as a stepping stone towards the separation of Karachi from the rest of Sindh. Thus, the Tokyo model may not work here. Recommendation of the CPLC about revamping of the police, especially modernising it, could be implemented without creating a separate police force for Karachi.

(*d*) De*weaponization of the City*

Since the beginning of turmoil in Afghanistan in late 1970s, the city of Karachi has been awash with weapons of all kinds and politicians were quick to exploit this. Jam Sadiq Ali himself issued 20,000 licenses to MQM activists. The number of illegal arms is now much higher. According to the former Interior Minister, Choudhry Shujaat Hussain, 600 illegal weapons were discovered from 28 October to 30 November 1998.[106] This was just the tip of the iceberg. It is estimated that there are about 80,000 illegal weapons of all kinds, available to criminals and terrorists in the city, which enables them to outgun the police in their activities. There is an urgent need of making Karachi a weapon free city. First of all, licensed arms should be temporarily surrendered to the police, who should make a careful scrutiny of the character of their owners. License of the people with dubious character could be cancelled. Secondly, rigorous efforts, including a house to house search in the most volatile parts of the city such as Karachi centre and east should be made to seize illegal arms. Nobody should be allowed to display weapons in public or bring weapons, legal or illegal, to the city. Law enforcing authorities should carry arms for the purpose of protection of citizens.

(e) *Keeping Karachi a Sindhi City*

It has been observed that two contradictory trends have played a significant role in criminalisation of politics in Karachi. One is the attempt of most of Urdu speakers, mainly those who subscribe to the idea of a distinct nationality, to separate Karachi from the rest of Sindh. Second is the attempt of successive rulers of Islamabad, to make Karachi a federal enclave and rule it by remote control? The first category of persons needs to realise that Karachi is physically a part of Sindh, depending even on the supply of water from the river Indus. Its gas and petrols extracted from Sindh.

The second category of persons has to realize that neither Sindhis nor the Urdu speakers will allow Islamabad to make Karachi a federal enclave, for different reasons. As a creation of the MQM demonstrates patronizing non-Sindhis will result in creation of militant organizations with separatist aspirations. Thus, for both Urdu speakers and the people of the upcountry, the Sindhis act as a balancing factor. Sindhis checkmate both extremes of the spectrum ranging from over-centralization to the secessionist. This Sindhi pivotal position should be recognized by all ethnic groups interested in the maintenance of peace and tranquility in Karachi. It is a good omen for the ethnic balance of the city that many Sindhis are settling in Karachi in a significant number. Sindhi cap which was anathema in Karachi, is remarkably visible in Karachi and the Sindhi cultural days and political functions are organized in Karachi. All these events are indicators of Sindhi presence in Sindh. More the Sindhis are settled in Karachi, more ethnic balance will be maintained, resultantly more criminalization will be curbed

(f) The External Factor: The alleged Indian Involvement

The external factor in the Karachi problems is treated as the final section of this article. While it is clearly not as important as the issues dealt with earlier, it is by no means a minor factor. Indeed, there was a glimmer of hope of an accord in February 1999 during the Lahore Summit, when the Prime Ministers of Pakistan and India, Nawaz Sharif and Atal Bihari Vajpayee, reportedly reached an understanding about resolving the Kashmir dispute. As a part of this deal, according to Prime Minister Vajpayee, Pakistan promised to stop its support to the Kashmiri militants.[107] Unfortunately, Lahore peace process was derailed by the army high command of Pakistan by sending infiltrators to Kargil area in Kashmir in May of the same year. Kargil crisis almost led to a war between India and Pakistan two months later. After international pressure, Pakistan was forced to withdraw its regulars from other side of the line of control. The plot of 2007 Mumbai bomb blasts was reportedly hatched in Karachi by ISI and its auxiliary religious organization, Lashjkar-e-Tayeba. MQM-A, has been declared as a terrorist organization by the Canadian Immigration Tribunal, equivalent to High Court.

Terrorism and counter-terrorism, posed by MQM and its opponents, not to mention the fundamentalists as well as ordinary criminals and the secret services, could be reduced significantly if Pakistan reorients its foreign policy towards the east. The resulting peace dividend of India could help Pakistan divert its resources from defence to development.

At present Pakistan rated as the 138th poorest country on the International Development Index,[108] spends 24.75% of its budget on defence.[109] If only half of its defence expenditure is diverted to development, it will give a huge boost to the economy, which will inevitably help reinvigoration of the industry in Karachi. If more jobs were created in Karachi for the people of Karachi and its surroundings, it is likely that rate of crime in the city would be reduced very substantially and collaterally the criminalisation of its politics.

Karachi has earned notoriety for politically motivated target killing too. In 2002, South Asia bureau chief of the *Wall Street Journal,* Daniel Pearl was killed by Maulana Masood Azhar and his disciple, Omer Seed Sheikh of the Jiash terrorist organization,[110] which subsequently assumed the title of Lashka-i-Tayeba. The Shia scholar, Hassan Turabi was killed in 2006 by Wahabi sectarian organization, Sipahi Sahaba. In May 2007, MQM allegedly killed more than 50 persons who were on their way to receive the then deposed chief justice of Pakistan, Iftikhar Choudhry. One week before this incident, many advocates were killed in an arson attack unleashed by MQM. Even now, political killings, land grabbing and extortion collection continue, with full knowledge of the state apparatus. The city can be called "City on Fire". Only an honest, and strong government, enjoying confidence of all citizens of Sindh in general and its capital, Karachi, in particular, can tender this fire. And this appears to be a farfetched scenario.

References and Notes

1. "Hit List: Karachi The City of Death," special map in *Herald,* monthly Karachi, Annual issue of 1995 and Jameel Yusuf, the

Chief of Citizen Police Liaison Committee (CPLC), Karachi, in an interview with the author, on 10 February, 1999.

2. *Ibid.*

3. Mehtab Ali Shah : The Emergence of Muhajir Quomi Movement (MQM) and its Implications for Regional Security, *The Round Table*, (Oxfordshire: Carfax Publishers, 1998) pp 512-514.

4. Shahida Wizarat : Karachi: An Economic Perspective, Hamida Khuhro and Anwer Mooraj (eds.), *Karachi: Megacity of Our Times*, (Karachi, Oxford University Press, 1997), pp. 154-169.

5. *Ibid.*

6. Yusuf Haroon, in an interview with this author, in Karachi, on 16 February, 1999.

7. *Ibid.*

8. Ghazanfar Hussain Hidayatullah, in an interview with this author, in Karachi, on 21 September 1998.

9. BB's Murder: Text of UN Commission's Report, *Dawn*, 18 April 2010.

10. H. Khuhro : The Capital of Pakistan in Khuhro and Mooraj, *op.cit.*, pp. 100-102.

11. Mahbubul Haq and Khadija Haq, *Human Development in South Asia, 1998*, Karachi, Oxford University Press, 1998, p. 16.

12. Syed Ali Dayan Hassan : City of Life: A Special Report on Karachi, *Herald*, September 2000, p. 80.

13. Khuhro, *op.cit.*, pp. 100-102.

14. A Zaidi, in *ibid.*, p. 385

15. *Ibrat,* daily, Sindhi, (Hyderabad), 14 April, 1997.

16. ASB Jafri, "Crime: Karachi's Fastest Growing Industry," *Dawn*, Sunday Magazine, 13 December, 1998, pp. 1-20.

17. Reported in *Awami Awaz,* daily, Sindhi, Karachi, 10 February, 1999.

18. Ibid.

19. Sabihuddin Ghousi : The Aliens Registration Plan Shelved, *Dawn,* 5 March 1999. In addition, Yusuf, *op. cit.*

20. *Dawn,* 20 January, 2001.

21. *Dawn,* 27 January, 1995.

22. *Hila e Pakistan,* daily, Sindhi, (Karachi), 7 July, 1997.

23. Brigadier AR Siddique, *Pachas Sal Ka Safar,* Urdu, (A Journey of Fifty Years), (Lahore: Enterprising Publishers, 1998), pp. 55-6, 93-6.

24. Ghaznfar Hussain Hidyatullah, *op.cit.*

25. Jammel Yusuf : Stolen Car at Khuzdar, letter to the Editor, *Dawn,* 24 March, 1999.

26. 24.*Dawn,* 3 March, 1999.

27. Jafri, *op.cit.*

28. *Dawn,* 4 March 1999.

29. An interview with late Syed Ghulam Mustafa Shah, then editor of *Sindh Quarterly* and an octogenarian Sindhi intellectual, Karachi, 9 February, 1999.

30. Compiled from *Dawn,* 6 February, 1997.

31. *Ibid.*

32. Oskar Verkaik, *A People of Migrants: Ethnicity, State and Religion in Karachi,* Amsterdam, VU Press, 1994, pp. 39-40 and Siddique, *op.cit.*

33. Taking a u-turn Altaf Hussain, leader of MQM has apologised to Sindhis and offered a hand of friendship to them for launching the basic document a joint struggle for the maximum provincial autonomy to the federating units, promised to them under the Pakistan Resolution of 1940, which led to formation of the country by federating units. *Dawn,* 14 January, 2001.

34. Mehtab Ali Shah, "The Ethnic Tension of Sindh and its Solution," *Contemporary South Asia,* Vol. 6, No. 3, 1997, Oxford, Carfax Publishers, 1997, pp. 263-264.

35. Hamayoon Gowher, Karachi Province?, *Political and Business Weekly,* 25 July 1995, pp. 29-30 and "Altaf Demands More Provinces in Pakistan," *Dawn,* 4 May, 1998.

36. Late Ashtique Azher, once number two in MQM hierarchy and then a dissident, disclosed this information in an interview with the *Herald,* November-December 1998, p. 45.

37. A Special Report on MQM in *Umat,* daily, Urdu, (Karachi), 27 July, 1998. *Takbir,* weekly, Urdu, (Karachi) 24 December 1998, pp. 12-23.

38. *Ibid.*

39. *Ibid.*

40. *Ibid.*

41. Idrees Bakhtiar : The Return of the Death Squads, *Herald,* July 1997, p. 27.

42. Compiled from various issues of *Newsline,* monthly (Karachi).

43. Azhar Abbas : Where Do We Go From Here? *Herald,* November 1997, pp. 23-29.

44. Sindh Government Home Department Report, released through the CPLC, 1995.

45. Statement of Choudhry Shujat Hussain, then Interior Minister of Pakistan, *Dawn,* 5 January, 1999.

46. Various Reports of the Home Department of Sindh Government.

47. Idress Bakhtiar : Shock After Shock, *Herald,* August 1998, pp. 47-49.

48. Choudhry Shujat Hussain, *op.cit.*

49. Nisar Khuhro, the Provincial chief of the Pakistan Peoples Party, *Ibrat,* 5 December, 1998.

50. Salim Asim : Sindh: Nothing Happened, *Dawn Review: 1997,* 1 January 1998, pp. 16-18.

51. Idrees Bakhtiar, *op.cit*

52. *Ibid.*

53. *Ibid.*

54. *Ibid.*

55. Jameel Yusuf of the CPLC and the statement of the then Governor Moinddin Hyder, *Dawn,* 11 February, 1999.

56. *Ibid.*

57. Hassan Mansoor : Conflict of Interests, *Herald,* September 1998, pp. 112-115.

58. Ishtiaq Azhar, *op.cit.*

59. This information was given to me by a resident of the area requesting anonymity because of possible threats to his job and life.

60. Shiraz Sidhva : Blood and Money, *Far Eastern Economic Review (Hong Kong)*, 4 March 1999, pp. 36-39.

61. Ishtiaq Azhar, *op.cit.*

62. This sort of petty bribe all over South Asia is called "Chai Pani", palm greasing. This explanation was given by a police officer sitting in the office of DIG Police (establishment division), Rahoo Khan Brohi, on 9 September, 1998.

63. Jameel Yusuf, *op.cit.*

64. Jameel Yusuf : The Fragile Peace, *Herald*, September 2000, pp. 102-103.

65. Mohammed Hanif : Terror in the Streets, *Newsline*, November 1990, p. 83.

66. Hassan Mujtaba : Corruptocracy, *Newsline*, May 1997, pp. 55-56.

67. *Ibid.*

68. Samina Chonars : Sitting Targets, *Herald*, February 1994, p. 34.

69. Arif Hassan : The Growth of Metropolis in H Khuhro and A Mooraj (eds.), *op. cit.*, p. 173.

70. *Kawish*, Sindhi, 17 March 1999, and also *Riasat*, Urdu, Karachi, of the same date.

71. *Awami Awaz*, 19 February, 1999.

72. *Dawn,* 17 March, 1999.

73. Mansoor Khan : Karachi: The Fire Within, *Herald,* February, 30-35.2010.

74. Staff Reporter : Alleged Land Grabbers Injure Three, *Daily Times : Karachi*, 30 April 2010.

75. *Financial Times,* (London) 13 November, 1991.

76. M H Askari : The MBL Scam, *Dawn,* 27 April, 1994.

77. Zaffar Abbas : The Mother of All Scandals," *Herald,* October 1997, p. 33.

78. Zaffar Abbas : The Swiss Connections, *Ibid* pp. 33. President Zardari is still accused of money laundering in the Swiss banks, but till he holds his official position, he enjoys immunity from the prosecution.

79. *Ibid*. pp. 33-45.

80. 79. *Dawn,* 26 February, 1999.

81. *Dawn,* 28 February, 1999.

82. http// en. Wikipedia. org./wiki /corruption-perception. Index, lat accessed 3rd May 2919.

83. *Dawn,* 19 February, 1999.

84. Sharmeen Obaid : The New Drug Culture, *The Dawn Review,* 4 February 1999, pp. 4-10 and *Dawn,* 28 February, 1999.

85. *Dawn,* 19 February, 1999.

86. Zigham A Khan and Naveed Zaffar : Life After Life, *Herald,* March 1999, p. 70.

87. An interview with late Dr. Zaki Hassan, a prominent psychiatrist of Karachi, on 6 March, 1999.

88. An interview at the office of the Pakistan Federation of Commerce and Industry, at Karachi on 6 March, 1999.

89. Farhan Bukhari : The Ripple Effect, *Herald,* August 1992, pp.12-14.

90. *Dawn,* 10 March, 1999.

91. Haroon, *op. cit.*

92. Yusuf, *op. cit.*.

93. *Dawn*, 5 January, 1999.

94. *Ibid.*

95. *Awami Awaz,* daily, Sindhi, Karachi, 14 March, 1999.

96. *Dawn,* 16 January, 2001.

97. S Akber Zaidi : Heart of the Matter, *Herald,* January 1999, pp. 138-139.

98. Mansha, *op. cit.*

99. Paul Kennedy : The Pivotal States and the US Strategy, *Foreign Affairs,* Vol. 75, No. 1, 1996, pp. 33-51.

100. *Dawn,* 10 March, 1999.

101. This information was given by a policeman of the interior of Sindh, who was posted in Karachi Central, the hotbed of MQM activists.

102. Jammel Yusuf, *op.cit.*

103. A Policeman, *op.cit.*

104. These alleged killers of Mir Murtaza, the brother of late Benazir Bhutto have higher positions in the federal government of President Asif Zardari.

105. Azhar Abbas : The Columbian Connections, *Herald,* November-December 1998, p, 45.

106. Shujat Hussain, *op.cit.*

107. "Pact will End Proxy War in the Valley," Vajpayee, *Dawn,* 11 March,

108. Human Development Index, http://hdrstats.undp.org/en/countries/country_fact_sheets/cty_fs_PAK.html ,last accessed 5th May 2010.

109. *Window on South Asia:* The Newsletter of Regional Centre for Strategic Studies, Colombo, Vol. 5, No. 1, January 2010.

110. Wilson John, *Karachi: Terror Capital in Making,* (New Delhi: Rupa & C, 2003) p. 44.

(This paper, entitled, "Criminalization of Politics : Karachi : A Case Study", was published in *Ethnic Studies, Report,* (Kandy : Sri Lanka, 2001) Vol. XIX, No : 1, 2001. This is its updated version)

6

Anti-Sindhi Policies of General Zia-ul-Haq

The Zia rule (1977-88) is considered as the bleakest period in the post-partition history of Sindh. Zulfiquar Ali Bhutto, the then genuinely elected Prime Minister of Pakistan (1972-1977) was ethnically a Sindhi. His hanging in 1979 by Zia evoked a strong reaction against Punjabi army dominated federal government. In 1983 Movement for Restoration of Democracy (MRD) was launched, which momentum mainly in Sindh. It was crushed as an "enemy inspired insurgency". Later on Pakistani establishment persistently attempted to divide Sindh on ethnic, clannish and sectarian lines. Although Zia is dead, the legacy of his regime still continues in one way or the other. Developments, which took place during his rein and their long-term implications on Sindh, are still felt. It dwells upon the measures, which can be helpful in launching the process of de Ziafication by the new Pakistani government and civil society.

Sindh, the southern province of Pakistan is one of its borderlands.[1] The Arabian Sea is to its South and the Indian states of Rajasthan and Gujarat to its east and south-east. The same ethnic groups straddle its land and maritime borders, which are the borderers of Pakistan as well. This geostrategic position gives it the *locus standi* in the Indian Ocean trade routes and South Asian politics. Historically speaking, there are four principal landmarks in the history and political processes of post-Partition Sindh. First, the creation of Pakistan in 1947, followed by huge transfer of population that marked huge loss of ownership of the ancestral homeland to the Sindhis.[2] Second, the amalgamating of four provinces of Pakistan in one administrative unit called, the One Unit in 1955, which subjugated Sindh to the numerically superior Punjab.

Third, separation of former East Pakistan and creation of Bangladesh in 1971, establishment of numerical superiority of Punjab in remaining Pakistan, rise of Zulfiquar Ali Bhutto as the prime minister of Pakistan in 1972, his overthrow and subsequent hanging. Fourth, Zia era (1977-88) whose legacy, arguably still continues and that is the principal subject matter of Zia's ascent to power, his policies towards Sindh and their repercussions on it are highlightened here after.

Sindh before Zia

After creation of Pakistan and formation of one-unit in 1955, there was a deep sense of alienation among the Sindhis, who felt being completely marginalised in Pakistani state apparatus, dominated by the civil-military bureaucracy, principally hailing from Punjab and India. In 1970 elections, Sheikh Mujeebu-ur Rahman, leader of the Awami League in Art Pakistan,won with landslide victory. He was supposed to be the next Prime Minister of Pakistan. From West Pakistan, Zulfiquar Ali Bhutto's Pakistan Peoples Party (PPP) won the highest number of seats in the National as well as Sindh and

Punjab Provincial assemblies. Instead of being the leader of opposition in a united Pakistan, Bhutto conceivably, wanted to be the prime minister of the remaining Pakistan.

After separation of East Pakistan in 1971, Bhutto first became the civilian-martial-law administrator and then prime minister of the remaining country. Although Bhutto was educated at Berkley and Oxford, he spoke Sindhi with a peasant's diction. Thus, he was very popular among all sorts of Sindhis, especially the poor. It can be said about most of the Punjabis. He gave a new constitution to the country in which, the civil rights were protected and provincial autonomy was promised though it was less in quantum than promised in the 1940 Lahore Resolution.[3] Karachi, separated from the hinterland Sindh in 1948, once again became the capital of Sindh.[4] Being the provincial capital and the only port city, many Sindhis from the interior of Sindh, started resettling in Karachi. Thus, Sindhis once again became markedly visible in Karachi, especially in offices.

Pakistan's military dictator, Ayub Khan (1958-69) shifted the capital of Pakistan from Karachi to Islamabad in 1960. From 1960 to 1972, there were hardly any Sindhis in Islamabad. Bhutto's rule attracted many job seeking Sindhis to the capital. Some of those Sindhis, who were already in the bureaucracy, were promoted to the rank of joint secretaries in the federal secretariat. One of Bhutto's lieutenants, Barrister Abdul Hafeez Pirzada, first became the law minister and then finance minister of Pakistan. Bhutto's cousin Mumtaz Ali Bhutto, became federal minister of communications and shipping. He gave jobs to the Sindhis in railways and Karachi Port Authority (KPA). Thus, Sindhis who were previously the rare species, became quite visible in Islamabad, which gave them a sense of participation in political processes of Pakistan though only token.

Before Zulfiquar Ali Bhutto's rule, Sindhi felt colonized by the Punjabis and migrants. But after his advent to power, this feeling markedly changed. Sindhis developed a sense of participation in the state apparatus and perceived to be the citizens of Pakistani state. The veteran Pakhtun leader, late Khan Abdul Wali Khan, leader of the National Awami Party (NAP) angrily dubbed him as "Raja Dahar", the 8th century AD Brahmin ruler of Sindh whose domain stretched from Kashmir in the north to Kutch in South and Balochistan to the west. In other words, the present day Pakistan, whose cultural roots are in the Indus Valley Civilization, after Raja Dahar, became domain of Bhutto and the Sindhis prided over it.

Balochistan is next-door neighbour of Sindh. There are intermarriages between Sindhis and Balochs.[5] Many Baloch leaders such as late Mir Ghous Bux Khan Bizenjo, Sardar Attaullah Khan Mengal and Nawab Akber Khan Bugti, who was murdered under the instructions of General Musharraf in 2006, were educated in Karachi. In Karachi, there are strong old Baloch localities in Lyari and several other goths (villages). Sindhi is understood and spoken by almost all Balochs. Sindh and Balochistan have cordial relations.

In 1948, Balochistan was annexed to Pakistan by military action. Since the resources of Balochistan are allegedly not in the possession of Balochs, there had always been autonomist even separatist movement in Balochistan. In 1973, the trouble started in Balochistan between the Punjabi settlers and the Baloch tribesmen. Bhutto's central government dissolved the provincial government of Balochistan. In protest, the NAP government resigned in NWFP. On the advice of then army chief, General Zia Haq, Bhutto took military action in Balochistan.[6] Since Bhutto was a Sindhi, his military action in Balochistan psychologically hurt Balochs. Since then traditional Sindhi-Baloch political amity still appears to be in the doldrums.

In 1977, elections were rigged by the PPP *Jiyallas* (activists). A political non-entity, Jan Mohmmed Abbassi, of Jamait-i-Islami, (JI), Larkana, who wanted to contest elections against Bhutto, was kidnapped by *Jiyallas*. Such an incident provided the JI with oxygen of propaganda against Bhutto. Muhajir Punjab-Pashtun Ithad (alliance) of Nawab Muzafar and Nawab Yamin Khan of Hyderabad, joined the JI. Bhutto, was facing a nationwide agitation launched by the 9-party Alliance. After many rounds of talks, 9-Party alliance and PPP government reached an understanding for holding new elections. But at the midnight of 9th July 1977, General Zia promulgated martial law in the country. He arrested Bhutto and after a prolonged trial with casting vote of the chief justice Anwar-ul-Haq, of supreme court of Pakistan, who also hailed from Zia's home district, Jallandher, Zulfiquar Ali Bhutto was hanged on 4th April 1979. According to Justice Dorab Patel, a leading jurist, such a hanging was the "judicial murder in 1979".[7] One of the convicting judges, Justice Naseem Hassan Shah, made a confession on television that four Punjabi judges including himself acquiesced to Zia ul Haq for hanging Bhutto, whereas the three non-Punjabi judges acquitted him.[8]

Sindh During Zia

Bhutto's hanging was a shock to Sindhis. After it, those Sindhis from the interior who used to go to Islamabad in the search of jobs were reluctant to do so. It was widely regarded by them as "the city of conspiracy and death". Zia was considered as the enemy of Sindh and Sindhis. At that time, two sons of Bhutto - Murtaza and Shahnawaz-were in England. His widow mother, Nusrat and eldest daughter Benazir, were put under house arrest and even in jail for sometime. Unfortunately, they are dead now. Once again a deep sense of alienation gripped the Sindhis. This grief and calm were misperceived by the intelligence agencies as the acceptance of the martial law by Sindhis.

Meetings with Pseudo Sindhi Intellectuals

To gauge the mood of the Sindhis, immediately after hanging Bhutto, Zia convened the meeting of the Pakistan Writers Guild, an official body of Pakistani writers, poets and intellectuals. All the Sindhi invitees, except the two- late Professor Zaffar Hassan, a political geographer at Sindh University and Ali Baba, a story-writer-participated in it.[9] This huge participation of "Sindhi intellectuals" made Zia to propagate that the Sindhis have forgotten Bhutto's murder and they were happy with his martial law. It is noteworthy that despite the passage of three decades, many of the Sindhi participants of this convention, still hold important positions in the governmental and semi-governmental institutions. Former director of Institute of Sindhology, in Sindh University, was one of them.

Promoting Extremism, Madrasahs Drug and Crime Culture

Zulfiquar Ali Bhutto was hanged despite clemency appeals from all over the world. As a reaction to the indifference to these appeals, economic sanctions were imposed on Pakistan by the West. But the former Soviet Unions' invasion of Afghanistan in December 1979, made Pakistan "the front line state". Aid to Mujahideens, (holy warriors), the forerunners of Taliban, was funneled into Afghanistan through Pakistan. The West condoned Zia's martial law. President Ronald Reagan granted $3.2 billion dollar as an aid. The Arab states and China followed suit. Thus, the Soviet invasion of Afghanistan turned Zia's fortunes. Now he was a "statesman" in the western capitals.

Being the son of a Maulvi (preacher), Zia had strong leanings towards religious bigotry that made him a blue-eyed boy of the Gulf and Saudi rulers, who adhere to the obscurantist Wahabi brand of Islam. Since he wanted to send recruits to Afghanistan and extract money from the oil-rich Arabs, Zia launched the programme of Islamization of society. It was rejected in the country as whole. Sindh has special aversion to Islamization process for two reasons. Firstly, the Sindhis by nature are secular in their religious outlook whereas Zia promoted the Wahabi Islam. Secondly, about twenty per cent Sindhi belong to Shia sect[10], which has severe anathema towards Wahabism. Thus, besides resentment over Bhutto's hanging, being adherents of the liberal Sufi Islam, Sindhis became visibly upset about the process of Islamization in the country more than any other ethic groups in Pakistan. Zia's cultivation of military, political and economic linkages with the West and its allies, made him confident about tackling the Sindhis or anybody else at home.

The reactivation of political-military linkages with the United States emboldened him to start his clandestine nuclear programme and also supported the Kashmiris and Sikh insurgencies in India in the 1980s.[11] Since he was from East Punjab, he knew well how to exploit Sikh religious sentiments and implicitly supported the Sikh insurgency in the Indian Punjab aimed at creating a Sikh religious state, Khalistan, another land of the pure[12]. By doing so, Zia wanted to settle old scores with India for intervention in East Pakistan in 1971, which led to the creation of Bangladesh.

As a result of so-called Arab-American patronized Jihad in Afghanistan, about 3.6 million Afghan refugees settled in Pakistan.[13] Since Karachi is the port city and a transit point to travel aboard, at least half a million of them settled in Karachi.[14] Suhrab Goth, an area originally owned by Jokhio Sindhi tribe in Karachi, became an Afghan township. Many of these Afghan refugees started transport business in Karachi and interior of Sindh. Some of these transporters bought Russian, American and Israeli weapons from the Afghan Mujahidden living in refugee camps in Balochistan or NWFP or from Darra Adam Khel, the Federally Administered Tribal Territory (FATA), where local arms are manufactured. Afghan transporters sold these smuggled weapons to the terrorists in Karachi and Hyderabad. Suhrab Goth became the Dane of drug dealers and human traffickers to the Middle East. Thus, the Pashtuns became a factor in politics of Sindh.

Afghan drug and arms dealers sold weapons also to outlaws in the interior of Sindh. According to one theory, due to glut of weapons in the rural Sindh, the petty criminals were helped by the intelligence agencies in becoming bandits and kidnappers just to keep the Sindhis worried about their daily life, instead of thinking about their political problems.[15] From 1983 to 1985, there were at least three jailbreaks, which conceivably took place with the connivance of the jail staff in Dadu, Qambar and Sukkur.

Drugs, arms and Wahabi Madrasahs patronized by Gulf States, especially Saudi Arabia and Zia government were the gifts of Zia regime to Pakistan that markedly changed the political culture of Sindh more than the other provinces of Pakistan. And as a reaction to this phenomenon, Sindh was simmering with dislike for Zia regime and waiting to vent its anger.

Crushing of the Movement for Restoration of Democracy (MRD)

The Movement for Restoration of Democracy (MRD) was formed by a seven-party alliance in 1982. The PPP was its major component. Its activity was confined to issuing press releases on different occasions. On 14th August 1983, MRD leaders especially, Ghulam Mustafa Jatoi, of PPP, Rasool Bakhsh Palejo, Maoist leader of Sindhi Awmai Tahrik (Peoples Movement), gave a call for launching a movement for the restoration of democracy and release of detained political leaders.[16] Demonstrations and strikes were launched throughout the country. However, they took a serious turn in Sindh.

As stated earlier, Sindh was simmering with the anti-Zia and anti-marital law feelings; MRD call fanned the flames. Urdu speaking population distanced itself from demonstrations. But Sindhis hailing from villages and towns came on the streets. They dislocated railways tracks, set on fire trains, banks and other government property as the symbols of the state power.[17] Moro, Sakrand, Halla, Badin, Kahripur Nathan Shah, Meher, Dadu and several other towns of Sindh, became focus of national as well as international media, specially the BBC Urdu Service.[18]

Shrine of Shah Abdul Latif Bhittai, the saint-poet of Sindh (in Hyderabad, who gave the message of nationalism and universalism, became the rallying point of revolutionaries. Similarly, Makdoom Bilalwal, a 16th Century AD religious scholar, who issued an edict against the Central Asian Arghaun invaders of Sindh, was resurrected as a hero of the land.[19] Likewise, the grave of Doolah Darya Khan, Sindhi commander, who resisted the Arghuns and was buried in the vicinity of Dadu, was once again frequented by local MRD activists.

The veteran Sindhi leader, G.M. Syed who opposed the state of Pakistan till his death in 1992, has had enormous impact on the minds of the Sindhis. Though during the MRD movement Sindhi were fighting under the banner of the Pakistan Peoples Party, its activists were imbibed with the nationalist ideas of GM Syed.

During MRD movement, Pakistani flag was replaced by Peoples Party flag at Deputy Commissioner's office in Dadu. That was a something akin to the East Pakistan situation in 1970-71 when the Awami League flag was hosted instead of the Pakistani flag on the government buildings. In Dadu, the police refused to obey the orders of the superiors to open fire on the demonstrators and were disarmed. According to the then martial law administrator and the Governor of Sindh, Lt. General Jahanadad Khan, three divisions of the army, the

Frontier Constabulary, a paramilitary force of Pashtun soldiers Hur battalion,[20] Sindhi followers of Pir Pagara, who without reservations claims to be on the Army's man, were deployed in Sindh in general and Dadu district in particular.[21]

Demonstrators and army clashed at several points, especially in Khairpur, Nathan Shah and Sakrand in the central Sindh. The Frontier Constabulary burnt villages in Katcha (area) near the river-bed of the Indus in the vicinity of Dadu town. Air force for the second time in history of Sindh, bombed Sindhi villages. First time, it was used by the British to crush the Hur rebellion (1942-1945) in Thar Desert of Sindh in 40s, era coinciding with the Second World War.[22] For the second time, air force was used against the Sindhis the Village Lakhat, in Nawab Shah District on the pretext of weeding out dacoits and anti state elements.[23] It is ironic that during Hur revolt, Punjabi and Pathan soldiers of the British-Indian Army were arrested, tortured and killed Hur men and maltreated their women folk."[24] However, during MRD, the Hur battalion allegedly did the same with the fellow-Sindhis[25] on behalf of a Punjabi General. During the course of MRD, according to American expert on South Asia, Selig Harrison, 300 Sindhis were killed and about 10000 were incarcerated and tortured.[26]

Since Zia was already interfering in the Indian administered Kashmir and Indian Punjab, he conveniently shifted blame to India and the former Soviet Union for interfering in Sindh to disintegrate Pakistan.[27] Indian Prime Minister, Indira Gandhi's pro-Sindhi statements in the meetings of Sindhis and in the Indian parliament, "for not remaining indifferent to the atrocities committed by the military regime against the Sindhis"[28], were quoted by Zia to project the MRD as an anti-state and separatist movement supported by India.[29]

Apparently, GM Syed distanced himself from the MRD for considering it a strong and centre orientated movement,[30] but he did not remain aloof from the plight of Sindhis for whose rights he fought throughout his life. He appealed to the UN Amnesty International and Mrs Indira Gandhi, to at least express concern over the genocide of Sindhis by the armed forces.[31] Mrs. Gandhi's statements about the situation in Sindh were probably in response to Syed's appeals.

Pir Pagara supported the establishment in crushing the MRD. The urban Urdu speaking population, on the whole, maintained the benevolent neutrality in favour of Zia. If these forces had supported the MRD along with GM Syed, Sindhis would have either got their own state or they would have got maximum rights within a confederal or federal Pakistan. But because of the lack of support from these quarters, the MRD became moribund by the end of 1984.

Mushahid Hussain Syed, political commentator, presents another perspective on the failure of MRD. According to him, in order to pressurize Zia to continue war in Afghanistan, Americans patted the back of PPP leader, Ghulam Mustafa Jatoi to challenge the military regime, but when they felt that Zia was not wanting in playing the role of proxy for them, they signaled Mr Jatoi to stop the movement. Hence, the MRD failed. Although MRD did not succeed in dislodging military rule, the image of Sindhis as timid, docile people washed away.

Launching of Muhajir Quomi Movement (MQM)

One of the ironies of Pakistan is that its formative Muslim League leadership came from the Hindu majority areas, having no roots in the areas where Pakistan came into being.[33]

In order to create their constituencies, Muslim Leaguers, by social engineering, settled the Indian migrants principally in the urban centres of Sindh, such as Karachi, Hyderabad, and Sukkur, where they became a majority.[34] Mohammed Ayub Khuhro, then chief minister of Sindh wanted to thwart these designs. On the advice of prime minister and real power wielder Liaqat Ali Khan, the governor general of Pakistan, Qauid-i-Azam Mohmmed Ali Jinnah, dismissed Khuhro. Karachi, the capital of Sindh, was separated from the hinterland in 1948. Thus, Karachi became the first base of the migrants.

The idea of creating a separate niche for migrants was there from 1947 onwards, but in 1985, it was given a kick-start by the formation of Muhajir Quomi Movement (MQM) (Migrants National Movement) under the leadership of a demagogue, Altaf Hussain. MQM, according to an Urdu speaking analyst, Brigadier retired, AR. Siddique, was formed and nurtured by General Zia ul Haq.[35] its main demands were the attain to status of a "nationality" for the migrants and separation of Karachi from the rest of Sindh.[36]

The demand for Karachi *Suba* (province) was/is seemingly aimed at ultimately expanding it into the *Muhajir Suba* (province) *or* even an independent *Urdu Desh* (state) comprised of Karachi, parts of the Thatta, Badin, Hyderabad, Sanghar and Tharparkar districts. It is noteworthy that Thatta, Badin, Sanghar and Tharparkar District share either the maritime or the land boundaries with the Gujarat and Rajasthan states of India. Moreover, being the people of Indian origin, MQM activists are proud of it.[37] These cross-border kith and kin relationships of MQM create the identical perceptions of Sindhis and a section of the establishment, otherwise the bad-fellows, about its real or imagined intentions of MQM for dividing Sindh and breaking away from Pakistan.[38] Ostensibly, for tactical reasons, MQM has postponed this demand for a separate province till an appropriate time, but it still strictly adheres to the demand of a nationality.[39] In order to do so Altaf Hussain insists his followers to buy the latest weapons on one or the other reason.[40]

Although MQM subsequently developed its own agenda, General Zia supposedly created it for two principle purposes.

Firstly, like many of his predecessors, sensing Sindhi's disappointment with the over centralized, military cum Punjabi-migrant dominated Pakistani state and their resultant craving for creating a Sindhi state, by breaking away from Pakistan, he checkmated them with the formation of MQM whose constituents are settled in the big cities. Without these cities, an ideal *Sindhudesh* (independent Sindh) cannot be created.41

Secondly, since MQM is one of the largest parties of the country, with violent tendency and its street power in Karachi and parts of Hyderabad, no party ruling Sindh can afford to ignore it. It has to be co-opted in formation of coalition government. Thus, arguably, Zia gave it a veto power over the governance of Sindh. In 1986, it destabilized the Sindh government of chief minister, Ghous Ali Shah, a Zia's favourite, by launching an attack on Suhrab Goth. Next year, it unleashed terror on Sindhis in Karachi and Hyderabad for the purpose of ethnic cleansing. Now there are no houses of Sindhis in the Latifabad locality of Hyderabad, whose land was donated by Mirs, the descendents of pre-British rulers of Sindh to rehabilitate the "Muslims brethren from India."

Because of its vote bank, MQM formed governments in Sindh twice with the PPP support in 1988-90, 1993-96 but turned on against it. PPP was forced to take action against its activists by arresting them for their alleged terrorist activities. In 1990-93, 1996-97, prime minister of Pakistan, Mian Nawaz Sharif, found himself in the same position and took the same action. From 1999 to 2007, when Musharaff, a fellow Urdu speaking military dictator was in power, MQM whole heartedly supported him.[42] As a quid pro quo, Musharaff gave it virtual control over the city governments of Karachi and Hyderabad. It is ironic that during the Musharaff era, while the five districts of Karachi were merged into the Karachi city government, four new districts were created out of the Hyderabad District. The control of the Hyderabad city, fell into the hands MQM. The purpose of this gerrymanderism was to give mastery over two main cities of Sindh to MQM.

In 1999, General Musharaff appointed an MQM activist Dr Isharat-ul-Ibad, as Governor of Sindh province. Dr. Ibad is reportedly implicated in the murder of Hakim Saeed, the philanthropist and one time governor of the province in 1998. Such a controversial appointment demonstrates that Musharaff also condoned the MQM's terrorist activities such as extortion, land grabbing, and destruction of the hundreds of year old Sindhi villages for constructing new plazas by the land and builder mafias in Karachi and its suburbs.[43] On 12 May 2007, during the arrival of deposed Chief Justice of the Supreme Court of Pakistan, Justice Iftikhar Chowdhry,[44] MQM allegedly murdered forty eight persons in Karachi. Musharaff called it the "show of people's power against the politicized judge."[45]

In October 2007, US brokered a deal between PPP and General Musharaff. According to its terms, along with late Benazir Bhutto and her husband, Asif Ali Zardari, 700 MQM leaders or workers got indemnity from prosecution.[46] In 2008, PPP once again formed coalition with MQM in Sindh. In a surprising move of appeasement, it exempted the local Governments of Karachi and Hyderabad from the auditing procedure, which takes place all over the world for the purpose of financial transparency and accountability.[47] It is ironic that Nawaz League, which refused to talk to MQM because of its alleged terrorist character in 2007, hobnobed with it to unseat the coalition government of the PPP both in Sindh and the centre.[48]

Despite partnership with the centre and Sindh provincial governments, MQM restarted its gory drama. In November and early December, 2007 at least 50 persons were killed[49] in the riots between the Pashtuns and MQM constituents. Most of the causalities are believed to be cobblers, roadside hotel owners and daily wage earning Pashtuns[50]. At least about 50 Pashtun owned hotels were also gutted. In another incident, 40 Siriaki speaking from Rahim Yar Khan, Southern Punjab squatters in North Karachi were burnt alive.[51] MQM apparently provided relief to the victims but some quarters opine that the fire was set ablaze by its arsonists to force Siraiki slum dwellers to leave the plot which could be allotted to the MQM backed builder mafias.[52]

Studying the pattern of the ethnic riots in Sindh, it is apprehended by informed Sindhis that next target of MQM terror is likely to be the Sindhis again.[53] This apprehension appears to be quite plausible, because people from the upcountry may be frightened to return to their respective places. However, being the sons of soil, it is the Sindhis only, who will fight for their motherland. Moreover, it is the Sindhis who are main obstruction to conceivable MQM's ultimate goal of dividing Sindh into pieces. Thus, arguably, Zia had put a perpetual grinding millstone on the neck of Sindhis by creating MQM.[54]

Launching of the Depoliticization Process

In order to keep people away from any political affiliations, Zia had launched the process of depolitcization of society. Since Sindh was his main vulnerability, he adopted more repressive measures against it. For the support of his regime, he co-opted Mullahs, whom he called *Mashaikhs* (scholars), retired bureaucrats, glorified as "technocrats" and above all, the waderas (feudal) who own big tracks of land in the interior of Sindh. Zia nominated them as the members of the *Majlis-i-Shura* (consultative body) in 1981.

As for as, Waderas are concerned, usually they jump on the bandwagon of any political party which they feel will win elections and return them to the assemblies. One of the apparent purposes of formation of *Shura* was to introduce Islamization process in the society, which then sounded sweet to the American ear. But in reality, it was aimed at depoliticization of the society by strengthening power of Waderas in their respective constituencies. Most of them were previously the PPP members of national or provincial assemblies.As like a case in the point, scores of other waderas, Amir Bukhsh Junejo and Mohmmed Bakhsh Jamali, both from Dadu were among the members of *Shura*. As a bribe for co-opting with the regime, waderas got development funds and jobs for their relatives and cronies. Now instead of any party leader, masses were thinking of their powerful waderas for jobs and help in the petty matters in government departments.

Going a step further in his policy of depoliticizaton and projecting his better image to the American legislators, Zia held the non-party polls in 1985. As an engineered poll rigging bid, Zia's cronies won the national provincial assemblies' elections. Mohammed Khan Junejo, a small time politician from Sindh became the Prime Minister. To Zia's anguish, when Junejo asserted himself and convened an all-party conference on Afghanistan Crisis, attended by the opposition leader, Benazir Bhutto, and later on signed the Geneva Accord on Afghanistan in 1988, Zia became furious with him. In fact, Junejo wanted to curtail the powers of the armed forces in running the country. In 1988, there was a fire in the arms depot at Ojhri near Islamabad, Junejo ordered the inquiry into the causes of the fire, which was allegedly ignited by the army men themselves to bluff the visiting American military delegation to probe into reports of smuggling the Stinger missiles to Iranians.[55] Now a "docile Junejo" became unacceptable because he in Zia's words, arrogantly behaving like his Sindhi predecessor Bhutto, by challenging the authority of the army. Ultimately, Zia unceremoniously dismissed him in the midair on his way back from China in 1988. After Junejo's dismissal, the general impression in Sindh was that whether an "assertive Zulfiquar Ali Bhutto" or a "docile Junejo" both Sindhis, were unacceptable to Punjabi migrant dominated establishment of Pakistan.

Encouragement to Jirga System

Zia also encouraged the promotion of Jirga culture in Sindh. In parts of tribal societies of Balochistan and the Pakhtunkhaw, where the state's writ hardly runs, disputes are settled by congregation of the tribal chiefs, Sardars or Maliks (chiefs) forming a *Jirga.* In Sindh, there were hardly any Sardars except in the Jaccobabad District abutting Balochistan. But after becoming the members of Zia's *Majlis-i-Shura*, provincial and national assemblies, many waderas assumed the title of Sardars of their *Bradari* (clan) or tribe. They formed Jirgas, parallel to law courts for resolution of disputes, related to murder and fornication cases.

In some cases, Jirgas marry off even 5-years old girls from a murderer's family to the murdered family's 50 years old men as a compensation. This was called the "Sangh Chatti". Similarly, a man and women having allegedly illicit relationship, are declared as *Karo Kari* (guilty) by Jirgas and punished with death penalty. Sometimes the women accused of adulatory were buried alive or thrown to the dogs.[56] According to the Asian Human Rights Commission Report, in 2007 900 women were killed in Pakistan on adulteration charges and most of them were from Sindh.[57] According to another report released by Karachi-based Aurat (Women) Foundation in 2008 a human right watch dog concentrating on the plight of women folk, 30 Jirgas were held in Sindh. On their decisions 400 women and 80 men were killed on the charges of "Karo Kari" and 17 women were given as "Sangh Chatti"[58]. Zia is dead with his *Shura,* but the obscurantist jirga system encouraged by him still persists and thrives both in Pukhten Khan and Sindh. Even those Sardars who had presided over these inhuman Jirgas are federal and provincial minister in the present government.

Damaging the Higher Education System

The principal purpose of dictators is to prolong their rule. Students and academics all over the world are the sensitive parts of society. They offer resistance to dictatorship. General Zia-ul-Haq like his predecessors, Ayub, Yahya Khan successor and Musharaff were aware of this threat. In order to control the students, Zia banned student unions, erected wall around the student hostels and appointed the Vice Chancellors, who followed his instructions. Intelligence moles were planted among the students, teachers and university bureaucracy.

Sindh University is considered as the hotbed of Sindhi nationalism. All other universities of interior of Sindh are its off springs. One can argue that he who controls this university, will control the higher education of the interior of Sindh. According to the Cambridge historian, Ayesha Jalal, Pakistani establishment has been allowing the dropping of standards of education of Sindh University with the purpose that Sindhis should not compete with any other ethnic group of the country.[59] By damaging Sindh University, Zia presumably wanted to destroy the higher education of the area systematically.

Zia, in order to monitor and crush the secessionist movement in Sindh, installed an intelligence wing in Sindh University. He significantly accelerated the pace of declining of its standards. In Sindh University, students and teachers were frequently frisked by army and police. An army major, Habibulah Niazi was appointed as a Superintendent of Police (SP) of the area with special responsibility of surveillance of the University. In May 1983, the police, without permission of the then Vice-Chancellor Professor Ilyas Abro, stormed a hall of residence and killed a student, Ahsan Memon.[61] Police claimed it to seize arms, but the students refuted such a claim. In a general body meeting of the students, teachers and the then Vice-Chancellor, condemned the police action.[62] London School of Economics trained Professor Abror was replaced with a bureaucrat of the income tax group, Mazharul Haq Sissique, with a Master's degree from the army owned National Defence

College (NDC) [63] where, besides the officers from the three services and the intelligence agencies, bureaucrats are trained to govern the country. Like his predecessor, the new vice-chancellor followed the dictates from the army. Despite opposition from the students and teachers, he banned the student union, erected walls around the student hostels, restricted their movements and made the campus look like a concentration camp.

In October 1987, students belonging to Jaiy Sindh Students Federation (JSSF) were going by the University buses to Larkana to participate in their convention. Some chowkidars (guards) also boarded the buses. On behalf of the vice-chancellor, the then Additional Registrar, Saleh Rajar reported to the army that some armed thugs disguised as students had hijacked buses, should be intercepted. Near Thorhi railways-crossing, District Dadu, Army besieged the buses and killed two students and one Chowkidar,[64] the sole breadwinner of his extended family.

Like his predecessor, this non-academic vice-chancellor, did not participate in the condolence meeting and closed the University for some time. Moreover, on the one hand, he created an atmosphere of harassment and on the other, encouraged culture of cronyism by bribing the students and giving additional charges to teachers so that they co-opted with him. As allegedly desired by intelligence agencies, the standards of education started falling markedly during his incumbency.

It is ironic that despite his retirement from the bureaucracy, the same person was appointed vice-chancellor by Musharaff regime in 2001. He chose the same registrar again, a retired person to assist him in running the administration. The vice chancellor's cronies held multiple additional charges.[65] Instead of merit, patronage based management of the University precipitated, marked decline of the standards of education.

Sindh University was one of the five top universities of the pre-1971 Pakistan. It ranked 11, out of 23 teaching-cum research public sector universities of the country by the Higher Education Commission of Pakistan in year 2007.[66] University administration has so badly failed in managing the university affairs that in order to settle a dispute between some rouge students and two chowkidars, it held a jirga of Sardars to resolve it.[67] For doing so, it was condemned by academics and other sections of the civil society. But since the vice-chancellor and registrar are reportedly linked with army and intelligence, the PPP government seemed happy with it. Thus, the process of Ziafication still persists in damagingly the higher education of Sindh. This affects the very fabric of educational system as a whole in the province.

Conclusion

It has been argued that in the 80s, Zia by taking advantage of Pakistan's geopolitical location, renewed relationship with the United States. By cultivating these political military linkages, he wanted to remain in power indefinitely. At home, he initiated the processes of Islamization, over-centralization and reinvigorated Punjabi migrant relationships. These policies played havoc with Sindh. Arguably, if Zia had not staged the coup'd tat and hanged Zulfiquar Ali Bhutto, democracy would have been consolidated in Pakistan and the estranged Sindh could have been brought in the mainstream of Pakistani politics. But Bhutto's murder pushed it away from Pakistan's mainstream political, social and economic life.

One can argue that with 2008 elections the President and Speaker of National Assembly are Sindhis and the complains of sense of deprivation are unfounded. However, if one looks at the mechanism of the real power structure in the country, the things are quite opposite. Even the Senate members of the PPP from Sindh, including Rahman Malik, the adviser to the federal interior ministry and Zardari's muscleman, are non-Sindhis.

Moreover, Pakistan's refusal to handover the alleged terror plotters Hafiz Saeed and Maulana Masood Azhar of the Bombay bomb blasts of November 2008 aswell, of the extremist Jamait-i-Dawa organization to India for investigation or to send the ISI chief for investigation,[68] demonstrate that instead of civilian government of President Asif Ali Zardari, Army and its intelligence wing, ISI and Military Intelligence (MI) are still the real power wielders in the country.

As far as the fiscal autonomy is concerned, Sindh is at the receiving end. The resources of Sindh, especially, oil, gas, coal, two sea-ports, the Karachi International Airport, excise, taxation and land revenue generated out of Sindh, make 70 per cent resources of Pakistan altogether.[69] Central grants are allotted mainly on the population basis. Accordingly to 7th National Financial Award, distributing income between provinces and the centre announced in 2009, Punjab will get 51 percent and Sindh 24.55 percent from the federal pool. Seaports, airports, and mines, gas, petroleum and value added tax(vat) will still remain federal property,[70] controlled by Punjabis and migrants. Due to this disproportionate distribution of funds, 50 per cent of Sindhi, especially in the rural Sindh, live below poverty line.[71] In this scenario, Zardari is just a showpiece engaged in attaining personal benefits in the name of Sindh.

If Zia had not encouraged the formation of MQM, this terrorist organization could not have been there. Because of its street power and killing gangs, it is widely perceived as a threat to democracy, unity of Sindh and even to the integrity of Pakistan. One can argue that the restive section of urban Sindh, might have organized itself into a militant party without Zia. However, from 1947 to 1977 this restive portion of the migrant community was not as strong as it became after the advent of Zia. Thus, he played a significant role in nourishing and nurturing the MQM. His military successor, General Musharaff taking a leaf from him, supported the MQM more vigorously.

It was Zia's party-less polls, which encouraged the formation of the jirga and the biradari systems in Sindh. Because of these callous-medieval systems, many women have lost their lives on the pretext of honour killing. Many young girls have been forcibly married to elderly persons, which is a gross violation of human rights.

In order to make the Sindhi youth incompetent, since the creation of Pakistan in general, and Zia advent in particular, intelligence agencies chalked out a plan to lower down the standard of Sindh's higher education. Zia accelerated this process further. Ironically, his anointed officials in Sindh University are still in the saddle. Presumably, they continue with his mission of lowering down the standards of higher education, which will ultimately sink the ship of education in the interior of Sindh.[72]

In the final analysis, process of Ziafication in Pakistan in general and Sindh in particular, is so strong that the trends he set, are still operating despite the passage of more than twenty years and change of successive governments. Indeed, 9 years of Musharaff regime, gave a new lease of life to it. Thus, there is a need to state a process of deziafication in the realms of the domestic politics and foreign policy, which will save Pakistan from disintegration.

Political and economic autonomy to Sindh and three other provinces, will strengthen federation and check the centrifugal tendencies on one hand and the Talibanisation on the other. Sindhi, Baloch, Pashtun and Punjabi nationalists are secular in their orientation. They opposite extremism in the country. The good neighbourly relations with immediate neighbours, especially India, will be helpful in eliminating the process of Ziafication in its manifestation such as over-centralization, militarization and extremism, which are poisonous, not only for Sindh but for the country as a whole.

References

1. Pakistan is one of the unique states in the world that all of its provinces: Sindh, Balochistan, Punjab and Pakhtunkhaw are its borderlands. The same ethnic groups straddle across its international borders. In case of Sindh, Sindhi Muslims live across border and many Hindu Sindhis migrated to all parts of India. Similarly, after Partition, many Urdu, Gujarati, Kutchi speaking Muslims who migrated to Pakistan, were principally settled in the big cities of Sindh. Indeed, the Urdu speakers from Delhi, Uttar Pradesh (UP) and Bihar make the bulk of immigrants. They are active in politics and have considerable representation in bureaucracy and armed forces. General Musharaff was one of them. For composition of migrants: Brigadier AR. Siddique, *Partition and the Making of the Muhajir Mindset: A Narrative,* Oxford University Press, (OUP), Karachi, 2008, pp. 119-121.

2. Sarah Ansari, *Life After Partition: Migration, Community and Strife in Sindh: 1947-1962,* OUP, 2005, pp. 46-73.

3. 1973 Constitution has two lists of the portfolios: the federal list, and the concurrent list. The concurrent list was supposed to be transferred to the provinces after 10 years. But it has never happened. The 1940 Resolution, which laid the foundation of a Muslim Home Land, promised the creation of sovereign autonomous Muslim homelands in the Muslim majority areas where, with exception of defence, foreign affairs, communication and currency, all the remaining portfolios will be given to the provinces. Hassan Askari Rizvi, "Lahore Resolution and Muslim Identity", *Dawn,* special edition, 23rd March, 2009.

4. Late Mahmood-ul-Haq Usmani of the leftist National Awami Party was one of the enlightened Urdu-speaking intellectuals, who also supported the return of the Karachi to Sindh.

5. Sindhi is Sardar Ataullah Khan Mengal's mother tongue.

6. Selig Harrison, *In Afghanistan's Shadow: Baluch Nationalism and the Soviet Temptations,* Carnegie Endowment for Peace, New York, 1981, p. 3.

7. Muhammad Ali Siddiqi, An Expat's Question, *Dawn,* 27 March, 2009.

8. *Geo News Channel,* 21 December, 2007.

9. Zaffar Hassan's Diaries, Sindhi, self-publisher, 2000, p. 198.

10. Sir Morrice James (Lord Saint Brides), edited with introduction by Peter Lyon, Pakistan *Chronicle, C.* Hurst, London, 1993, pp. 159-160.

11. Ahmed Rashid, *Descent into Chaos,* Allan Lane and Imprint of, Penguin, London, 2008, p. 146.

12. Mark Tully, *Amritsar: Mrs. Gandhi's last Battle,* The Books, London, 1985, p. 212.

13. Nasreen Ghufran, Repatriation of Afghan Refugees, in Moonis Ahmared, *Challenge of Rebuilding Afghanistan,* 2nd edition, Karachi University Press, 2006, p. 126.

14. According to the Home Minister of Sindh, 516519, Afghan refuges and Pashtuns illegally live in Karachi, *Daily Time: Karachi,* 7th February, 2009.

15. Imam Bux Ghuryani Advocate Dadu is the main proponent of this idea, who as a counsel of a dacoit, Qurban Chandio produced

a certificate in Sindh High Court, with the signature of an army major allowing him to do his "business as usual".

16. Kaleem Omar, "Pressure Cooker Politics: Waiting for Explosion, *Monthly Herald,* Karachi, September 1993, Ayeaz Amir, Dark Forces at Committee Chowk", *Herald,* September 1993, p. 12, Ayeaz Amir "And So, On to 84". *The Herald,* 1984, pp. 43-47.

17. Kaleem Omar, *Ibid.*

18. *Ibid.*

19. GM. Syed, *Sindh Ja Soorma: the Warriors of Sindh* (translation from Sindhi), G.M. Syed Academy, Sann, district Dadu, 2000, pp. 22-23.

20. Lt. General Jahand Dad Khan, *Pakistan: Leadership Challenges,* OUP, 1999, pp. 253-4.

21. *Kawish,* 26th December, 2008.

22. HT Lambrick, *The Terrorists,* Ernest Benn, London, 1972, pp. 47-48.

23. Lt. General Jahand Dad Khan, *op.cit.,* pp. 1723, and Daily *Hilal-Pakistan,* Sindhi, Karachi, 15 September, 1983.

24. Imam Zadi Wasan : Hur Tahrik Meen Urtun Jo Kirdar : "The Role of Women in the Hur Movement", (translation from Sindhi), Monthly, Sindhi, *Sanghar (Awakening),* Hyderabad Sindh, March 2006, pp. 27-30.

25. Interview with the inhabitants of the village Jhalo near Dadu town.

26. Selig Harrison : Ethnicity and Political Settlement in Pakistan in Ali Banuazizi Myron Weiner, eds, *The State, Religion, and Ethnic Politics in Afghanistan, Iran and Pakistan,* Syracuse

University Press, Syracuse, 1986, pp. 278-289. S. Harrison : Ethnic Conflict and the Future of Pakistan", in Wilson John, ed, *Pakistan Struggle Within,* Pearson: Longman, Delhi, 2009, p. 27.

27. Mushahid Hussain Syed, *Pakistan's Politics: The Zia Years,* Progressive Publishers Lahore, 1990, pp. 434, and General K.M. Arif, *Working with Zia: Pakistan's Power Politics: 1977-1988,* OUP, 1995, p. 201.

28. General Arif, *Ibid.*

29. *Ibid.*

30. Mushahid Hussain, *op. cit.*

31. MS. Korejo, *GM. Syed: An Analysis of His Political Perspectives,* OUP, 2000, p. 83.

32. Mushahid Hussain, *op.cit.*

33. Sarah Ansari, *op. cit.,* p. 212.

34. *Ibid.*

35. AR Siddique, *op.cit,* pp. 127-29.

36. *Ibid.*

37. Balraj Puri, *Indian Muslims since Partition,* Gyan Publishing House, New Delhi, 2007, pp. 92-93.

38. Mehtab Ali Shah : The Emergence of the Muhajir Qaumi Movement (MQM) in Pakistan And Its Implications For Regional Security", *Round Table,* Number 346, Carfax Publishers, Oxfordshire, 1898, pp. 514-515.

39. There had frequently been rows among the leadership of the MQM over the issue of "armed struggle for liberating *Urdu Desk*

comprised of Karachi and Hyderabad". Anwar Khan, Saleem Shahzad and Khalid Maqbool Siddiqi time and again have raised this demand but the MQM chief, Altaf Hussain has snubbed them on the grounds that the situation is not ripe for launching such a movement. Laurent Gayer : History of Violence: Ethnic and Sectarian Conflicts in Karachi (1985-2005), in Sindh *Through History and Representations: French Contribution to Sindh Studies,* Michel Boivin, ed, OUP, 2008, pp. 58-59.

40. In order to please America and Britain, from his London headquarters, the MQM boss, has created the bogy of the Talibanization of Karachi and its takeover by the Pashtun settlers. His claims have been refuted by the Sindhi and Pashtun political parties, including the PPP provincial interior minister, Dr. Zulfiqaur Mirza. *Daily Kawish,* 1st November 2008, and Fariha Aziz, "Region of Terror", *Monthly Newsline,* Karachi, December, 2008, pp. 52-53.

41. Ansari, *op. cit.,* and MS Korejo, *A Testament of Sindh: Ethnic and Religious Extremism: A Perspective,* OUP, Karachi, 2002, pp. 120-121.

42. Laurent Gayer, *op. cit.,* p. 59.

43. For the criminal activities of the MQM, Mehtab Ali Shah : The Criminalization of Politics: Karachi a Case Study," *Ethic Studies Report,* Colombo, Vol. XIX No: 1, January 2001, pp. 99-138, and J, Wilson John, *Karachi: A Terror Capital in Making,* Rupa & Co, in association with the Observer Research Foundation, New Delhi, 2003, pp. 5-14, and Moosa Kaleem, "May 12:A Script Gone Away", *Herald,* June 2007, pp. 64-73.

44. In November 2007, Chief Justice Chowdhry was dismissed by General Musharaff and after a prolonged struggle by lawyers and the other members of civil society, the PPP government was forced to reinstate him in March, 2009.

45. *Daily Times: Karachi* 14th December, 2007.

46. Irfan Hussain, Pakistan Politics as Greek Tragedy, *Dawn,* March, 21, 2009.

47. *Kawish,* 20th November, 2008.

48. *Daily News,* Karachi, 24th February, 2009.

49. *Dawn News Channel,* 15th December, 2008.

50. *Daily Times: Karachi,* 5th December, 2008.

51. 22 children Among 40 Killed in Fire, *Dawn,* 10 January 2009, and *Kawish,* 10th January, 2009.

52. The Press Release of the Siraiki Nationalist Party Karachi Branch, *Daily Khabroon,* Sindhi, Karachi, 14th January, 2009.

53. Dr. Mir Alam Marri: Karachi Mein Talibanization jo Khouf Cho Pakhriji Rahyo ahi? Sindhi: "Why the Fear of Talibanizatoin is spreading in Karachi"?, *Kawish,* 7th December, 2008.

54. Korejo, *op.cit.,* pp. 123-125.

55. Mehtab Ali Shah : *The Foreign Policy of Pakistan: Ethnic Impacts on Diplomacy: 1971-1994,* I.B. Tauris, London-St. Martin, New York, 1997, p. 153.

56. Women's Magazine, *Daily Kawish,* 19 December 2008.

57. *Asian Human Rights Commission (AHRC): Pakistan Chapter,* Clear-Cut Publishing and Printing Co., Hong Kong, 2007, pp. 231-232.

58. "Karachi Saw 194 Rape Cases in First Nins Months of 2008, Says Report," Dawn: *Metropolitan,* 6th January, 2009. Also Zubeida Mustafa : Women Decide to Fight Back, *Dawn,* 25th February, 2009.

59. Ayesha Jalal, *Democracy and Authoritarianism in South Asia,* Cambridge University Press, 1995, pp. 230-231.

60. AG. Noorani : Academic Freedom in Kashmir and Elsewhere, *Economic and Political Weekly of India,* Mumbai, 8 September 2007, pp. 3600-3602.

61. Daily *Hilal-i-Pakistan,* , 27th May, 1983.

62. *Ibid.*

63. The one-year NDC Masters degree is considered inferior to the 2-years normal Qauid-i-Azam University, Islamabad's Masters degree by political analysts, Ayesha Siddiqa : The Development of Strategic Studies in Pakistan" in Inayatullah *et. al.*, editors, *Social Sciences in Pakistan: A Profile,* Council of Social Sciences Pakistan, Pisces Enterprise, Islamabad, 2005, p. 57.

64. Jahandad Khan, *op. cit.,* p. 267, and *Hilal-i-Paksitan,* 19th October, 1984.

65. Mohammed Hanif Rahmoon, Shagird Siyasat and Intazamia jo Kirdar: "Criticism against the Student Politics and the Role of Administration" (translation from Sindhi), the letter to the Editor, *Kawish* 19th January, 2009.

66. "Public Sector Universities Ranking 2006-7 Report by the Higher Education Commission (HEC), *Daily Jang,* Urdu, (Karachi), 6 April, 2007.

67. "Jirga in Sindh University Condemned", *Dawn: Metropolitan,* 28th March, 2009.

68. Zahid Hussain, "Pakistan's Hour of Reckoning", *Newsline,* December 2008, pp. 21-25.

69. "Balochistan Package" editorial in *Dawn,* 30th March, 2009. Naseer Memon, Oil and Gas Resources and the Rights of

Provinces", *Economic and Business Report: Daily Dawn,* 3rd October, 2008.

70. Punjab Makes Room For Historic NFC Accord", *Dawn,* 12 December 2009.

71. Naseer Memon *op. cit.*

72. Nadeem Panhwar, "The Universities of Sindh Run by the Retired Bureaucrats", English translation), *Kawish: Educational Page,* 7th February, 2009.

PART - II
SECTARIANISM AND COMMUNALISM IN SOUTH ASIA

7

Cramped Styles of Schismatic Denominations

Introduction

Religious composition of Pakistan is almost 97% Muslim, principally divided into Sunni and Shia sects. The Sunnis comprise about 80% and the Shia about 20% of the Muslim population.[1]

Paradoxically, although Pakistan is a Sunni-majority state, its founding father, Muhammed Ali Jinnah and the first Prime Minister, Liaqat Ali Khan, were from the Shia minority. Before and immediately after the creation of Pakistan in 1947 there were no marked Sunni-Shia sectarian differences. These emerged later in the 1950s and became sharp from the 1980s onwards.

Although Pakistan was created in the name of Islam, Jinnah was a non-practicing Muslim. In a speech made on 11 September 1947 he declared that, after the creation of Pakistan, Muslims and non-Muslims would cease to be Muslims and non-Muslims in political terms. This speech can be interpreted as an indication that the *Qauid-e-Azam* (Father of the Nation) was secular in his personal and political outlook. He was completely against theocracy as a form of government. The question then arises: which forces, for what purposes, have been attempting to push Pakistan towards the establishment of theocracy, leading to conflict not only between Muslims and non-Muslims but also among the Muslim community, as well as to increased discord with Pakistan's neighbours, especially India and Iran?

What are the reasons for polarization between Sunnis and Shias and impact on human and national security of Pakistan and approaches and methods that might bridge these differences? The emergence of sectarianism is closely connected with the political processes taking place in Pakistan. Zia period (1977-88) is arguably the turning point in the history of Pakistani sectarianism.

Germination of Sectarianism (1947-77)

At the time of the creation of Pakistan, there were no strong manifestations of sectarianism in the country. There were two main religious parties, the Jamait i Islam (JI) and Jamait i Ulama e Islam (JUI). The former was operating in both wings of the country, whereas the latter was confined to the North West Frontier Province (NWFP). The JUI was indigenous in its nature. JI supporters were mainly drawn from immigrants of East Punjab. Ironically, the JI, which had opposed creation of Pakistan, became a champion of the ideology of Pakistan after 1947 and correspondingly, of the imposition of its own brand of Islam. JI was vehemently opposed to Qadiani/Ahmedi sect, whose adherents, it maintained, denied the finality of the Prophet Mohammed. Thus, Qadianis were regarded as *Kafirs* or non-believers and thus not entitled to any high office. However, the Qadianis were well entrenched in Pakistan's military and bureaucracy. The first foreign minister, Sir Zafrullah Khan, was a Qadiani.

He was responsible for arguing Pakistan's case over Kashmir in the United Nations. Declaring him a non-Muslim would have harmed the Pakistani case at a critical moment. The launch of a movement against the Qadianis by the JI and other Sunni religious parties created a problem of law and order in West Pakistani province of Punjab. Any agitation against the Qadianis indirectly damaged the fragile government of Khawaja Nazimuddin, who came from East Pakistan. He imposed martial law in Lahore in 1953. This was the first imposition of martial law in the country, aimed at curbing sectarianism. After that, sectarianism was unheard of for many years. There was, however, a marked struggle between the forces of over-centralization and decentralization.

In 1958, General Ayub Khan assumed power after getting clearance from USA and UK. Pakistan, with its British trained army and strategic location, became a US partner in military alliances, such as South East Asia Treaty Organization (SEATO) and Central Treaty Organization (CENTO). Within the country, Ayub Khan's main constituency was the army. In addition, he co-opted the bureaucracy as his junior partner. Despite the support of these two powerful institutions, Ayub Khan was facing resistance from democratic forces, specially from what was then East Pakistan. In order to checkmate these in 1962, he formed his own faction of Muslim League, the Council Muslim League. He also created the Islamic Ideological Council, to re-interpret Islam according to the needs of the time and to give legitimacy to military rule. At one stage, Pir Ali Mohammed Rashdi, a journalist-cum-politician, advised Ayub Khan to wear the mantle of the *Amirul Momneen* or *Kahalifatal Mulemeen* (the Caliph) for his entire life. With his Sandhurst secular background, Ayub Khan declined such a preposterous suggestion. However, from time to time, he convened meetings of the *Ulmahs* and *Mashikh* (Mullahs and Pirs or self-appointed holy men), who made speeches calling for his long life and prolonged rule. Ayub never co-opted the Mullahs[2] in his power sharing scheme. In 1962, during the month of Muharam, a procession of mourners was stirred up by Mullahs of the extremist Wahabi3 sect in the township of Thahri, near Kharipur Mirs, Sindh. However, this local conflagration was easily controlled by the district administration.

In 1969, Ayub Khan handed over power to another military dictator, General Yahya Khan. He is rightly stigmatized for harsh military action in East Pakistan and for latter's separation from the rest of the country. He was, however, the only ruler in the history of the country to conduct fair general elections, in 1970. Yahya Khan had no political ambitions. He wanted to return to the barracks after the transfer of power to the politicians, an objective in which he badly failed. Yahya Khan's principal and exclusive constituency was the armed forces and he had no plans to create any other. He completely ignored the Mullahs. There was no sectarian discord during his rule.

After the disintegration of the country in 1971, Zulfiquar Ali Bhutto became head of the state. After producing a new constitution in 1973, he faced a number of problems. On the insistence of the army chief, General Zia, military action was taken in Balochistan against Baloch nationalists, who were pressing for more provincial autonomy. This was dubbed a separatist movement by the federal government. Bhutto also faced difficulties posed by Sindhi and Punjabi nationalists[4]. With Bhutto isolated, the Mullahs became active. Punjab and the urban centres of Sindh were their main bases.

Arguably, in their heart of hearts, Mullahs were unhappy with a secular Sindhi politician, with Shia leaning being at the helm of affairs. They were looking for an excuse to topple him. The Mullahs launched a nationwide agitation for the acceptance of their demands, including declaring the Qadianas as a non-

Muslim minority, replacing Sunday by Friday as the weekly holiday and banning liquor shops. In 1974, Bhutto made many concessions to the Mullahs, giving a great boost to their morale. They then looked for a bigger target — Bhutto's removal. A vigorous Mullah-military alliance emerged, culminating in General Zia's military coup against the Bhutto government in 1977.

Advent of General Zia (1977-88)

In 1977, apparently unassuming and apolitical General Zia ul Haq, who had been promoted Chief of Army Staff, out of turn by Bhutto, staged a coup against him. Bhutto was the most assertive elected prime minister of Pakistan. He was a charismatic figure, loved and respected by a considerable section of the population. Although Bhutto propounded the programme of 'Islamic Socialism,' he was secular in educational and political outlook. His mother and two wives were reportedly Shias. In contrast, Zia came from a humble Sunni background. His father was a village Mullah, with a narrow vision of the world and of Islam, Zia took after his father. He had strong inclinations towards the teachings of Maulana Mouddidi, founder of Jamait-i-Islami and exhibited his Islamic piety.[5] Zia had also long maintained connections with his fellow East Punjabi, Moulana Tufail Ahmed, the second *Amir* (chief) of JI. For its part, the party had well established links with Saudi royalty and USA. In 1950s, USA was perceived as the defender of free world against communist infidels. Tahreek-Khatamumi-Nabuwati (defenders of the finality of Prophet Mohammed), a group of Wahabi maily Pashtun Mullahs of Balochistan, also became undeclared allies of the Zia regime. In 1978, they demanded that the Zikris of Makran district be declared non-Muslims.[6] They believed that Zia would support their bid. However, the secular and nationalist Baloch leadership was, and is, seriously opposed and Zia did not want to antagonize it over this issue.[7] After the Qadianis, the Zikris were the second target of religious fanaticism/sectarianism. However, the Shias were, of course, the most significant target.

As was widely expected, in 1979 Zia sent Bhutto to the gallows. His action received worldwide condemnation. Then US President Jimmy Carter was already unhappy about Pakistan's clandestine nuclear programme. Under the Symington Amendment, he stopped aid to Pakistan, treating it as a pariah state. But the rapidly changing geo-political scenario brought Pakistan and Zia to the centre of the world political stage.

In Iran, after a long struggle against the pro-American Shahdom, the clerics came to power under the leadership of the Grand Ayatollah Khomeini. They proclaimed a revolutionary Islamic Republic in December 1979. Like any other revolutionary power, Iran began to export ideas. Since most neighbouring states were pro-American Sheikdoms, with their regimes and their patron, USA, perceived the revolutionary Iran and its policies as a threat to their vital interests, especially in oil resources.

The Central Asian states, before the disintegration of USSR in 1990, were considered a soft underbelly, because of their predominantly Muslim and non-Russian population. They were vulnerable to internal dissonance instigated by outside interference, which subsequently, spread to the Russian Republic itself. From the 19th century onwards, Afghanistan had been a buffer state between Russians and British Empire in India (including what is now Pakistan). After the Islamic Revolution in Iran, Russians feared that the Central Asian states and Afghanistan would be overrun by Islamic fundamentalism, with covert or overt support from the West. In order to avert this scenario, Soviet troops invaded Afghanistan in late December 1979.

The West, especially USA, interpreted this as a reinforcement of the old Soviet policy of advance towards warm water ports and occupation of oil fields[8]. The situation brought huge benefits to Zia. USA, Saudi Arabia, China and Iran all started supporting *Mujahideen* (holy warriors) in Afghanistan. The main task of engineering a *Jihad* was given to the Pakistani army, especially its intelligence wing, the ISI. The Pakistani religious parties, which had a strong base in the areas bordering Afghanistan (NWFP and the Pashtun belt of Balochistan), started recruiting volunteers for *Jihad* in that country. Their *madrassahs* (seminaries), along with the Afghan refugee camps, became military training centers, where serving Sunni and Wahabi military officers trained recruits, principally underage pupils.

These religious parties already had links with Saudi Arabia but, thanks to the conflict in Afghanistan, they started receiving even more money from the Gulf States. A Saudi-sponsored Wahabi brand of Islam became the norm among the *Mujahideen.* The early warriors of Islam, revered only by the Sunni, such as Caliph Omer, Khalid bin Walid and Mouwiyah Bin Abu Sufyan, became the heroes of the Afghan *Mujahideen.* Training camps were named after them. It must be emphasized that it was with American assistance that volunteers from Southeast Asia, Egypt, Algeria and other Arab states started pouring into Pakistan in order to fight Russians. More importantly, Al-Qaeda (under Osama Bin Ladin, a Saudi millionaire) was founded and became operational in Afghanistan. Al-Qaeda became and still is the mother organization and sponsor of all sectarian and Jihadi groups in Pakistan.

Islamic Revolution in Iran slightly predated the Russian entry into Afghanistan. As stated earlier, it was perceived by USA and its allies as a big threat to the stability of Gulf. The revolutionary appeal of Islamic Revolution was perceived as Shia propaganda against Sunnis. In order to contain the influence of Iranian Revolution, at the instigation of USA and

Gulf sheikhdoms, the former ruler of Iraq, Saddam Hussein waged an eight-year war against Iran from 1980. Immediately after Iran-Iraq War, an extremist Wahabi group, Sawad-e-Azam (Greater Unity) came into being in Pakistan. With the implicit support of General Zia, this organization demanded that, as Sunnis were in the majority in Pakistan, it should be declared a Sunni state, whereas the Shia, like Qadianis and Zikris, should be declared non-Muslims. Immediately after this, in 1980, Zia promulgated the *Zakat* ordinance, under which all Muslims were supposed to pay this Islamic tax. Shias vigorously opposed this decree and laid siege to the National Assembly building. Zia was forced to give them an exemption. Sawad-e-Azam argued that, since only non-Muslims were exempt from *Zakat,* Shias should be declared non-Muslim. The Shias, under the leadership of Mufti Jaffer Hussain, formed their own political organization, Tahreek Nifazee Fqihi Jafaria (TNJF), for the protection of their religious rights. It included an alternative jurisprudence.

Zia period coincided with the mushrooming of *Deeni madrassahs* (religious schools). This was first time in the history of Pakistan that *madrassahs* received government aid, from the newly created *Zakat* fund. This aid was in addition to the charitable funds they received from private donors. A huge amount of money started pouring into the *madrassahs,* from Gulf official and unofficial sources. One way or the other, this supply still continues.[9] Besides the inculcation of religious knowledge at a primary level, *madrassah* pupils *(Talibs)* were, and still, are heavily indoctrinated in the notion of *Jihad,* holy war against the *Kafirs* (unbelievers). From their point of view *Jihad* is one of the fundamental duties of a good Muslim. According to this interpretation, Russians, Westerners, Indians, Iranians, Jews and Shias can all be seen as *Kafirs.* A chain of *madrassahs* was established in areas bordering Iran and Afghanistan, in all big cities and even in many villages. *Talibs* were also given military training and sent to different fronts, *i.e.,* to Afghanistan, India and the home front, against the Shias.

It is also interesting to note that Zia regime recognized the *Sanad* (certificate) awarded to graduates of *Deeni madrassahs* as an equivalent to the Bachelor and Masters degrees awarded by the country's universities. This was a glorification of *madrassah* education and led to the degradation of secular education. Illiterate or semi-illiterate Mullahs and Maolavis (clerics) were seen rubbing shoulders in legislative bodies of the country with Oxbridge graduates. This was the end of a liberal Pakistan as visualized by Jinnah. In *madrassahs,* hatred for other forms of Islam was spread. Arguably, the Iran-Iraq war (1980-88) was fought by proxy in Pakistan. And the process still continues.

Sawad-I-Azam gave birth to a terrorist Wahabi/Sunni organization, the Sipah-i- Saahaba (SSP — the soldiers of the Companions of the Holy Prophet). Its splinter group Lashkari-Jhangvi (LJ) also came into being and became quite active.[10] Impoverished Southern Punjab became the recruitment area of the sectarian Wahabi lashkers and Sipahs. Shia worshippers all over the country were targets, especially Shia doctors in Karachi. A Shia terrorist group, Sipah- i- Mohammed emerged in reaction.

In order to please Gulf sheikhs, Zia used the jargon and concepts of Sunni Islam in daily discourse. This emboldened Sunni Lashkars and Sipahs and enraged the Shias still further. In 1986, Zia settled Sunni Afghan refugees in Parachinar region of the NWFP, bordering Afghanistan. Arms were smuggled from there into Pakistan and distributed among the Sunni population. Presence of Afghan refugees and arms dumps was resisted by Shia Toori tribe of the area. Shots were exchanged. Shia leader, Allama Arif Hussain Hussani, was assassinated, allegedly on the instructions of the then governor of the NWFP, General Fazl ul Haq, a close friend of Zia. Shias vowed to avenge his murder. Within a few days, on 17 August 1988, Zia had been mysteriously killed in an air crash. He left behind him a legacy of ethnic and sectarian conflicts and a drug and Kalashnikov culture. His rule also coincided with the culmination of the Mullah-military alliance, which, still remains intact.

Zia to Musharraf 1988-99

This phase witnessed Pakistan's transformation from dictatorship to a fragile and dubious democracy. The two terms of Benazir Bhutto (1988-90, 1993-96) witnessed an uneasy relationship between the prime minister and the army, while the USA continued to hold the balance. The country was locked in ethnic tension especially between Urdu and Sindhi speakers in Sindh. Such tension had profound implications for national security and the armed forces were deeply implicated. Although Nawaz Sharif was a protégé of Ayub Khan and of General Zia and won the elections of 1990 and 1995 with the active backing of the ISI, he developed differences with the army and tried to assert his authority over it, resulting in his removal from office in May 1999 by General Musharraf.

During this 11-year period, the Mullah-military alliance remained intact. The army reportedly lent covert support to the religious parties and through them to sectarian institutions. There is a strange relationship between religious and ethnic tensions in Pakistan in order to keep its grip on the country's political processes. Whenever and wherever ethnic tension decreases, sectarian tension increases and vice versa. Most probably this relationship is manipulated by invisible hand of the army through its intelligence services.[11]

In accordance with this hypothesis, the second government of Benazir Bhutto had to deal with ethnic violence in Karachi in 1994-96. Taking advantage of the situation, heads of two JUI factions, Maualan Fazlul Rehaan (a coalition partner in the Bhutto government) and Senator Samuel Haq, planned to send some *madrassah* pupils to Afghanistan, supposedly to stop infighting between the warlords and to make the highways linking Pakistan and Afghanistan safer.[12] Desperately needing the support of armed forces to deal with the law and order situation in Karachi, Benazir Bhutto reluctantly approved the plan. However, the real purpose of the ISI was to capture Afghanistan through Taliban proxies. USA knew and approved because it needed an anti-Shia regime in Afghanistan, to the rear of Iran.[13]

One by one, Taliban began to capture the cities of Afghanistan. In 1996 they took Kabul and became masters of much of the country, which was in many ways similar to Pakistan. Taliban imposed the Wahabi, Pashtun and rural brand of Islam on Afghanistan. As mentioned earlier, Wahabis regard Shias as *Kafirs* (infidels) and Wajbul Qatil (liable for mass murder). After becoming masters of Kabul, Taliban took steps to implement their ideology. The Darri Speaking Shia Hazarajat, living in Kabul, became their first victims. Then they fought pitched battles with the Shias in Bamiyan province. After defeating the Hazarajat, Taliban killed many of their able-bodied male members and took their women and children as slaves.

Taliban became a role model for religious parties and sectarian groups in Pakistan. Their slogan was *Aj Kabul, Kal Islamabad Parsoon Srinagar aur Delhi* (Today Kabul, tomorrow Islamabad and day after tomorrow Srinagar and Delhi).[14] The main objectives of this plan was to bring about a Taliban model of Islam into Pakistan. In 1995 and from then on, they received active support from a strong faction of senior army officials led by Major General Zaheer ul Islam, Brigadier Muntaanser Billah and Colonel Inayuttal Khan.[15] The sectarian groups and other Jihadis were getting arms from Afghanistan and Taliban were gaining fresh recruits for fighting against the Northern Alliance, especially the Hajarajats. Killings of Shias in Pakistan took place under Taliban influence. Southern Siraiki belt in Punjab became a hotbed of sectarian organizations.

Nawaz Sharif, in both his terms of government, attempted to quell sectarian violence in Punjab, even though sectarian terrorists were receiving military training and sanctuary in the Al-Qaeda-run camps in Taliban Afghanistan. The sectarian organizations were causing havoc in Punjab. They were so emboldened that Sipah-i-Sahaba exploded a bomb on Nawaz Sharifs route to his farm in Raiwand, near Lahore, in 1998. Sharif requested from Mullah Omar, the Taliban head of state. The extradition of the notorious terrorists Riaz Basra and Akram Lahore, the leaders of the LJ who were wanted for several murders. Until its end, the Nawaz Sharif government was locked in bitter encounters with the sectarian Lashkars. In all probability, factions within the armed forces were aiding the terrorists.

In October 1999, General Pervez Musharraf, the Army Chief of Staff, staged a coup. He used army to maintain good relations with Taliban, which provided Pakistan with strategic depth against India and a foothold in Central Asia. Taliban continued to aid and abet terrorists and outlaws, including Lashkars and Sipahs operating inside Pakistan. Like his predecessors, Musharaf, unsuccessfully asked Taliban to return fugitives from Pakistan. But nothing changed before 11 September, 2001.

The Post-9/11 Scenario

After the dropping of the atomic bomb on Japan in 1945, 9/11 is probably one of the most significant events of the modern age. USA, the sole superpower, was badly shaken when it was attacked on its home territory by non-state actors. President of United States, George Bush, announced a new kind of war on international terrorism. Al-Qaeda and its host organization, the Taliban were declared principal perpetrators of this unprecedented gory incident. The roots of these terrorists were traced to Afghanistan, where Osama Bin Laden, the Al- Qaeda leader, (once a blue-eyed boy of the CIA) was/ is based.

In his crusade against international terrorism, Bush was looking for allies all over the world. Out of pragmatism, Pakistani military junta joined the US-led coalition, especially against the Taliban. It gave air and naval bases to Americans from which to launch attacks on Afghanistan. In October 2001, aerial bombardment of Afghanistan began. Al-Sidique, Al-Umer, Al-Mouwiyah and Khalid Bin Waleed camps, where sectarian and Kashmiri militants were based, were destroyed like all other military training camps. In November 2001 the Taliban regime was ousted from Afghanistan.

Taliban and Al-Qaeda terrorists are widely dispersed within the Southern Pashtun belt of Afghanistan and the Pashtun areas of Pakistan, especially in the Wana area of South Waziristan and the Pashtun belt of Balochistan. There is intermarriage between Pashtuns and Arab militants. Arab militants have been in continuous receipt of money, through various channels from the Gulf. Thus they bring assets to their Taliban hosts. Central Asian and Chechnyan militants are of fair colouring. These ethnic groups mix with the local population in the Pashtun belt. Kashmiri militants were also present. Since they were fighting a war by proxy against the Indians in Kashmir, the ISI regrouped them within Pakistani-administered Kashmir after 9/11 and adjacent areas in the NWFP. Brown-skinned, less well funded, sectarian terrorists became a liability for the Taliban and Al-Qaeda.

In the aftermath of 9/11, special Police Department of Pakistan (commonly known as the CID) feared the return of militants to Pakistan and a new surge of sectarian killings. These fears were justified. In December 2002 General Musharraf outlawed sectarian organizations such as Sipahi Sahaba and Lashkar-i-Jhangvi, but they were active under new name, *e.g.,* Miliat i-Islamia.

In February 2002 Musharraf, like Zia before him, held a referendum to validate his rule for the next five years. In July of that year, he held well orchestrated general elections. One of the conditions was candidates should have at least a university Bachelor's degree or its equivalent. Taking a leaf out of Zia's book, Musharaff regime recognized the *Sanads* of *Madrassahs* as equivalent to a university degree. Thus, many Mullahs qualified to contest the elections. In another move, some Mullahs, implicated in serious crimes, were released and they too stood for election. As a result of this manoeuvring, many Mullahs, including Maulana Azam Tariq, principal leader of the LJ (implicated in several murders) became members of the Provincial and National Assemblies and upper house of parliament, the Senate. For the first time in the history of Pakistan, a grand alliance of Mullahs, Mutahida Majlis Amal (MMA) (United National Alliance) became the third largest force in parliament. Surprisingly, there was token representation of Shias, but they lacked clout. Mullahs won 45 of 324 seats in the National Assembly and 22 out of 100 seats in the Senate. Mullahs formed provincial governments in Balochistan and the NWFP.

General Musharraf's implicit tilt towards Mullahs had two main objectives. First, block the chances of popular political parties of Benazir Bhutto and Nawaz Sharif form government at central or provincial level. Second, and more significantly, to pass a message to USA that his military government was the only alternative to a fundamentalist takeover of a nuclear-capable Pakistan and thus to further instability and nuclear proliferation. This message was successfully conveyed to Bush administration, which continued to support Musharraf against the backdrop of mounting criticism in USA itself and abroad. In addition to US support, Musharraf was repaid by the Mullahs with the passage of the 17th Amendment and Legal Frame Work Order (LFO), which allowed him to retain the post of Chief of the Army Staff till the end of December 2004.

Religious parties apparently kept a distance from the so-called Jihadis. However, Jihadis were their offshoots and enjoyed their tacit blessing. It is fair to say that, after 9/11, the army's mind was with the Americans but its heart was with Mullahs and Jihadis. With these ambiguities, sectarian organization became fairly active in 2003-04. Militant organizations such as the Lashkar-i-Tayeba,[16] and Hizbul Mujahideen, fighting against Indian forces in Kashmir, are in fact, principally Wahabi Punjabis. They depend heavily for their interminable supply of fresh manpower on the sectarian groups, especially the LJ.[17]

After the Kargil Crisis of 1999 (which brought India and Pakistan quite close to a nuclear war) and 9/11, the Kashmiri militants started establishing new military training camps in Gilgit and Baltistan, abutting the Line of Control (LoC) dividing Indian and Pakistani administered Kashmir. Subsequently, they were joined by some sectarian activists.

Local population of this area is mainly Shia of Mongoloid descent, whereas the outside militants are Pashtun and Punjabi Wahabis. Thus, local population resented the substantial presence of newcomers. Militants on their own, forced the feeble Northern Areas local authority to teach only Sunni *Fiqah* (Islamic jurisprudence) in schools and to use textbooks published in NWFP, where a Sunni/Wahabi government was in power. This conflict over the school curriculum took a bloody turn in which the outside militants sided with local Sunnis. There was a siege of Shia villages by law enforcement agencies in which, Shias were killed. Since then, ethnic and sectarian conflicts have become blurred in many parts of the country.

From 1947 onwards, many migrants from Ladakh, Gilgit and Baltistan have trickled down to Karachi. These people have established their residential area, Ladakhi Colony in Malir area of the eastern part of the city. These Gilgits and Baltistanis have had socio-economic and cultural clashes with Punjabi (mostly Sunni) migrants. LJ has a strong base in the area. Consequently, the Gilgits and Baltistanis are also allies of the main factions of Mutahidi Quomi Movement (MQM[18], principal political party of the Urdu-speaking section of the population of Sindh, which has many Shia activists in its ranks. Arguably, because of seemingly interminable clashes of the MQM factions and the involvement of other ethno-sectarian groups therein, in two separate attacks on Shia Masjid (mosque) and, shops nine persons were killed in February 2004. No culprit was arrested.

Quetta, the provincial capital of Balochistan, is quite close to Afghan border. It has a multi-ethnic and multi-sectarian population, with cross-border affiliations. Kandahar with Mullah Omar, is the hotbed of Taliban resistance to pro-US Karzai government of Afghanistan. After 9/11, Taliban regrouped and reorganized themselves in the Pashtun belt of Afghanistan and Pakistan. There are many Afghan refugee camps in the suburbs of Quetta. Teachers at the Wahabi *madrassahs* openly deliver anti-American, anti-Karzai and anti-Shia sermons. Audio-videotapes of these inflammatory sermons are still played in roadside hotels and buses.

The Taliban regard the Hazaras as *Kafirs.* Like their cousins in Afghanistan and Iran, Hazaras in Pakistan are predominantly Shia and look to Iran for support and guidance in temporal as well as spiritual matters. From the outset, Hazaras and Afghan *Mujahidden* (later the Taliban) despised each other. In 1998, when the Taliban massacred Hazaras in Afghanistan, Pakistani sectarian groups collaborated. For their part, as partners of the Northern Alliance, Afghan Hazaras collaborated with the Americans in ousting the Taliban from power. After the fall of Kandahar in 2001 relations between Pashtuns and Hazaras deteriorated further in Pakistan.

In 2003, 11 Hazara police recruits were gunned down and no killer was traced.19 During Muharam, the Shia month of mourning commemorating the martyrdom of Imam Hussain (the grandson of the Prophet Mohammed), a Shia procession in Quetta was attacked and 57 mourners killed. These incidents coincided with deaths of more than 200 mourners by mysterious firings and bombings in the Iraqi holy cities of Karbala and Kazmiyan. More than 30 Shia mourners were killed in Parachinar in NWFP. On another occasion, 44 Shias were killed in a Quetta mosque. The coincidence of killings in Quetta and Iraq provided an easy excuse for Pakistani, particularly the Urdu press, to place the blame squarely on USA. Investigations transpired that at the instigation and with financial support from the top LJ terrorist, Riaz Basra,[20] it was Daud Badani, an active member of LJ, along with 10 accomplices, who carried out these attacks on Shia in Quetta, Sectarian troubles in Quetta continues, albeit on a smaller scale. On 17 September 2004, Professor Atiqual Hassan Naqvi, a retired university professor, was gunned down near the Balochistan University Campus. A year earlier, his son had met the same fate. Civil Society in Quetta held rallies in protest at the killing of Shias[21].

Karachi is the hub of economic activity in Pakistan. Despite its cosmopolitan culture, it is riven with ethnic and sectarian conflicts, which flare up from time to time. Because of its intensity and the fact that bombs and remote-controlled devices are being used, the sectarian conflict appears as deadly as ethnic. In other parts of the country, sectarian clashes usually take place in the month of Muharam. Violence reached a new level in 2004. According to figures released by the Citizen-Police Liaison Committee (CPLC), in three interconnected incidents in May, a semi-autonomous organization, one Sunni cleric, Mufti Nizamuddin Shamzai, was assassinated and 46 Shias were killed.[22] In the first incident on 7 May, Akber Khan, a police constable on duty at the Haideri (Shia) Mosque, located within the premises of Sindh Madrasatul Islam, Jinnah's *alma mater,* blew himself up with a bomb and killed[23] Shia worshippers. The constable had strong ideological links with LJ.

Mufti Nizamuddin Shamzai was killed on 30 May 2004 by unknown assassins. He had been a teacher of Mullah Omar, and his staunch supporter. Men in the street believed that, because of his pro-Al-Qaeda stance, Mufti Shamzai was killed by some foreign agency or that he was killed because of infighting between members of the Benori *madrassah* administration, which he headed. Such a killing of a teacher at the same seminary had taken place a few years earlier. The immediate reaction to the Mufti's murder was mass vandalism in central Karachi by his *madrassah* pupils and their sympathizers. Then, on 31 May, a remote-controlled bomb exploded in the Masjd-i-Ali Raza (a Shia mosque) in MA Jinnah Road in the heart of Karachi, killing 23 worshippers. Initially, the Governor of Sindh province accused anti-state elements of these wanton killings. However, as in Quetta, the Sindh police proved the involvement of LJ.[24]

Musharrf to Zardri : (2008 onwards)

With the change of Mushararf regime with Zardari Government in 2008, sectarian violence remains undiminished. Like every year, there were two bomb blasts in Karachi during Muharam, in December 2009, and January 2010, in which about 100 persons died. Although Taliban and Junduallh, a Baloch nationalist-cum Wahabi group, were suspected responsible, for heavy loss of life responsibility, the Federal Investigation Agency (FIA) cast doubts on an ethnic party, the MQM as well[25]. Similarly there were clashes in Parachinar area of NWFP taking the toll of 8000 persons in the two years.[26] On the day of Eid MIladu Nabi (according to Sunni sect the birthday of Prophet) there were clashes between Sunnis and Wahabis in the town of Dera Ismail Khan, the hotbed of Wahibi Islam, in which about

40 lives were lost. Thus, along with other facades of religious extremisms, sectarian killings remain unabated in Pakistan making highly damaging impact on society and state.

Influence of Sectarianism on Human and National Security

Because of mass killings, members of Shia community have almost lost faith in state's ability to protect their lives, dignity and property.[27] Many Shia doctors and civil servants have been targeted. Many more are emigrating, which affects the working of hospitals and services structures in Pakistan. Shia businessmen have been kidnapped for ransom. Farooq, the son of Hameed Bhojani, a leading Karachi businessman and philanthropist, was kidnapped on his way to school and subsequently killed.

Foreign investors avoid Karachi. The murder of American journalist Daniel Pearl and of French engineers, Iranian diplomats, engineers and military personnel, with the attack on American Consulate-General in 2002, have frightened off foreign investors. This stoppage in the flow of fresh money, has badly hit local industry. Local businesses shut down earlier than their normal closing hours. In June and July 2004, shops were closed in the main shopping areas of the city, such as the Saddar and Tariq Rood. The city then wore a ghostly look. In early 2005, matters were gradually returning to normality in Karachi but citizens lived from day to day. According to Dr Haroon Ahmed, leading psychiatrist of the city, about 60% of them are under stress from violence-related tension and constant fear of becoming a victim[28]. Some Shias prefer to be part of India and live peacefully with their kinsmen on the other side of the international border. The Hazaras of Balochistan feel that the state of Pakistan cannot defend them against the Taliban/LJ onslaught. They look to Iran, Iraq or further afield, even to Hizbollah of Lebanon, for some protection and fraternity. Punjab is the central province of Pakistan. Chakwal and Jhelum are recruiting centre for the army. These areas are riven by sectarianism. So are Lahore and other parts of the central Punjab, as well as the Southern Siraiki belt, which for centuries, before 1970s, used to be the most peaceful part of the region.[29]

At present, interior of Sindh only is, remarkably spared from sectarian infection. However, there is a chain of Wahabi *madrassahs* operating in Hyderabad city, Tando Adam, Dadu, Nawab Shah Sukkur, Theri[30] and many other big and small towns in the interior, which could ignite the flames of sectarianism, if their activities are not monitored and controlled by the state and civil society.[31] Interior of Sindh is saved primarily because of the tolerant and universalist teachings of Sindhi mystics, especially the Shah Latif of Bhit. These Sufi teachings have created an atmosphere of tolerance, mutual respect and fraternity and deprived fanatics of open sympathizers. This could become a model for the rest of the country, if state and civil society were willing to apply it.

Even if Shias do not form an 'influential minority'[32], they do form a sizeable minority. If such a visible minority, whether ethnic, religious or sectarian, loses faith in a state, then the very existence of that state is jeopardized. It comes close to being a 'failing state'. Moreover, sectarian tensions and the alliance between sectarian and Jihadi organizations have adversely affected Pakistan's relationships with three out of four of its immediate neighbours: Iran, Afghanistan and India. In the West, Pakistan is considered a state that aids and abets fundamentalists and terrorists. In other words, sectarianism has divided Pakistani society internally and isolated it internationally.

Terrorism in the name of sect or religion was a byproduct of General Zia's promotion of drug and Kalashnikov culture and his adoption of so-called Islamization. The process of

Islamization was, in effect, a process of Ziafication of the Pakistani state and its society. Mullahs and military were the twin pillars of the Zia regime. A combination of internal and external forces nurtured and nourished the culture of intolerance, militancy and violence which gave birth to terrorism of all kinds. Consequences for Pakistani state and society and for the international community, are horrendous. These problems must be tackled for the sake of cohesion of Pakistani society, the security of state, and stability of the international community, as the London based prestigious weekly, *The Economist*, correctly suggests.[33]

During his tenure, General Musharraf launched his programme of "enlightened moderation", aimed at curbing extremism and terrorism in the country. However, Ijazul Haq, the son of dictator Zia ul Haq, was Minister of Religious Affairs in his cabinet. Ijazul Haq, acted as a strong link between reportedly fundamentalist section of the armed forces, the civilian facade of the military-dominated political establishment and the Mullahs. He dealt directly with M*adrassahs,* the breeding grounds of terrorism and sectarianism. He symbolized the legacy of Zia. During 2002 elections, Musharraf engineered the results in such a manner that the Mullahs formed two provincial governments and they had a marked presence in both houses of parliament. After two attempts on his life in December 2003, Musharraf had apparently taken a hard line with the terrorists but the power of Mullahs appears intact. He has not broken contact with them. On the contrary, Musharraf never missed an opportunity to woo them. Keeping in mind the post-2004 scenario, he assured a group of M*adrassah* heads that there would be no interference in their affairs.[34] This was an explicit recognition of the power of the Mullahs.

Religious/political parties apparently deny their links with the terrorists but are generally disbelieved. All captured and killed terrorists had been educated in *madrassahs* and maintained links with them.[35] These linkages with seatrain outfits by ruling parties of the country, protect and embolden the former in killing Shia and non-Muslim minorities, especially Christians in Punjab. This is the reason sectarianism as a form of extremism, remains intact. Presently, Rana Sanuallah, the law minister of Punjab, who is the member of the ruling Muslim League Nawaz group, reportedly maintains links with LJ, which is banned in Pakistan under the anti-terrorism law.[36] Such a hobnobbing with the sectarian outfits will give them lease of life and political influence in their area of operation, such as the Siraiki belt.

Because of the military operation in Waziristan and other parts of the Federally Administrative Area (FATA), Mullahs and military appear to be at loggerheads. This tussle may be short-lived, because, as just stated , sectarian organizations are one of the faces of religious zealotry. Americans, who have given 7.5 billion Dollars aid for five years to Pakistan under the Karry-Lugar Law of 2009, are skeptical about Pakistan's links with Taliban. In an interview to the London financial *Times,* U.S. special envoy to Afghanistan and Pakistan, who conducts diplomatic contacts with the Afghanistan, Pakistan and India said, he was "agnostic" about Pakistan as decisively turned against the Afghan Taliban.[37] Arguably, one cannot draw a line between Afghan Taliban and Pakistani Taliban. And till Pakistan's intelligence services maintain contacts with the Al-Qaueda and Taliban, nexus between the Al-Qauida, Taliban and the sectarian organization will remain intact, because they are interdependent on each other.

It is also worth mentioning that infiltrators who allegedly operate in India, are based and trained mainly in camps in Azad Kashmir. These so-called Kashmiri Jihadis get fresh recruits from the sectarian organizations, especially the Lashkari Jhangvi and Sipahi Sahaba.[38] And besides Mullahs, Pakistan Army appears too adamant to retain its clandestine links with the Lashkar-i-Tayeba. It is this organization which is implicated by Indians for the Mumbai bomb blast of November 2008. And Zardari Government in Pakistan under pressure from right wing political parties and the Army is unwilling to extradite Hafiz Saeed to India, to stand a trial there. He allegedly masterminded the attack on Mumbai, This is one of the most soaring points in Indo-Pak relations. Thus, arguably, handing over the leaders of Lashka-i-Tayeba leaders to India will be helpful on two accounts. It will facilitate the improvement of Indo-Pak relations, on the other hand, it will put cracks within the ranks of the extremists including the sectarian outfits, because one group depends on the other.

In addition, if a liberal and tolerant society is to survive, *Madrassah* education should either be discouraged or monitored, because Madrasshahs are the nurseries of all kinds of religious terrorism. In order to support Musharraf's above mentioned programme of modern enlightenment, $ 3 billion were given to the Madrassahs to reform their education system by introducing English language and internet skills. The whole scheme proved to be counterproductive. A new group of Mullahs with knowledge of English and information technology emerged. Will they be a catalyst of change for the better? Or will they strengthen worldwide terrorist networks? After all, many terrorists are well educated. Sheikh Ahmed Omar Saeed, who allegedly masterminded the murder of Daniel Pearl, was educated at the London School of Economics. He had only a brief education in a *Deeni Madrassah* but that proved more formative than the liberal LSE. Tanzanian-born Ahmed Khalfan Ghaliani, Naheem Noor Khan and Amjad Farooqi (all involved in sectarian killings and *Jihad* in Kashmir and Afghanistan), were reputedly well versed in computer science. One could argue that knowledge of computers or geography or physics will not be of much help in changing the mindset of *Madrassah*-educated students because exclusiveness, bigotry and militancy in the name of *Jihad* are taught to pupils at a very young age. Liberalization of Mullah mentality appears near impossible. It would be better to isolate the Mullahs than to woo them. Money should not be spent on the *Deeni madrassahs* but on public sector universities and on government-run schools imparting liberal knowledge. Job opportunities should be created for young and able graduates. Then poor parents will prefer to send their children to these schools, rather than dumping them in M*adrassahs* where they are prepared to become cannon fodder of sectarian and other terrorist organizations.

In traditional rural societies of Sindh and Punjab before Zia era, Mullah was confined to the *Masset* (mosque). He was called upon by the people only on three occasions: the birth of a child, a marriage or a death in the family. It was only in the Zia era and onwards that Mullahs assumed a more general leadership role. This role should now be challenged in both urban and rural areas.

Liberal folk culture should be promoted. Urban intellectuals and village folk should sit together in the *Mellas* (festivals) where the fakirs (disciples of the saint) and folksingers sing the songs of Shah Latif, Khuwaja Ghulam Farid, Bullah Shah and Das Kabir. Poetry of these saints preached human brotherhood instead of bigotry. Their message should be popularized at all levels. It is hearting that *Kalam or Risalo* poetry of Latif is being sung at home and aboard.[39] Its translation is presented to the audience in the local languages and English. Thus, gradually, the world in general, and Pakistan in particular, are becoming familiar with the message of inter-communal harmony and international peace propounded by Latif and other mystics. This appears to be a societal change which will operate as a mechanism for curbing extremism of all kinds including sectarianism. The combination of above stated measures will be conducive in achieving this noble goal, which will be good for its civil society, state of Pakistan and international community.

References

1. Amin Lakhani, 'Why sectarian violence must end', *The Daily Dawn* (Karachi), 19 August, 2004.

2. Word *Mullah* takes on different meanings in different contexts. In Iran, it is used for a person who knows jurisprudence and leads the congregation. Before the Islamic Revolution in Iran in 1979 *'Mullah'* was used in this sense. After the revolution, it was replaced by such titles as *Ayatollah* and *Hujatul.* In Afghanistan and rural areas in Pakistan *'Mullah'* denoted a congregation leader. Shia *Mullahs* follow Iranian usage. Their Sunni and Wahabi counterparts prefer to be addressed as *Mufti* or *Moulvi Sahib* or *the Moulani,* but still use the term *Mullah* for themselves.

3. Founder of Wahabi sect was Sheikh Abdul Wahab from the Najid province of present day Saudi Arabia. He interpreted Islam as a puritan religious movement owing much to the Bedouin tradition. The Sheikh supported the Arab rebellion against the Turks during the First World War. Thereafter, the Wahabi brand of Islam enjoyed the official patronage of the British in the Gulf. After the installation of the Saudi dynasty in 1922, Wahabi Islam became the undeclared official religion of Saudi Arabia. Since the emergence of Al-Qaeda in the 1980s, a triangular relationship between Al-Qaeda, Saudi clergy and the Saudi royal family developed which enjoyed American patronage till 11 September 2001. The Wahabis of the subcontinent call themselves Daobandis, after Daoband, in the suburbs of Saharnpur. All the Wahabis of the subcontinent were originally educated there. Thus, the Sindhi Wahabis, who have many *Madrassahs* in Thahri, call themselves Daobandis but the common people address them as Wahabis and this popular term has been used here.

4. For the Bhutto—nationalist tussle and the situation exploited by Mullahs and military, see Mehtab Ali Shah, *The Foreign Policy of Pakistan: Ethnic Impact on Diplomacy, 1971-1974,* (London: I. B. Tauris, 1977), pp. 137-138.

5. Sir Oliver Forster, the British High Commissioner to Pakistan in the mid-1980s, narrated an interesting story about Zia's pretensions to public piety. At one stage, Margaret Thatcher, then British prime minister, along with her Foreign Secretary, Sir Geoffrey Howe, visited Torkham, the border crossing between Afghanistan and Pakistan. Zia suddenly said that he should be excused from conversation because he had to offer noon prayers. While he was offering his prayers not far from the guests'. Sir Geoffrey commented on what a devout Muslim he was. Mrs Thatcher instantly retorted what a good friend of the West he was.

6. Ian Talbot, *The History of Modern Pakistan,*(Lahore: Vanguard, 1999), p. 252.

7. Interview with Kachkol Ali Baloch, advocate, the leader of Opposition in Balochistan Provincial Assembly, Quetta, 28 May, 2004.

8. Fred Halliday, *The Making of the Second Cold War,* (London: Verso, 1989).

9. B.Raman, "The Saudi Connections", *Weekly Outlook,*(New Delhi) 7th March, 2010, pp. 10-14.

10. London-based prestigious think tank, International Institute of Strategic Studies, (IISS) considers these sectarian organizations as terrorist groups. *The Military Balance* 2009 (London: Brassy, 2010), p. 331.

11. I have borrowed this idea from the late Professor F.S. Northedge, who spoke of "the blob of tension" in the

international context. According to him, conflict is a perennial factor in the international political system: whenever it recedes in one region of the world, it increases in another. For details, Northedge, *The International Political System,(* London: Faber and Faber, 1976), pp. 265-266. From the Northedge viewpoint balance of conflict, like the balance of power, is something natural which functions automatically in the international political system. I have applied this model in the context of Pakistan's domestic situation. However, the relationship between ethnic and sectarian tension in Pakistan is not automatic but manipulated by the army in order to gain greater leverage in national politics.

12. Ahmed Rashid, *Taliban, Islam, Oil and the New Great Game in Central Asia*,(London and New York: I. B. Tauris, 1992) pp. 17-81.

13. John J. Coolley, *Unholy Wars: America and International Terrorism,*(London: Public Press, 1999), pp. 222-223.

14. Azmat Abbass, 'Return to sender', *The Herald:* Karachi, December 2001, pp. 26-27.

15. Masoud Ansari, 'Divine mission', *Newsline:* Karachi, July 2004, pp. 46-52.

16. Hafiz Seed, the leader of Lashka-i-Tayeba, who reportedly masterminded the Mumbai bomb blasts is from Bahawalpur.

17. Zaffar Abbass, 'Action replay', *The Herald,* December 2003, pp. 56-57.

18. *Dawn* 5th, November 2009.

19. Azizullah Khan, 'Clueless in Quetta', *The Herald,* April 2004, pp. 31-33.

20. The *Daily Dawn,* 21 September 2004; and *The Daily Times* (Lahore), 22 September 2004.

21. *The Daily Dawn,* 17 September, 2004.

22. *Comparative Casualty Figures: Killed in May 2004,* study compiled by the CPLC. Also Syed Shoib Hassan, 'Fear over the city', *The Herald,* June 2004, pp. 64-67.

23. Conversations with four different Karachi taxi drivers.

24. Zahid Hussain, 'Cover story', *Newsline,* August 2004, pp. 19-40.

25 . *Dawn: Metropolitan,* 21 February, 2010.

26. "Parachinaar Under Curfew", *Dawn,* 6th March 2010.

27. Amin Lakhani, 'Why sectarian violence must end'. *The Daily Dawn,* 19 August 2004.

28. *Dawn Thursday Review,* 10 June, 2004.

29. In one spate of violence, 25 Shias were killed in Sialkot, bordering the Jammu region of Indian Jammu and Kashmir, four Shias were killed in Lahore and 46 followers of the LJ were killed in Multan. *The Daily Dawn* on the different dates of October, 2004.

30. Amjad Farooqi, an Al-Qaeda terrorist, who twice attempted to murder General Musharraf was a member of Sipahi Sahab and Lashkar- i- Jhangvi, with a price of Rs. 20 million on his head. He was killed in Nawab Shah and his accomplices were arrested in Sukkur and Mir Pur Khas. These arrests demonstrated that there is a strong network of religious terrorists present in the interior of Sindh. *The Daily Dawn,* 27, 28, 29 September 2004.

31. *Dawn,* 8 September, 2004.

32. Arnold Toynbee coined and defined the term 'influential minority' for a group of persons who cannot be ignored while

making decisions about a community. Toynbee, *The Study of History: An Abridgement,* (London: Chatham House Publications, 1977), p. 77.

33. Shias are Targets in Pakistan Too", leader, The *Economist*, 4th March 2004, pp. 36-37.

34. *The Independent* (London), 21st October 2004.

35. *The Independent,* 28 September, 2004.

36. Zulqaranin Tahir, "Contact with Banned Outfit: Tasser Asks Shahbaz to Remove Rana", *Dawn,* 6th March 2010.

37. Baqir Sajjad Syed, "Pakistan's Tactical Moves Displeases the U.S.", *Dawn, 6th* March 2010.

38. B. Raman, "Blast After Blast", *Outlook:* 14-21 March, 2010.

39. Fakir Juman Shah, the main singer of Latif is singing at different places in the world. His latest performance was in Jaipur, Rajasthan during the 5th Literary Festival held in March 2010.

(This is the updated version of the article "Sectarianism-A Threat to Human Security : A Case Study of Pakistan" in *The Round Table,* Vol: 94, Issue: 382, October, 2005, Rutledge Journals, Francis and Taylor, Carfax, Oxfordshire, 2005. I acknowledge the source with thanks to the Publishers.)

8

Punjabi Dominated Pakistan Army behind Kashmir Imbroglio

There is no unanimity among Pakistanis over the idea of the accession of entire Kashmir to Pakistan. It also suggests that in different provinces of Pakistan, the idea of an independent Kashmir, generally known as the 'third option', is gaining momentum.

The four provinces of Pakistan—Punjab, the North-West Frontier Province, Sindh and Balochistan have different geopolitical locations on the map of Pakistan and South Asia Principal inhabitants of these provinces, Punjabis, Pashtuns, Sindhis and Balochs, have attended different levels of participation in the decision-making processes of Pakistan over the last four decades.

The geostrategic locations of these four provinces, *vis-à-vis* Kashmir and their level of participation in the governance of Pakistan, have a great deal of influence on the views of the principal inhabitants of the provinces over the solution of the Kashmir dispute.

To examine these views on Kashmir, as a part of a bigger research project, this author conducted interviews with some of the major spokesmen from four provinces. Although in many cases, these spokesmen on Pakistan's domestic and foreign policy might not necessarily be the elected representatives of four provinces, they enjoy a considerable degree of popularity in their respective provinces. Besides interviewing these informed opinion-makers, the coverage of the newspapers published in vernacular languages from four provinces about Kashmir dispute was also studied by this author.

A Punjabi perspective of the Kashmir problem

The Punjab is the biggest province of the post-1971 Pakistan. It comprises about 56% of the population of Pakistan.[1] The bulk of Pakistan's military hails from Punjab.[2] Similarly, according to Charles Kennedy, an American academic interested in bureaucratic structure of Pakistan, the biggest chunk of Pakistani bureaucracy, about 60%, also comes from Punjab.[3] It is this civil-cum-military bureaucracy which has directly or indirectly ruled the country over its 60 year history.

Punjab has a common border of about 280 kilometres with the Pakistani administered part of Kashmir. In fact, Punjabi city of Sialkot touches the J & K territory. All the rivers of Punjab flow from Kashmir. Kashmir is an area from where free flow of rivers to Pakistan, is the main determinants of prosperity of Pakistan. Many prominent Punjabis, such as Allama Iqbal and Mian Nawaz Sharif's ancestors, were Kashmiris. There are large Kashmiri settlements in Lahore and other major cities in the Punjab. A great many Kashmiris are also recruited in armed forces of Pakistan.[4]

Punjabis, after Kashmiris themselves, are more interested in this dispute than anybody else in Pakistan. To the majority of Punjabis, Kashmir represents the letter *K* of the word *Pakistan*. Without its accession to Pakistan, the Muslim homeland in north India would be incomplete.[5] For proximity and blood relationship with Kashmiris, the Punjabis shout loudly and repeatedly the slogan of *Kashmir Bane ga Pakistan*.

Ending of Indian control of Kashmir, instability of India in Kashmir and East Punjab, according to Selig Harrison, an American specialist on South Asia, were the policy objectives of the Zia regime.[6] There appears to be no change in this policy as far as Kashmir is concerned. Lahore based Jamaat-i-Islami calls guerrilla warfare in Kashmir a *Jihad* (holy war) and openly admits to arming and training Kashmiri militants, especially, *Hizbi Mujahideen* and *Al Umer,* guerrilla organizations.[8] The terrorist band, Lashkar-e-Tayeba, which operates in India, is headquartered in Muridke, near Lahore. Because of anti-Indian insurgency launched by the Jamati Islami utterances, Indians feel that they are fighting a war by proxy in Kashmir against Pakistan-backed rebels.[8]

Ironically, while the overwhelming majority of the Kashmiris living on both sides of the Line of Control in Kashmir, and abroad, are demanding unification of the whole of Kashmir into a single state and its independence from both India and Pakistan.[9] the Punjabi opinion makers, in concert with their co-ethnic policy makers, still play incessantly on the tune of *Kashmir Bane ga Pakistan.* When Mushahid Hussain Sayed, the former editor of the Islamabad based English language newspaper, *The Muslim,* and latter an adviser to the former Punjabi Prime Minister of Pakistan, Nawaz Sharif and now a leader of the army funded Muslim League-Qauid-i-Azam(Q), was asked to comment on Pakistan's reaction to the idea of an independent Kashmir, he said:

Pakistan would never subscribe to such an idea. To Pakistan, independence means the freedom of the Srinagar valley from Indian control and its subsequent accession to Pakistan.[10] I.A. Rahman, a leading human rights campaigner, columnist and left wing Lahore-based intellectual, when interviewed on this subject, was also evasive in his exposition. He suggested that:

> A loose Indo-Pakistani condominium that could provide a higher degree of freedom of movement to the Kashmiris, would be a more practical solution and Pakistan may accept it. Because it would be easier to recognize the present *de facto* partition into a *de jure* one, than the recognition of Kashmir as an independent state.[11]

Thus, most of Punjabis, leftists and rightists, do not support the idea of an independent state, which could be one of the internationally acceptable solutions of the Kashmir dispute.[12]

One could argue that besides the Indian intransigence on considering Kashmir as its integral part, keeping the Kashmir dispute alive also serves Punjab's interests within Pakistan. This problem maintains hostility with India intact. It provides a major justification for keeping a huge military machine which, according to its critics, has been used as the iron hand of the Punjab to tighten its grip on the smaller provinces.

A Pashtun Perspective of Kashmir Problem

Most of the Pashtuns live in the North-West Frontier Province. The Province of Balochistan has its own sizeable portion of Pashtun population. Both Pashtuns from the NWFP and Balochistan form the second largest portion of civilian-military bureaucracy of Pakistan.[13] Here views of Pashtuns from the NWFP only are studied on Kashmir problem. Views of Pashtuns from Balochistan are almost identical with their cousins from NWFP on Pakistan's internal and external affairs.

Aftab Ahmed Khan Sherpao, leader of the provincial branch of the Pakistan People's Party, now his own faction of the Pakistan Peoples Party, commenting on the Kashmir problem as a part of Indo-Pak relationship said:

The idea of an independent Kashmir appears to be untenable, because if an independent state of Kashmir was created by uniting the Indian and Pakistani parts of the former princely state, it would not be economically and politically a viable state, So the whole of Kashmir must accede to Pakistan.[14] Mr. Sherpao's line of thinking shows no marked difference from the Punjabi dominated Islami Jamhuri Itihad (IJI) policy position on Kashmir.

Awami National Party (ANP) is one of the oldest and well organized political parties of NWFP. It was led by Late Khan Abdul Wali Khan and Ajmal Khatak, the two radical leaders of entire Pakistan. As the successor of the Khudai Khudmitgar and later the National Awami Party, ANP professes to cherish the Gandhian ideal of non-violence. Often NAP and its present offspring the ANP, are accused of being pro-India.[15] Wali Khan always advocated the normalization of Indo-Pak relationship. However, for a settlement of this chronic dispute between India and Pakistan, which mars their relationship badly, Wali Khan did support the idea of the maintenance of the *status quo.*[16]

The only singular Pashtun politician with a voice of dissent on Pakistan's policy over India in general and on the Kashmir dispute in particular, is Mr. Afrasyab Khatak, the Secretary General of the Pashtukhaw Quomi Inqlabi Party, who has rejoined the ANP. His views are summarized as following:

Pakistan should support the idea of an independent Kashmir instead of its present moribund policy of the accession of Kashmir in Pakistan which is out of tune with Kashmir aspirations. Pakistan certainly has a hand in the Sikh insurgency which does not go well in its own interests. One sitting in the house of glass should not throw stones at others. Pakistan must give top priority in improving its relations with India than with the other countries around it.[17] Afrasyab Khatak's position represents a minority Pashtun view on India. The rest of the Pashtun opinion makers, most conspicuously the ANP, from the late 1980s onward, tend to agree implicitly with the Punjabis dominated IJI and other political parties on the Kashmir issue.

One can argue that if Pashtuns did not have a substantial share in both the bureaucracy and army, then their perceptions about India would have been markedly different. Since the army needs an enemy, the Pashtun officer corps in their own interests supports the perpetuation of enmity with India.

Sindhi Perceptive of the Kashmir Problem

Sindh is the southernmost province of Pakistani union. It is situated about 2000 kilometers from Kashmir. Native Sindhis are the principal inhabitants of this province. However, a considerably high number of the Urdu speaking descendants of the migrants who came from India after 1947), also live in big cities of Sindh province.

"The Muhajir politics", according to Altaf Hussain, leader of one of the factions of *Muhajir Qoumi Movement (MQM)* orbits around jobs and the other related problems faced by this community in the big cities of the Sindh Province.[18] After the creation of Pakistan, Urdu speaking migrants formed the backbone of the bureaucracy of Pakistan and they still comprise a considerable portion of it. Being a substantial part of the ruling elite of Pakistan, most of the migrants used to share the perceptions of their Punjabi and Pashtun counterparts on the national and international affairs of Pakistan. There are hardly any comments available, suggesting that most of the migrant politicians and intellectuals support the idea of an independent

Kashmir. Hence, one can assume that being a part of the ruling elite, the migrant community on the whole shares the Pakistan official position on the Kashmir dispute, the accession to Pakistan.

In contrast with the migrants, Sindhis from 1947 to 1993 in general and from 1977 to this date in particular, do not enjoy any considerable influence in the decision-making processes of Pakistan. They feel a deep sense of deprivation in the management of the state of affairs of Pakistan. Execution of Zulfiquar Ali Bhutto, the first Sindhi Prime Minister of Pakistan by the Punjabi dictator of Pakistan, General Zia-ul-Hq in 1979, inflicted deep wounds on the Sindhi psyche. Similarly the subsequent dismissals of two other Sindhi Prime Ministers, Mohammed Khan Junejo (1988) and Benazir Bhutto (1990) by General Zia and his successor, Ishaq Khan (a retired Pashtun bureaucrat) respectively, have added insult to the injury of the Sindhis. Their sense of deprivation is so deep, that most of them see the Punjabi-Pashtun-Muhajir dominated Pakistan as a manifestation of an internal colonialism which deprives them of their own natural resources in their own ancestral homeland.[19]

Most of the informed Sindhis do not share the foreign policy perceptions of the ruling elite. Pakistan People's Party led by Benazir Bhutto is an exception. Besides Sindh, PPP has support bases in the Punjab and the NWFP also, which it cannot afford to lose at all. Lending any support to the cause of an independent Kashmir might further erode the PPP support bases in the Punjab and the NWFP. Thus, to retain its dwindling popularity in these provinces, the PPP leadership sticks to the old policy of 'right of self determination' for the Kashmiris.

Although the PPP was the main political party, but not the exclusive platform of the Sindhis on which they express their views. In Sindh, there are many political parties which have started supporting the idea of an independent Kashmir instead of its accession to Pakistan.

It is also worth mentioning that the geographical remoteness of Kashmir from Sindh makes it a less sensitive issue for the Sindhis,[20] as it used to be for the Bengalis before 1971.[21] In Sindh, unlike Punjab, there are no substantial pockets of Kashmir population. Nor are there any intermarriages or a high degree of contact between Sindhis and Kashmiris, which might make the Kashmir issue something emotional for the Sindhis.

Kashmiris working in Sindh, especially at Karachi airport, in the Pakistan International Airline (PIA), Karachi Development Authority (KDA), steel mill or the law enforcing agencies, mainly hail from Mirpur in area under Pak occupation and are mostly believed to be ethnically Punjabi[22] and thus hardly distinguishable in their attitude from the Punjabis to a Sindhi onlooker. Thus, at an individual level, Sindhis perceive Kashmiris settled in Karachi as aliens who have impinged on their resources. Prime Minister of Pakistani Kashmir, Sardar Abdul Qayoom Khan, makes things worse for Kashmiris. Whenever there are Sindh-Muhajir riots in Sindh, Sardar Qayoom visits Sindh and makes inflammatory speeches against Sindhis.[23] Sardar Qayoom's rhetoric against Sindhis creates a bad impression of the Kashmiri people in Sindh.

However, Sindhis of almost all political persuasions consider Kashmiris having own ethnicity. It should be made emphatically clear that despite Benazir Bhutto's deliberate ambiguity on the interpretation of the right of 'self-determination' for the Kashmiris, probably not a single Sindhi leader supports the idea of the accession of the Indian held part of Kashmir to Pakistan. Sindhis support the idea of the 'third option', propagated by the Jammu and Kashmir Liberation Front (JKLF) led by Amanullah Khan, which insists on the unification of the two parts of Kashmir into a single state and then its independence from both India and Pakistan.[24]

Asif Baladi, a young Sindhi student leader of Jiaye Sindh Students Federation (JSSF), sees the slogan of *Kashmir Bana ga Pakistan,* as a ploy of Punjabis to impose centralization in Sindh in the name of confrontation with India over the Kashmir issue.[25]

Rasul Bux Palejo, leader of Marxist Sindhi Awami Tahrik (Sindhi People's Movement) which played a leading role in the Movement of the Restoration of Democracy (MRD) in 1983, believes that :

Kashmiris are a mature people and would not be swayed by obscurantist parties such as the Jamaat-i-Islami to join a Pakistan in which they would find themselves suffocated and exploited by the Punjabis. There is little choice for Kashmiris to select between either an India or an obscurantist Pakistan. If they have to exercise their right of self determination, they must strive for an independent state. And they, in fact, are going in that direction. Let us support them in that endeavour.[26] G.M. Sayed a seasoned Sindhi leader spent about 50 years in detention fighting for the cause of Sindh. He is considered by the Pakistani establishment as the enemy of Pakistan. But most of the Sindh youth and intellectuals revere him as their unquestionable leader[28] addressed as the Seen (Sir) by most of the other Sindhi leaders, even by his political rivals.

G.M. Sayed saw the accession of Kashmir to Pakistan as unrealistic and dangerous for smaller nationalities in Pakistan. He saw Indo-Pak relations on the one hand, and Sindhi-Punjabi (centre-province) relations on the other, as zero sum games. Any loss for India resulting from Kashmir if it accedes to Pakistan, would be a gain for Pakistan. By this logic, any gain to Pakistan which he calls Punjab would be a loss to Sindhis.[28] From G. M. Sayed's point of view, accession of Kashmir would encourage Punjabis to pursue a policy of expansion more vigorously and in order to do so they would be more repressive to Sindhis. He preferred the maintenance of the *status quo* between India and Pakistan on Kashmir, rather than the accession of the whole of Kashmir to Pakistan.[29]

Barrister Abdul Hafiz Pirzada, a former Law and Finance Minister of Pakistan during the Bhutto era (1972-1977), well known expert on constitutional law was the General Secretary of Pakistan National Party, which had a strong political base in Sindh and Balochistan. Pirzada perceived the Kashmir issue from the point of view of realpolitik. He argues that:

Under no international pressure India is going to budge over the Kashmir issue by allowing Kashmiris to join Pakistan. Nor could Pakistan grab Kashmir from India militarily. To make a favourable environment in India and the world at large, Pakistan must support the Kashmiris for the creation of their own state rather than joining the union of Pakistan.[30]

Thus, the overwhelming majority of informed Sindhis support the idea of an independent state, rather than the accession of the Kashmir into Pakistan as advocated by the government of Pakistan. There is a strong opinion among informed Sindhis that after the independence of Kashmir, Pakistan would have the best possible relationship with India. This amity would facilitate a drastic cut in the defence expenditure of Pakistan, which would in turn reduce the level of the exploitation of Sindh in the name of national defence. From a Sindhi point of view, an independent Kashmir could be a harbinger of an internal change in the structure of the union of Pakistan and its foreign policy, which could be equally true for India as well.

Baloch Perspective of the Kashmir Problem

Balochistan is located at the western fringe of South Asia. Kashmir is physically far flung from Balochistan. Unlike

Punjabis, Balochs have no racial and cultural bonds with the Kashmiris. Moreover, there is a deep-rooted resentment against the Punjabi-Pashtun-migrant domination of Pakistan in Balochistan province. In the past there has been a number of full-blown insurgencies against central government of Pakistan in interior of the province of Balochistan. Most significantly, the insurgency which drew international attention took place in the mid-1970s during the Bhutto era when an over centralized federal system was imposed on Balochistan.[31] This over centralized system of the government, according to the Baloch accounts, was imposed to deprive them of their own natural resources.

Balochs as an ethnic group, are still completely marginalized in the decision-making processes of Pakistan. And as a reaction to this marginalization, Balochs have strong reservations about the whole range of Pakistan's domestic and external affairs, including the Kashmir problem. Likewise the Sindh leader GM Sayed, many Baloch leaders, especially, Sardar Attullah Khan Mengal, the former Chief Minister of Balochistan, perceived any gain of the Pakistani rulers as a loss for Balochs.[32] In his words :

The Kashmir dispute with India has been exploited by the Punjabis to keep conflict alive with that country in order to keep a huge Army intact. This Army is not only a major source of their earning but also gives them a clout over the smaller nationalities. The maintenance of the *status quo* or minor territorial adjustments are required to settle the Kashmir dispute once and for all.[33]

Chief of Baloch Student Organizations (BSO), late Ghulam Mohammed Baloch, opposed the slogen of *Kashmir Bane ga Pakistan*. On the contrary, he strongly supported the idea of the creation of an independent Kashmir state.[34]

Thus, the informed Balochs do not support Pakistan's policy of the accession of Kashmir to it. Such a policy, from an articulate Baloch point of view, is aimed at an expansion of Punjabi power for which Sindhis and Balochs should not pay any political or economic price.

As discussed earlier, because of the attainment of different levels in the decision making processes of Pakistan and because of their variant geopolitical location from Kashmir, the principal ethnic groups in Pakistan do not share any common policy on the major issues of their country's foreign policy, including the Kashmir problem. Most of the Punjabis and Pashtuns who comprise the chief component of Pakistani establishment, support the official views on this crucial issue. Most of the Muhajirs also jump the bandwagon of Punjabis and Pashtuns. Conversely, most of the Sindhi and Baloch intellectuals and politicians support the idea of the creation of an independent, secular, demilitarized and neutralized, Austrian model Kashmir. From their perspective, an independent Kashmir would help India and Pakistan to improve their relations and divert their resources from defence to development, which is badly needed by the people of these states. Incidentally, such an idea is gaining currency in the world.[35]

References

1. Population of Pakistan. For an overall population of Punjab within Pakistan, see *Pakistan Yearbook 1991,* p. 11. And for the claims of the Siraikis, see *The Siraiki People's Charter of Demands,* Siraiki Lok Sangh (mass awakening) (Islamabad: 1989), pp. 20-22.

2. Stephen Cohen, *The Pakistan Army,* (Berkeley: University of California Press, 1984), pp. 44-45.

3. Charles Kennedy, 'Table 8.3: Officers of the Federal Bureaucracy by Districts of Domicile', *Bureaucracy in Pakistan* (Oxford: Oxford University Press, 1986), p. 196.

4. GS Bhargava, *Benazir: Pakistan's New Hope,* 1990, p. 130.

5. Kuldip Nayar, 'Kashmir: Rereading its Past in order to Proffer a Practicable Solution, *The Round Table,* Vol. 323, July 1992, p. 305.

6. Selig Harrison, 'South Asia and the United States: a chance for a fresh start', *Current History,* Vol. 91, No. 563, March 1992, p. 97.

7. 'Kashmir: the rocky road ahead', *Herald,* monthly, (Karachi), February 1990, pp. 82-90; and *Takbir,* weekly, Urdu, Karachi, 25 April 1991, pp. 31-32.

8. Ramesh Vinayuk, 'The battle spills over', *India Today (New Delhi),* 30 September, 1992, pp. 42-43.

9. Harinder Bajva, 'Amanullah Khan speaks: an interview', *India Today,* 20 December 1992, pp. 66-67. And also, Zaffar Khan, the diplomatic representative of the Jammu and Kashmir Liberation Front (JKLF) in an interview with this author, at the Institute of Commonwealth Studies, London, 27 July, 1993.

10. An interview with the author in Islamabad, on 3 October, 1991.

11. I. A. Rahman, in an interview with this author in Lahore on 30 September, 1991.

12. Stephen Cohen, 'Kashmir: the roads ahead-III', *Frontier Post,* 16 September, 1992.

13. C. Kennedy, *op. cit.*

14. An interview with the author in Peshawar on 10 October, 1991.

15. *Jang,* London edition, 12 July, 1992.

16. *Ibid.*

17. An interview with the author in Peshawar on 8 October, 1991.

18. *Jang,* daily, Urdu newspaper, London edition, 25 September, 1993.

19. GM Sayed, *Sindho Desh: A Study in its Separate Identity,* (Karachi: G. M. Sayed Academy, 1991), p. 401.

20. Asif Baladi, an interview with this author in Jamshoro Sindh, on 16 October, 1991.

21. Leo Rose and Richard Sisson, *War and Secession: Pakistan, India, and the creation of Bangladesh* (Berkeley: University of California Press, 1990), p. 107.

22.s Ashutosh Varshney, 'India, Pakistan and Kashmir: antinomies of nationalism', *Asian Survey,* Vol. XXXI, No. 11, 1991, p. 1004.

23. Awami Awaz, daily, Sindhi, (Karachi), 14 December, 1988.

24. 'A question of national identity: Kashmir', an editorial in *The Economist,* 15 February 1992, pp. 13-15.

25. Baladi, interview with this author at Jamshoro Sindh, on 16 October, 1991.

26. Palejo, in an interview with this author, at Hyderabad, Sindh, on 19 September, 1991.

27. Zaffer Abbass, 'GM Sayed: sinner or the saint', *Herald,* February 1992, pp. 24-25.

28. G.M. Sayed, an interview with the author, at Hyder Manzil Karachi, on 1 August, 1991.

29. *Ibid.*

30. Pirzada, interview with the author on 28 August, 1991 at Karachi.

31. Probably the best account on Balochistan and its political developments could be found in Selig Harrison's *In Afghanistan's Shadow: Baluch Nationalism and the Soviet Temptations* (New York: Carnegie Endowment for International Peace, 1981).

32. Sardar Attullah Khan Mengal, an interview with this author at Warrington, UK, on 27 April, 1991.

33. *Ibid.*

34. Late Ghulam Mohammed Baloch, an interview with this author at Quetta, Balochistan, on 4 September, 1991.

35. 'Kashmir: a question of identity', an editorial in *The Economist,* 15 February 1992, pp. 13-14.

(This original version of this article, entitled, "The Kashmir Problem : A View from Four Provinces of Pakistan', was published in The Contemporary South Asia, (Oxfordshire : Carfax Publishers, 1995) Vol : 4, No: 1, pp. 103-112)

PART - III
FOREIGN POLICY OF PAKISTAN

9

Kashmir Tangle: The Solution within

Barry Buzan, the well-known social scientist, defines the state as a some whole of the people, territory, government and society.[1] If international system is shelved off, then the state still remains major organization of human beings. According to the newly developing concept of human security, vogue in academia, people have precedence over anything else. However, totalitarian states still give precedence to their respective systems of government over their peoples. They also try to shape society according to their ideologies. Pakistan comes into this category.

Question is whether the state emanates from its society and reflects its wished and aspirations or is society, the offspring of a particular form of the government shaped according to its designs? Any student of political science knows that the first and far most element of statehood is the people. Professor Northedge, speaking in the context of international relations, defines the state as the organization of peoples for the purpose of participation in the international system.[2]

Pakistan for most part of its 63 years of existence has been ruled directly and indirectly by the military rulers, generals and the intelligence services. Some of these military dictators, especially General Zia-ul-Haq (1977-88), heavily relied on the conservative religious parties, commonly known as the Mullahs, for legitimacy and support. Others like, General Musharraf, maintained a liaison with Mullahs for their survival. The military and Mullahs had joined hands in their attempt to model the society according to their common ideal, militancy and *Jihad.*[3] It should be pointed out at the outset that Pakistan army, which has ruled the country for most of its life, had till recently made Kashmir as the core cause of conflict with India. The army has facilitated the siphoning of the natural resources of the country and imposing a centralized Punjabi dominated state structure on Pakistan. Relationship between Pakistan's over-centralized military dominated state structure and a decentralized, heterogeneous, multi-dimensional Pakistani Society vis-a-vis Kashmir dispute is one of the most crucial determinants of Pakistan's domestic policy.

The Nature of Pakistani Society

For analytical purposes, Pakistanis could be divided into the following categories: firstly, rich and poor individuals, regions and districts secondly, liberal and conservative segments, thirdly, urban and rural areas; fourthly and more significantly, on an ethno-geographic basis. Division between these different segments of the society, is theoretical and they certainly overlap in practice. However, through these divisions, we can understand dynamics of societal perceptions of the resolution of Kashmir dispute.

Rich and Poor Sections of Society

Wealth in Pakistan, according to *Pakistan Human Development Report-2005,* is unevenly distributed. Some individuals, some regions and even some localities are very poor.[4] Richest citizens of Pakistan are concentrated in its capital, Islamabad. Most of the richest persons of Islamabad are active and retired top civil servants, generals and former spymasters and their offsprings. They enjoy all the amenities of life including education, healthcare and sanitation. They live in the posh areas of the town. They are part of the establishment. Ignoring the view of the general Pakistani society, these privileged few support views of the establishment on all national and international issues of Pakistan[5]. These affluent individuals, view Kashmir dispute as the "Core Issue" between India and Pakistan that should be solved according to the wishes of Pakistani establishment.

Majority of Pakistanis, especially in the rural areas of Sindh, Balochistan and Southern Punjab, are very poor. They do not have easy access to healthcare, education and even drinking water. Their children go barefooted to school, functioning under a tree. Higher education and professional job opportunities for youth of the poor are inaccessible. This is one of the reasons, poor parents in Southern Punjab to dump their children and other orphans in Madrassas, where they become *Jihadis* subsequently. Otherwise, majority of the people of Pakistan are extremely poor. Their priorities are medicines, schooling and a better future. Their perception of security is the protection against hunger, diseases, poverty, unemployment, and indignity. They care little about Indian missiles, nuclear weapons and conventional superiority.[6] However, the reasonably educated among this class of citizens feel that instead of wasting their money on armaments, Pakistan must spend its resources on clinics, good schooling and job opportunities. For them, Kashmir dispute has no meaning and it should be resolved according to the wishes of Kashmiris themselves.

Liberal and Conservative Segments of Society

Conservatives are a group of people who avoid abrupt change, or a group of persons who are rigid in their views and feel that their ideas have a heavenly mandate. From this perspective, religious parties and Mullahs appear conservative in their outlook; rest of Pakistanis are liberals. They are liberals in the sense that they accommodate new ideas and new trends in their thinking. If one applies this paradigm to the Kashmir dispute, only members of a religious party *Jamaat-i-Islami*, stubbornly refuse to change their attitude towards India and Kashmir dispute. Sectarian groups such as *Laskkar-i-Jangvi, Sipahi Sahaba, Lashkar-e-Tayeba* and *Hizbul Mujahadeen* are offsprings of Mujahideen, who fought against Soviets in Afghanistan during the 1980s. And Subsequently Taliban, turned against any rapprochement with India. These *Jihadis* fight as the proxy of their paymasters. Their overall influence in the society is markedly decreasing. In the 2008 general elections, religious parties demonstrated their poor showing. Out of 332 seat in the National Assembly, alliance of religious parties, Mutahida *Majlis-I Amal Pakistan (MMA-P)* Joint Action of Pakistan, won only 8 seats[7]. Unlike the recent past, they failed to form any provincial government in the country, which indicates that Pakistanis are liberal not conservative in their outlook. Correspondingly, they are not war mongers. Pakistanis, especially from rural areas, revere saints such as Shah Abdul Latif Bhittai, Baba Farid and Baba Bulleh Shah who preached peace and fraternity among the human beings irrespective, of their caste, creed and religion.

Urban and Rural Segments of Society

65 percent of Pakistanis live in the rural areas and remaining 35 percent live in urban areas like Karachi, Lahore, Rawalpindi, Faisalabad, Quetta, Peshawar, Hyderabad and Sukkur. Urban and rural overview are sharply contrasting. Availability of a clinic, school, water, fertilizers, pesticides, markets and law and order are among the major priorities of the village dwellers. They rarely discuss the issues like nuclear deterrence and LoC. These issues are the realm of a few city dwellers.

The urban population has its own life style. Many people have migrated to big cities from their villages. Finding a job and niche are principle problems of inner-migrants. Industrial and construction labourers and other daily wage earners only think of three meals for their families. Attitude of low salary government employees is almost the same. Small business community is also engaged in daily business matters. Big business is worried about different acts of terrorism such as payment of *bhatta* (extortion money) to the party *Dadas* (bullies), kidnapping and murder, fluctuation in stock exchange and other matters related to money making. However, due to a wider exposure to the modern world and western education, the business community wants to open trade with their eastern neighbour. Many business leaders who migrated from India are particularly interested in opening trade routes with their neighbor (India). In big cities, academics, intellectuals, journalists, and other professionals discuss the issues of national and international importance while rest of the citizens are busy with their daily life.

Ethno-Geographic Segments of Pakistan and their Perceptions of Kashmir Dispute

Pakistan is the combination of four provinces: Sindh, Balochistan, Punjab and the North-Western Frontier Province (NWFP), recently renamed as *Khyber Pakhunkhaw*. The location of these provinces vis-a-vis Kashmir, their main inhabitants and experience within Pakistan's political development, shape their outlook towards the Kashmir dispute and India.[8]

Sindh

Sindh has two major ethnic groups within its bounds: the native Sindhis and Urdu speaking migrants who mainly live in the big cities. Although migrants came from different parts of India, the Urdu speakers form their social-political core and have provided leadership to them. These Urdu speakers primarily live in the urban centers of Sindh. These are the people, who have an emotional attachment with their relatives who live in India. This feeling of kinship partially shapes their opinion about the place of the Kashmir dispute in an overall ambit of Indo-Pakistan relationships.

Sindhis have no significant participation in the decision-making processes of Pakistan. Three Sindhi Prime Ministers of Pakistan, namely Zulfiquar Ali Bhutto, Mohammed Khan Junejo and Benazir Bhutto were dismissed by military generals of Pakistan. Infact, Zulfiquar Ali Bhutto was hanged in 1979 by General Zia-ul-Haq, and General Musharraf is widely believed to be one of the main plotters of Benazir Bhutto's assassination in December 2007.[9] Thus, Sindhis usually, do not share any of the Islamabad's perception on Kashmir dispute. Sindhis, of their perspective, have remained the main victims of military rule. Military rule has facilitated the Punjabi dominated process of over centralization. Sindhis consider the budget spent on national defense as not only wastage of money but also a factor for military domination in the country[10]. Moreover, quoting official figures, Sindhis claim that Sindh is producing about 70 percent of the income of the country, which goes to the arms race and maintenance of the army. They feel that in order to cut the defence expenses, Pakistan has to improve its relations with India by resolving all disputes with it including Kashmir. The best method of the settlement of the Kashmir dispute, from a Sindhi point of view, is to covert the LOC into the international border.[11]

Mr Iqbal Akhund, a senior diplomat and adviser to Benazir Bhutto on national security, believed the idea of an independent Kashmir appears to be impracticable. India and Pakistan will not agree to cede their respective parts of Jammu and Kashmir. Thus, the only solution may be ultimate wish of the people on both sides of LOC.[12]

Pakistan People Party, whose founding leader Zulfiquar Ali Bhutto signed the Simla Accord with Mrs Indira Gandhi in 1972, suggested establishing of "soft borders" between the Indian and Pakistani parts of Kashmir. This supports the Indian point of view that the Line of Control (LoC) should be converted into an international border.

This author for a long period of time held the notion of an independent Kashmir. After 9/11 he has changed his position due to the changing realities.[13] Pakistan has never supported the idea of an independent Kashmir. It has always supported the accession of Indian administered Kashmir into its own territory, which is unacceptable to India, the international community and the Kashmiris living on the both sides of the dividing line. This is the biggest fault line in Pakistan's policy on Kashmir. Moreover, by encouraging non-Kashmiris like Arabs, Pashtun, Afghans, and other Central Asian militants, to fight as the proxies in Kashimr, Pakistani intelligence agencies have arguably, bungled the whole affair. After 9/11, Kashmiri militants are considered by the international community as Islamic terrorists fighting a democratic India. Thus, there is no international support to Kashmiri militants. In these circumstances I believe, converting the Line of Control into an international border only will resolve the dispute once for all. Ironically, Altaf Hussain, leader of the Mutahida Quomi Movement (MQM), after his Delhi *Yatra* (visit) supported the idea of temporally converting the LoC into an international border[14]. The resolution of the Kashmir dispute, according to Altaf Hussain, will be helpful in developing a good neighbourly relationship between India and Pakistan that will facilitate reunion of people of the Indian origin with their relatives living in India. Delhi born Pakistani dictator, General Musharraf reportedly in his famous "Out of Box Solution" supported the idea of converting Line of Control into an international boundary, giving maximum autonomy to the Indian and Pakistani Kashmirs within the constitutional frame works of India and Pakistan and free flow of people and goods between the two Kashmirs.[15]Therefore, Sindhi and Urdu speaking sections of the population of Sindh, are not sentimental about the resolution of Kashmir dispute. They see it as the economic burden on their resources created by history.

Balochistan

Balochistan is the most Western province of Pakistan, bordering on the Persian Gulf, Iran and Afghanistan. Different Baloch tribes are its principal inhabitants. It is quite remote from Kashmir or India. The nearest point of the Indian border may be around five hundred miles from the town of Sibi in Balochistan. Thus, Balochs are remotely concerned about the Kashmir dispute between India and Pakistan.

Balochs justifiably complain to have a bitter experience with Pakistani rulers. They pointed out that the Baloch territories were annexed into Pakistan in 1948 by the Pakistan army when the Qauid-i-Azam Mohammed Ali Jinnah was legal adviser to Khan of Kalat, the hereditary ruler of Balochistan. Balochs complain that in 1955, 1973-1977, and 2004, military actions were taken by federal governments of Pakistan. Their resources are being exploited by the federation. Mega projects such as Gwadar seaport, Coastal Highway, and Mirani dam are being constructed for settling the outsiders.[16] The only Baloch Prime Minister of Pakistan, Mir Zafarulah Jamali, was dismissed within one and half years of his tenure. There are frequent bomb blasts targeted at the armed forces in Balochistan. According to some reports Balochistan Liberation Army (BLA), a guerilla force, also exists in Balochistan for fighting with Pakistani armed forces and Punjabi settlers in the province. Thus, there is almost a complete antipathy between Baloch nationalists and the federation. Balochs see the Kashmir dispute from this perspective.

Balochs believe that Islamabad rulers of Pakistan want to prolong the Kashmir dispute with India just to keep a huge army and colonialism intact. This army, according to Sardar Attua Allah Khan Mengal, one of the senior most Baloch leaders, is being maintained to keep the grip tight on Balochistan and Sindh[17]. Otherwise, a professional force, which runs bakeries and sell petrol, cannot defend an inch of the land. Sardar Mengal, like other articulate Balochs[18] argues that only a dialogue between Kashmiris living all over the world can resolve the issue. Pakistan should stop drum beating of Kashmir. He insisted that it should be resolved as soon as possible.

If the rulers of Islamabad have any sense, they should stop manipulating the Kashmir issue. They should give attention to national integration, provincial autonomy issues in the state.

Khyber Pakhutunkhaw

NWFP or Khyber Pakhutunkhaw is one of the borderlands of Pakistan having common frontiers with both Afghanistan and the Pakistani administered part of Kashmir. Its main inhabitants are Pashtuns, but sizeable minorities of Hindu speaking Hzariwal live in the areas adjacent to the Kashmir. Islamabad, the capital of Pakistan and power centre of the country, is 150 miles away from Peshawar.

Arguably, in order to grab the property of Hindus and Sikhs in 1948, the then Chief Minister of the NWFP, Khan Qayom Khan, instigated rioting in the NWFP, which resulted in the exodus of non-Muslims from the NWFP.[19] By glorifying this act, Sardar Qayoom Khan with the connivance of Liaqat Ali Khan, prime minister of Pakistan, sent a Pashtun Lashkar in Kashmir to "liberate it from India". In this expedition, many Pashtun died in Kashmir and subsequently the *Jihadis* established a linkage between Pashtuns and Kashmir *Jihadis*, which is in the tact. Thus, unlike Sindh and Balochistan, one may find some quarters in NWFP, who now support the idea of *Jihad* in Kashmir and accession of the Indian administered Kashmir into Pakistan. However, the mass support to these notions is not visible in NWFP. The oldest party of the province, is the Awami National Party (ANP) of Asfadyar Wali Khan. He is the grandson of KhanAbdul Ghaffar Khan who supported the idea of a union between India and his NWFP and an independent Pakhunistan. Ghaffar Khan's successors continued to maintain good relations with India and refrained from seriously criticizing India or its policies in Kashmir. The ANP leadership advises Kashmiris to seek a solution within the broader framework of provincial autonomy envisaged in the Indian constitution. *Jamiat-i-Ulmai Islam* of Maulana Fazlul Rehman is the successor of the *Jamaat-i-Ulamai Hind* in Pakistan. It also maintains good relations with India. He had visited India and met the Kashmiri leadership and advised it to settle its difference within Indian union. It is only *Jamaat-I-Islami* that is hostile to India. Any party, which rules the province, can create serious problems for the federal government if it embarks on the path of the improvement of Indo-Pakistan relationships. Such an understanding was given by Kazi Hussein Ahmed to the West while addressing a seminar at the Woodrow Wilson Centre for Scholars, Washington sometime ago.[20]

Majority of NWFP is in favour of an early settlement of Kashmir dispute according to the wishes of inhabitants of valley. Hussain Shaheed Suharwrdy, a young faculty member of Department of International Relations, University of Peshawar expressed such an opinion in a conference in which he empathically rejected the notion of *Kashmir Banaga Pakistan.*[21] Suharwardy's views about Kashmir could be the reflection of general perceptions of younger generation of educated Pashtuns of NWFP and all over Pakistan.

Punjab

Punjab is the most populous and most influential province of Pakistan. About 57 percent of the total population of the country lives in Punjab. Pothowhari, Punjabi and Siraikis are the main languages of Punjab. Pothowaris of the northern Punjab are mainly soldiers and batmen of the army or truck drivers, cooks, etc. Siraikis of Southern Punjab have a psyche of *"Muthri"*, of being amongst the "marginalized groups of Pakistan". Their role in the decision-making processes of Pakistan has remained minimal. For the dwellers of *Rohi and Cholsitan,* desert areas of Southern Punjab, adjacent to Rajasthan, the paradise of Kashmir is as remote place as the heavens and so are the issues related to Kashmir.

For all practical purposes, Punjab means the Punjabi speaking central Punjab. It is the Punjabi Army, which makes about 80 percent of the Pakistani Army and a similar chunk of the bureaucracy that dominates the decision-making processes of Pakistan since its inception. The Punjab-based *Jamaa't-e-Islami* has been mainly setting the politico-religious agenda of the country. Usually *the Jamait* associates itself with the military oligarchy. On the other hand, it was the Muslim League Nawaz Group and the Pakistan Peoples Party, founded in the Punjabi city of Lahore, that offered stiff resistance to the military rule of General Musharraf. Thus, Punjab still sets agenda for the country as a whole and it probably will continue to do so in future.

Punjab experienced a bloodbath during its partition, which indeed, was the result of the partition of India in 1947. The Punjabi army's policies led to India-Pakistani wars of 1965, 1971 and the smaller Kargil war of 1999. Again, Punjab bore the brunt of these wars in men and material. Traditionally, Punjab had maintained a hawkish and uncompromising attitude towards India. Punjabi youth used to chant the slogan of *Kashmir Banaga Pakistan.*

Punjabi, like any other language has a magical effect on the psyche of its speakers. It unites all its speakers irrespective of their caste, creed and religion. Alongside geography, language makes history. Punjabi, like other languages, has mesmerizing effects on Muslims, Sikhs and Hindus. They sing the *Heer* of Waris Shah and revere Baba Bulleh Shah of Kasur for spreading his message of universal brotherhood.[22] Fort of Lahore is the common heritage of all Punjabis, which refurbishes the history of Punjabi state created by Maharaja Ranjit Singh and destroyed by the British in 19th century. Sikh holy shrines in Lahore, Nankana Sahib, and Hasanabdal, are as sacred for Sikhs as Mecca and Madina to Muslims. Sikhs from all over the world come to the *Yatra* of these places where they are usually well received by locals and the government.

It is worth mentioning that in Pakistan, one way or other, three smaller provinces, Sindh, Balochistan and Khyber Pakhtunkhaw or NWFP are not happy with Punjab's over bearing influence on the federation, especially over the controversial issues of the construction of the Kalabagh Dam and the quantum of provincial autonomy.

Siraikis of Southern Punjab are always complaining of lack of their adequate representation in the provincial as well federal structures. That state of affairs creates a psychological isolation of the Punjabis vis-a-vis other nationalities of Pakistan. In order to over come this psychological state of mind of Punjabis, the colingual Sikhs are their natural allies. Sikhs share the common history, culture, geopolitics and geo-economics imperatives with their Muslim cousins on this side of the Wagha border. To many Sikh intellectuals, Siraiki is not a separate language but a Multani or Riyasti (Bahawalpuri) dialects of the Punjabi language. Thus, the Lahoris have cultural allies in Sikhs in wake of opposition from the Siraikis.

The interplay of politics, language and economy became markedly visible in Punjab when in 1991, Nawaz Sharif became the Prime Minister of Pakistan. Pakistan was (still is) identified with Punjab because of the army's composition, its Punjab-centric strategic doctrine.[23] and the political role of province. Nawaz Sharif gave it a political face by becoming the first Punjabi Prime Minister in the post-1971 era. Punjab and Pakistan became practically synonymous with each other. Nawaz Sharif proved that this political dictum was correct. Nawaz Sharif was born in the Amritsar district in the Indian Punjab. He had an industrialist outlook and was sensitive about the requirements of the Punjabi farmers. Nawaz Sharif initiated his *Ostpolitk* and looked to the east for the expansion of his business interests, which he identified as Pakistan's economic stakes in India. Thus, the improvement of Pakistan's relations with India became Nawaz Sharif's top priority. During his first term of office (1990-93) he dealt with the icy Narasimha Rao and Deve Gowda of India. With them he developed a working relationship, which he felt, could have been established between the two states as well.

During his second term in office (1997-99), Nawaz Sharif had a sympathetic audience in Inder Kumar Gujral, the first Punjabi Prime Minister of India, who was born in Jhelum, now in Pakistan. Being an astute politician and a senior diplomat, as late DN Dixit, former National Security Adviser to the Government of Manmohan Singh, stated, Gujral had a conviction about maintaining peace with Pakistan for regional peace and stability.[24] Gujral, however, had grand designs about the role of India in world affairs, which at that time might have been obstructed by Pakistan. In order to avoid this he wanted to have better relations with Pakistan where he was born and educated. In Pakistan, Gujral had to deal with Nawaz Sharif. Gujral, met him several times at the SAARC, Commonwealth heads of Government meetings and the sessions of the United Nation. Chemistry of the language worked well and they started understanding each other's predicaments. Although they remained entrenched into their respective positions on Kashmir, they struck a happy note that business between India and

Pakistan was possible without settlement of Kashmir dispute. What they reportedly said: *"Kashmir noon Mati Pao"*, (put earth on Kashmir). The meetings with a high caliber leader like Gujral boosted the morale of Mian Nawaz Sharif in dealing with any future Prime Minister of India or any other country in the world, and of course, at home with his opponents and allies.

During Nawaz Sharif's second term his attention was once again focused on improving bilateral relations with India. His younger brother, Shahbaz Sharif, was Chief Minister of Pakistani Punjab. In order to give further boost to the agro-economy of Punjab, Shahbaz Sharif wanted to import good quality seeds, modern agricultural appliances and cheaper diesel oil from East Punjab. At international energy markets of the world, plans of linking Central Asia, Pakistan and India or Iran-Pakistan-India by gas pipelines were discussed. These proposed pipelines from Central Asia or Iran to India were supposed to pass through Punjab to India. Influential Ambani industrial family of Bombay was interested to lay pipelines from Central Asia and Iran to India. They were also pleading India for better relations with Pakistan. Similarly, Pakistani Punjab could have been a warehouse of the Indian goods to Central Asia. Thus, proposed barter of gas via Pakistan and diesel from East Punjab, for trade between Punjabi businessmen from both sides of the Wagha border, was discussed. Mian Nawaz Sharif was again in the saddles and he was the captain of the Punjabi businessmen. The BJP leader Atal Bihari Vajpayee was his opposite number in Delhi. The best person for approaching Vajpayee was Parkash Singh Badal, then chief minister of the Indian Punjab.[25]

Octogenarian Vajpayee, a poet, is temperamentally a man of peace. Vajpayee also favoured a wider and early rapprochement with Pakistan. In May 1999; Vajpayee paid his historic visit to Lahore where he made it emphatically clear that India considers Pakistan a viable state. He also retreated from the Indian official position that Kashmir is its internal affairs, by saying it is a dispute that would be solved at an appropriate time and in an appropriate manner. He also forestalled the possibility of a future India-Pakistani war. It is also reported that for settlement of the Kashmir dispute, Shahbaz Sharif suggested the transfer of Valley to Pakistan and Jammu to India.[26] Nawaz Sharif at Lahore with cooperation of Vajpayee and chief minister of the Indian Punjab, Parkash Singh Badal, paved the way for a wider understanding between India and Pakistan whose principle beneficiaries would have been Punjabis across the border. After Shimla Accord of 1972, Lahore Accord of May 1999 was another milestone on the road to India-Pakistan rapprochement.

In 1999, Pakistani army chief, General Musharraf launched his military operation in Kargil, conceivably, without knowledge of the prime minister, which completely derailed everything. It brought India and Pakistan twice (1999 and 2002) brink to a nuclear showdown. But after 9/11, the army top brass felt a need of curtailing their activities in Kashmir and improving relations with India. They brought Punjab in the forefront of cultivating people to people contacts between the two Punjabs. In 2003, chief minister of Indian Punjab and the scion of former prestigious princely state of Patiala, Captain Amrinder Singh, attended the World Punjabi conference. Captain Amrinder Singh and Om Parkash Chautalla, chief minister of Haryana, visited Pakistan. In November 2004, Choudhry Pervez Illahi, chief minister of Pakistani Punjab attended the International Punjabi Conference in Amritsar. He visited the Sikh Holiest Shrine, the Golden Temple and watched the month long Pan-Punjab Games. The exchange of visits between the chief ministers of Indian and Pakistani parts of the Punjab with their heavy entourage and the convening of the World Punjabi Conference, have been a yearly routine affairs which brings Punjabis further closer to each other.

To the fortunes of Pakistani policy makers, Dr Manmohan Singh is Prime Minister of India. Unlike, IK Gujral, Dr Singh lacks the political clout vis-à-vis the Indian polity. He is the symbol of Punjabi grandeur that boosts the morale of Punjabis in Pakistan. The literacy Programme, *Parha Lika Punjabi* (educated Punjabi) launched by the West Punjab government is replacing the derogatory image of the Punjab.

As mentioned, the Intrepreneurial Sikhs, living both in India and abroad, in collaboration with their Pakistani counterparts, some with their blood relations, considering Pakistani Punjab as a launching pad to Central Asia and Iran bought *Benami* (un named transfer) properties near the border in Lahore Defence Housing Society, owned by the armed forces[27] Pakistan estate agents, in many cases are the retired army officers.[28] In addition, warehouses and stores in these estates, will be constructed for transaction of goods from Central Asia to India via Lahore. Thus, according to the well known military analyst, Hasan Askari Rizvi, army believes that peace dividends with India, among other things, would improve Pakistan's economy, war against terrorism in South Waziristan and Afghanistan would obtain military and economic aid from United States.[29]

Cricket diplomacy of General Musharraf took him to New Delhi in April 2005. It allowed him to meet top Indian leadership including Dr Manmohan Singh and Mrs Sonia Gandhi. The track-II diplomacy was preceded by meetings between the Punjab Chief Ministers. If the General did not consider the Kashmir issue as the "Core Issue" but rather as one of the 'outstanding issues between the two countries' or if he had thought that the peace process was irreversible, then this could reflect the changing Punjabi mood towards India.

Perceptions of the informed Punjabis about India have significantly changed. The mentality of revenge and expansion has been converted into cultural and commercial cooperation with fellow Punjabis-not necessary leading to a reunified Punjab, as their detractors, especially Altaf Hussain of the MQM assert. That omens well for Pakistan as a whole, because the Punjabis are people whose writ runs large in the corridors of power in Islamabad. According to Fakir Aijazuddin, a leading Punjabi intellectual, whose great-grand father Fakir Syed Azizuddin, was the Grand Vazir of Maharaja Ranjit Singh, Kashmir is no longer the core issue of the people of Pakistan, but of the core commanders of the Pakistan army.[30] Discussing the relevance of Kashmir to the well being of the people of Pakistan, he says a billion and half Indian and Pakistanis should not allow themselves to be held hostage to the aspirations of 6.369 million registered votes of Indian held Jammu and Kashmir and less than half that number in Azad Kashmir.[31]

Arguably, Punjabis see aspirations and struggle of Kashmiris for independence as a liability. They propose that Kashmiris should be ditched away for making peace with India and capturing the border trade. This proposal of ditching away of Kashmiris or changing the properties is nothing new in history of *real politicks.* In 1938, the British Prime Minister Neville Chamberlain discarded the republic of Czechoslovakia to the Nazis. Winston Churchill, the pride of British realism, exploited millions of Ukrainian Cossacks, Volga Germans and Tatars, in the Second World War. Some of the Punjabi intellectuals are following a realist line towards India. But they have yet to come forward by suggesting the reduction of the size of Pakistani armed forces and the budget being spent on them.

If the Musharraf government had considered Kashmir as not the core issue but one of the important issues between India and Pakistan, it appeared to be the reflection of corporate Punjabi thinking at that time If General Musharraf had come forward in November 2004, with dividing Kashmir into seven zones based on geopolitical and ethnic lines and giving them autonomy, it was also in line with thinking of the army. Because according to this thinking, as Hassan Askari Rizvi points out, peace with India and war in South Waziristan would bring about military and economic aid from the U.S. which will reduce criticism on the defence expenditures.[32] PPP government which is in power since 2008, does not appear to be keen on the Kahsmir issue. Personally, President Zardari is reportedly more interested in improving trade relations with India than anything else.

For first time in history of Pakistan, perceptions of different social and ethnic groups have been almost similar on the Kashmir dispute. All of these groups believe that Kashmiris' inalienable right of self-determination should be supported by the government of Pakistan but not at their own expense. They are no far off from the official line which has been modified by overbearing influence of Punjab and radically changed international situation after 11th September 2001.

It has been argued at the outset that because of the diverse nature of Pakistani society its different segments have different perceptions of settlement of Kashmir dispute. These perceptions do not converge with the official thinking on this crucial issue of national security and foreign policy. However, especially after 11 September 2001, things at home and abroad have been changed dramatically and the military government of General Musharraf had brought about its policies on Kashmir dispute closer to the realities of the world and closer to the perception of the people of Pakistan. This similarity of perceptions may not be because of any altruism or statesmanship. It was because of the international pressures on his regime, mainly from the United States.

In Pakistan, this is the right time for different political parties, civil society organizations, think tanks and the universities to evolve a common policy on the Kashmir dispute that has remained the most crucial issue of both internal and external policies of Pakistan. They should publicize it and insist the government for its implementation.

It is also quite promising that in order to discus their common destiny the Kashmiris from both sides of dividing line have met for the first time formally in Kathmandu under auspices of the Pigwash group. Kashmiris were quite happy over the outcome of this meeting, which would ultimately bring them together in determining their common destiny. Newly launched Srinagar-Muzaffarabad bus service will also help reuniting the separated Kashmiris families with each other.[33] It operates as one of the confidence-building measures between India and Pakistan aimed at promoting good neighborly relations between them. A truck service also operates between Poonch and Mirpur, Azad Kashmir. Now Kashmiri leaders are meeting from time to time principally in Washington to understand each other's position.

Kashmir is a political problem of such a magnitude that cannot be solved with violent acts. All Indians, Pakistanis and Kashmiris, have stakes in the peace and prosperity of the subcontinent and South Asia. They are representatives of what late MB Bhandara, the Parsee member of the National Assembly of Pakistan, called "the critical mass of people of ethnic and lingual groups of India and Pakistan". They should unite together to remove a flashpoint of conflict[34]. Mr Ram Jaithmalani, a prominent Indian Lawyer of Sindhi origin and former Chairman of the Kashmir Committee of the Rajya Sabha, This momentous goal can be achieved based on a general goodwill, expressed by all for all.[35] His advice appears to be the central piece of the message of South Asian mysticism, imbibed in all religions of the world. This appears to be most appropriate method of conflict resolution.

References

1. Barry Buzan, *People State and Fear,* (Susex: Whetshelf, 1982) p. 60.

2. F.S. Northedge, *The International Political System*, (London: Faber & Faber, 1977) p. 17.

3. Stephen Cohen, *The Idea of Pakistan*, Pakistani edition, (Lahore: Vanguard Publishers, 2004), pp. 171-174.

4. *Pakistan National Human Development Report (PNHDR)* 2005-6, in *daily Dawn* (Karachi), 7 December, 2006.

5. An interview with a retired senior servant of Pakistan in Islamabad, in October 2007.

6. This observation is based on my own experience of sickness during 2001-2003 while talking to fellow patients in the Out-door Patient Departments (OPDs) of different government hospitals. When I asked questions about the nature of threat they faced from the Indian nuclear weapons, they looked at my face when I inquired from them whether they want proper diagnosis and treatment or the Pakistani nuclear arsenal for their security, the overwhelming majority preferred treatment not nuclear or conventional umbrella of Pakistan. An Indian rickshaw driver in Delhi also wanted a decent life not Indian arsenal in response to my query in 2007.

7. Masoud Ansari, "N.A. Winners", *The Herald*, March 2008, pp. 80-81.

8. Mehtab Ali Shah, "The Kashmir Problem: A View From Provinces of Pakistan", *Contemporary South Asia,* (Oxford, 1995) Vol. 4, No. 1, pp. 103-112.

9. Owen Bennett Jones, *Pakistan: Eye of the Storm*, third edition (London: Yale University Press, 2009) pp. 3-4.

10. Mehtab Ali Shah, *op.cit.*

11. Late Imdad Mohamed Shah, in an interview with the Sindhi causal paper, *Sanghah* (knowledge: Sindhi , Hyderabad Sindh, November, 2004) pp. 21-24.

12. Iqbal Akhund, The Resolution of the Kashmir Dispute", an unpublished paper in *Pakistan's Ethnicity, Security and Foreign Policy in the New Millennium, edited by* Mehtab Ali Shah.

13. Mehtab Ali Shah, *op. cit.*

14. *Dawn*, 30th December, 2004.

15. Ram Jethmalani, *Conscience of a Maverick,*(New Delhi: UBSPD, 20070) p. 312.

16. Saleem Shahid, "Balochistan Under Attack", Yearend Review: 2004, *Dawn,* January, 1, 2005, pp. 12-3.

17. A meeting with Sardar Attaullah Khan Mengal, Karachi, June, 27, 2004.

18. *Ibid.*

19. Ilyas Khan, "Low Priority", *Herald,* November 2004, pp.36-37.

20. *Dawn,* 20 January, 2003.

21. Comments by Syed Hussain Shaheed Suharwardy in a conference on *Human Security: Global and Regional Perspective*, (Jamshoro) August 31, 2004.

22. GR Puri and TR, Shigri, *Saen Bhullah Shah*, (Lahore : Fiction House, 2004).

23. Stephen Cohen, *The Pakistan Army,* (California: California University Press, 1982) pp. 44-45.

24. JN. Dixit, *India and Pakistan in War and Peace,* (London : Rutledge, 2002) pp. 301-302.

25. Kuldip Nayar, *Wall at Wagha : India-Pakistan Relations,* (New Delhi : Gyan Publishing House, 2003) pp. 197-222. Badal is now the Chief Minister of Indian Punjab.

26. *Ibid.*

27. Many Nakais, Bajwas, and Cheemas, Bhattis, both Sikhs and Muslims, have reestablished their prepartition familial relationships with each other. Many Punjab friends, both Sikhs and Muslim, gave this information to me. Some of them have established stakes in the real estate in near the border Lahore.

28. Zaffar Abbas, "is Punjab Ready for Peace" *The Herald,* November 2004, pp. 60-66.

29. An interview of Dr. Hassan Askari Rizvi, in *The Herald,* November, 2004, pp. 56-57.

30. Fakir Aijazuddin, alias Jaja Mian, the Key note speech given at the army own University, Comsat, Islamabad , 24th October 2006.

31. *Ibid.*

32. Dr. Hassan Askari Rizvi, *opcit.*

33. "India-Pakistan: Point of no Return", *The Economist*, 23 April, 2005, p. 28.

34. MB Bhandara, "Bilateralism and the Kashmir Dispute", *Dawn*, 2 January 2005.

35. Ram Jaithmalani, "Nothing Good, but Goodwill", *Dawn*, 7 October 2005.

(The earlier version of this paper was published under titled, "Gaps in State and Society : Approaches of Conflict and Conflict Resolution : A Case Study of the Kashmir dispute in Pakistan" in ed, Moonis Ahmar, DIFFERENT PERCEPTIONS ON CONFLICT RESOLUTION : NEED FOR AN ANALYTICAL APPROACH, Karachi : Karachi University Press, 2005)

10

Thaw in Indo-Pak Relations

In April 2003, Prime Minister of India, Mr Atal Bihari Vajpayee, while addressing a public meeting in Srinagar, offered an olive branch to the Kashmiri militants and Pakistan for the settlement of the longstanding Kashmiri dispute. He pronounced that a solution of the dispute is possible within the framework of "*Insaniyat* (humanity), *Jamhoriat* (democracy) and *Kashmiriyat* (Kashmiriness)."

He repeated same framework for improvement of Indo-Pakistani relationships in both houses of the Indian Parliament. Mr Zafarullah Khan Jamali, Prime Minister of Pakistan, welcomed the Indian goodwill gesture. He made a telephone call to his Indian counterpart. Both sides announced restoration of full diplomatic relations, reopening of rail road and air links and re-establishing the trade and sports ties between them. High commissioners between the two countries were exchanged. The goodwill delegations of Indian and Pakistani parliamentarians visited each others countries and held discussions with their opposite numbers and other prominent members of civil society. Mr Mani Shankar Ayer, a retired diplomat, author of the famous book, *Pakistan Papers* and now a Congress Party top intellectual, and Dr Asghar Ali Engineer, a Mumbai-based scholar, visited Pakistan. Congress, the main opposition party of India, endorsed Kashmir policy of the Vajpayee government. Above all, for the improvement of its overall relationships with India, Pakistan took a dramatic turn by proposing a "composite dialogue" on all outstanding issues, instead of sticking to its old stand of the settlement of the Kashmir dispute first and other issues afterwards.

The American Factor

Pattern of regional politics in any part of the world is shaped, to a great extent by currents of global politics. Although it has been denied by both India and Pakistan that United States has exerted any pressure on the both of them, the American involvement appeared visible in the new thaw in the Indo-Pakistani relationship since the Clinton era. A phase of high level contact (April 2003 onwards) between India and Pakistan took place before the visit of Mr Richard Armitage, Deputy Secretary of States for South Asia to this region. Before his visit, General Ehsanul Haque, the head of Pakistan's premier intelligence service, Inter Services Intelligence Agency (ISI) visited America. It is widely believed that ISI is one of the principal policy-making apparatuses in Pakistan, which has been directly or indirectly ruled by the military. Mr. Brajesh Mishra, Indian Prime Minister's National Security Advisor, also visited Washington DC and London. These influential policy makers, discussed the modalities for normalization of Indo-Pak ties with high ranking American official, including President Bush and Vice-President Dick Cheney. In May and June, high power delegation of India and Pakistan led by Indian Deputy Prime Minister, Mr. LK Advani and General Pervez Musharraf, also visited America and held bilateral dialogues with Americans. During all these meetings America was insisting on the Indian and Pakistani sides for normalizing their bilateral relations.

Because of its proximity with oil rich and conflict torn Middle East to resources rich Central Asia to China the potentials of becoming a huge market for American goods and investment, America has clear priorities in South Asia. Firstly, since 9/11 it is engaged in fighting against global terrorism. Secondly, the safety of its entrepreneurs residing or investing in the region, is also one of the US top priorities in South Asia. Thirdly, speaking in global geo-political terms in order to contain the rising power of China in South East Asia, United States intends to raise India as a counterpoise to it.

In early seventies to maintain an international order, Henry Kissinger, American scholar turned policy maker, wanted to create pro-American hegemons in various regions of the world. India was one of these regional candidates. In the post 11 September 2001 era, in order to maintain stability in South Asia, United States once again plans to see India as a preponderant power in the region, provided the hegemony may be accepted by its neighbours and they stop their bickering with it.

The regional stability and cooperation between South Asian states have been significantly marred by a strained Indo-Pakistani relationship over the Kashmir dispute. In 1998, the two countries acquired nuclear status, and South Asia has become a flash point. In 1999, during the Kargil Crisis and in December 2001 terrorist attack on Indian Parliament and the resultant troop deployment of two countries, India-Pakistan tension reached climax and only the US persuasion thwarted a nuclear war between them.

It is paradoxical that the United States intends to retain its nuclear capability and at the same time, propagates nuclear non proliferation. This nonproliferation or a nuclear freeze can be brought about in South Asia when India and Pakistan reach some understanding on the Kashmir issue. Besides, a stable nuclear relationship and combating terrorism, between India and Pakistan, is also one of the top US priorities in South Asia.

Terrorism can be brought to end in South Asia only when the *Taliban* and Al Qaida terrorist networks are destroyed in Afghanistan and Pakistani territory bordering Afghanistan. At the same time, Pakistan has to stop *Al Qaida* and Kashmiris militants, especially the reported ISI backed *Lashkar-i- Tayeba* from crossing the Line of Control (LoC) in Kashmir for fighting guerrilla warfare against the Indian forces. Thus, in its anti-terrorist strategy in the region, United States assigns a high priority to Pakistan.

Although India and Pakistan have denied any American pressure on both of them, America has been admitting that it only facilitates the two South Asian antagonists for a rapprochement. American paramountcy, particularly in the post-Iraq War scenario cannot be overruled by any state whether big or small. Both India and Pakistan, for different reasons are susceptible to the American pressures.

Indian Internal Environment

Indian expatriate scientists working in America are among channels of influence between India and the United States. In tune with their American hosts, these scientists have been urging the Indian government for a broader settlement with Pakistan so that the American investors in India feel safer.

The Bharatiya Janta Party (BJP) in India has been widely criticized by the media for its anti-Muslim policies in the Gujarat State, especially after the anti-Muslim riots of 2002. Mr. Atal Bihari Vajpayee, the top BJP leader did not condemned these riots. However, he wanted to go down in history as a peace maker a statesman of the high stature. In order to achieve this long cherished objective, Mr. Vajpayee, in his own words, once again for the "third and final time" has "offered a hand of friendship to Pakistan".

Pakistan's Internal Environment

Pakistan's principal ruling elite (the armed forces) for its own reasons and conveniences is bowing to the American pressures. Like any military ruler, General Musharraf knew that the survival and prolongation of his rule, heavily depended upon American patronage. Correspondingly, he faced legitimacy crisis, posed by the opposition parties and the civil society, to conform himself with the American wishes. Apparently, Pakistan has been cooperating with the United States in the latter's fight against terrorism in Afghanistan. Many influential members of the American Congress felt that General Musharraf was required by America in Afghanistan, and for sending Pakistani troops as a stabilizing force in Iraq. His utility might increase manifold if America attacked Iran, but one has to understand that America in its own interest, in the post-11 September 2001 era, in order to curb terrorism and to avoid a nuclear show down between India and Pakistan, needs the settlement of Kashmir dispute by a gradual process.

Looking from hindsight, it appears that in America's war on terrorism, ISI plays a double game. On the one hand, Arab members of the *Al Qaida* were captured in Pakistan and handed over to the Federal Bureau of Investigation (FBI), on the other, *Taliban* were being reorganized in Pakistani territory bordering Afghanistan, with full connivance of the ISI[1]. Moreover, the northern alliance, which wields a considerable degree of power in Afghanistan, is disliked by the pro-Pashtun ruling elite in Pakistan. Thus, ISI is creating an anti-Karzai, anti-Iran, anti-Indian axis in Kabul, which goes against the long term interests of America in Afghanistan. At the same time ISI plays the drum of the Pakistani encirclement by the Indians.

Immediately after General Musharraf, 9 day visit of United States, FBI accused the ISI of aiding and abetting the members of the *Kashmiri Jihadi* outfits, *Lashkar i Tyeba* in crossing the Line of Control (LOC) and fighting against the

Indian forces. The accusation of Pakistan by the FBI was clear indication of American lack of trust in the former, despite exchange of niceties between Bush and Musharraf.

After 11 September 2001 in general, and during the post-Iraq war scenario in particular, an undeclared alliance between America, Israel and India emerged. Both Israel and America supplied India with air and land surveillance devices such as Phalcon airborne surveillance planes and other devices for detecting the cross border infiltration. Bourgeoning political influence of *Mullahs* and their alleged links with the armed forces made Pakistan a common target of criticism by three countries stated above. Earlier the senior BBC correspondent, Humphrey Hawskley, in his political fiction, quite close to the ground realities, *The Dragon Fire,* depicted a crippled Pakistan's nuclear weapons and conventional capabilities[2]. One can add the Israeli factor in this scenario. If so, to thwart this real or imaginary threat, for strategic or tactical reasons, the military dominated ruling elite of Pakistan was inclined for a limited rapprochement with India. For them, the choice was between fire and fry pan. If in the post-Iraq war situation, Pakistan *were attacked jointly by India, Israel* and United States, Pakistan, in General Musharraf's words will be left alone for defending itself. In these circumstances, if Pakistan sought an overall rapprochement with India, majority of the political parties, especially, PPP, Muslim League Nawaz Group, Awai National Party (ANP) from the NWFP and, Balochistan National Party (BNP) would seek a drastic cut in the defence expenditure. If the defence expenditure is cut down to size, army will lose its political clout. But as a *fait accompli* it has no choice without exercising the second option. However, under this new scenario, settlement of Kashmir dispute was not at the top of the India-Pakistan dialogue. Such a settlement under a changed situation will be a time consuming exercise. Till the army under the pressure, agrees to the settlement, it will enjoy the privileged position in the political set up of the country. Most probably for this reason, in 2003, General Musharraf gave a green light to Prime Minster Zafarullah Jamali, an ethnic Baloch, for starting a dialogue with India.

Musharaff, the architect of Kargil Crisis of 1999, under the American pressures, and demands from the civil society, continued to improve relations with India. After the earthquake of 2005 in Pakistan, India gave aid to it aid to it, generously, which created an enormous goodwill for the latter. Sindh-Rajasthan railway route which was closed after the 1965 war, was reopened in February 2006. Through back-channel diplomacy, Musharraf reportedly reached close to the settlement of the Kashmir dispute by accepting the Line of Control as the International boundary between India and Pakistan. India and Pakistan relationship was gradually improving both at official and unofficial level. In February 2007, Lahore-bound Samjhota Express train was set on fire at Panipat railway station near Delhi. In this incident about 68 Pakistani lost their lives. Although, the Pakistan government remained cautious in its statement but the right wing parties in Pakistan created hue and cry on this incident blaming the Indian government for it.

In November 2007, Musharraf committed blunder of dismissing the chief justice of Pakistan, Justice Iftikahr Choudhry, which led to the nationwide lawyers movement against him joined by the civil society. This alongside Benazir Bhutto's assassination in December in the same year resulted into Musharaff's ouster in 2008. Benazir Bhutto's widower, Asif Ali Zardari became the president of Pakistan. He also reiterated his stand of improving trade and people to people relations with India. But without his knowledge and approval, the ISI sponsored *Lashkar-i Tayeba* operators launched a terrorist attack in Mumbai in November 2008, which resulted into the heavy loss of life, about 173 innocent persons were either killed or became injured . Pakistani government and civil society, like rest members of the international community condemned this wanton terrorist attack on India. However, when Pakistan refused to extradite the alleged main handler of the attack, *Lashkar i- Tayeba,* leader, Hafiz Seed, the relations between the two nuclear states were once again grinded to a halt. Pakistan on its own started accusing India of supporting the Baloch insurgents. However, due to British and American diplomacy, especially in the wake of Pakistan's war against *Taliban and Al Qauida* in Federally Administrative Area (FATA) and NATO operation in Afghanistan, persuaded India and, Pakistan to resume dialogue. The Indian Prime Minister, Dr Manmohan Singh met his Pakistani counter part, Mr Yusuf Raza Gillani in Egypt in 2009.

Reportedly under the US. pressures[3], on 25th of February 2010, Indian foreign secretary, Ms Nirupma Rao met her Pakistani counterpart, Mr Salman Bashir, in New Delhi for more than three hours. The India side suggested that before beginning of a composite dialogue on all issues, Pakistan should handover the perpetrators of the Mumbai bombing to it and dismantle the terrorist networks within its territory[4]. Understandably, Pakistan insisted on reopening the composite dialogue on all outstanding issues including Kashmir dispute, construction of Wulhar in Kashmir and Beglihar dams in India and demarcation of the Sir Creek maritime boundary between Sindh and Gujarat[5]. As expected earlier, the dialogue did not cut much ice with a vague promise to be in touch with each other. But *Dawn,* in its editorial optimistically analyzed the situation as a "chance given to peace".[6] One can argue that whether it is a composite dialogue or just terrorism-dominated single item agenda between the two countries. It is better than no dialogue at all. Commenting on the new round of limited dialogue, veteran Indian commentator, the A.G. Noorani opines that it is substance not form that matters and no subject should be excluded[7]. In diplomacy, it is said that jaw jaw is better than war war. People of India and Pakistan believe in this dictum. A slow but persistent pace of improvement of ties is required for good neighbourly relations.

Requirements of a Functional Approach for Indo-Pakistani Rapprochement

One of the architects of European Community, David Matronly, suggested a gradual approach for achievement of regional cooperation and settlement of disputes among the member states, what he called, "peace by pieces" or "Functional approach". According to this approach, peripheral issues between the states are resolved first and the core issues are discussed later. This method will be most appropriate for promoting Indo-Pakistan harmony. Focus of attention should be the promotion of amity between the people of the two countries, which will ultimately promote good neighbourly relations between India and Pakistan. People to people contact through Track-II and Track-III diplomacy, should be encouraged between India and Pakistan. The following steps could be taken in this direction.

1. Improvement and expansion of the travelling facilities

More the people of India and Pakistan visit each other's country more understanding will increase between them. This people to people contact will be quite helpful in the resolution of disputes between India and Pakistan in the long run. At the moment, there is a restricted flow of the people between India and Pakistan. Only one visa section works each in the high commissions of India and Pakistan. Karachi and Mumbai Consulate Generals remain closed. They should be kept open. In addition, the visa camp offices could be opened in Hyderabad and Sukkur for catering the needs of the more people of Sindh and its aforementioned neighbouring areas in India.

2. *Adoption of a liberal visa policy*

A liberal visa policy should be adopted by both the countries. Citizens of India and Pakistan have to visit just four places in the other country[8]. Many of them have to report to the police station at the time of their arrival and departure. This practice is nowhere in the world and should be given up. Like other countries, citizens of India and Pakistan should visit any part of the country. The time period of the visitor visa is usually ten to fifteen days. It should be extended for three months so that citizens of one country may see as many places as they can come into contact with citizens of the other country. Parliamentarians, Supreme Court and High Court judges and businessmen are exempted from obtaining visa in the two countries. Senior academics should be also included in this category. Their visits and exchange programmes should be encouraged.

Parliamentarians of India and Pakistan visited the two countries under the leadership of late Mr MB Bhandara of Pakistan and Mr Kuldip Nayar of India. They are trying to create a favourable atmosphere for the improvement of relations between these two beleaguered countries. Pakistani parliamentarians, especially from Sindh, should take a lead in inviting the influential Indian parliamentarians of the Sindhi origin, such as Mr LK Advani, Mr Ram Jethmalani and Mr. KR Malkani, a prominent BJP member. These parliamentarians are nostalgic for their birth places like Karachi, Shikarpur and Hyderabad, etc. Their visits to these places and to the Shrines of Shah Latif Bhitti and Udero Lal, etc, will soften their tough attitude towards Pakistan and be conducive to the improvement of India-Pakistan relationships. Similarly, the human rights activists and peace campaigners should make frequent visits to each other's countries. NGOs and governments of the United States, European Union and Scandinavian countries may be willing to sponsor such visits.

3. *Promotion of academic activities between the two countries*

More and more conferences and seminars should be jointly organized for the scholars and students of India and Pakistan to understand each other's point of view and narrow down their divergent perceptions. The Department of International Relations of Karachi University has taken lead in this direction. The Pakistan Study Centre of Jamia Millia, New Delhi, has not lagged behind in inviting Pakistani scholars on seminars and conferences. In 2009, Vidiapeeth, Ahmedabad, on its three-day *Sangethi* (conference) on Ghandiji's book, *Hind Swaraj* invited this writer. Its Vice-Chancellor, Professor Sudarsahan Iyenger and the Director of Peace Studies Centre, Dr Pushpa Motyani, a scholar of Sindhi origin, expressed a deep desire to establish academic linkages between Vidiapeeth and Sindh University in Pakistan. There is a need for establishing linkages between the Pakistani and the Indian universities. Visits and exchanges of students will be highly conducive in finding commonalities between the two people. Educational NGOs such as the Ford Foundation and the Hanns Seidel Foundation, for example, could provide generous donations for organizing Indo-Pak or South-Asian Politics orientated seminars and conferences. There should also be the joint publications by the scholars of the two countries.

4. *Direct Air Links with India*

At the moment, only Islamabad, Lahore and Karachi are connected with Delhi and Mumbai. But there are only two fights per week between Mumbai and Karachi, which geographically, historically and culturally appear to the twin cities. There are numerous similarities between them. Lot of people desire to visit their relatives and friends in the other cities. But the flights are limited. Their frequency should be increased. Hyderabad Sindh should be connected with Jaipur, Bhuj and Ahmedabad for the benefit of the people of Sindh and the neighbouring states of Rajasthan and Gujarat in India. Lahore may be connected with Amritsar and Chandigarh of the Indian Punjab also.

5. *Reopening of the Land Routes*

In pre-partition days, there were at least four land routes connecting Sindh and Punjab with their adjoining areas by railways and roads. After 1947, two railway lines, Khokhrapar-Monabao (Sindh-Rajasthan) and Wagha-Atari (Punjab) remained operational. After1965 war, the only railway link between Sindh and Rajasthan was closed. It has been reopened. But the train runs only fortnightly on this route. After the thaw in the Indo-Pak relations, bus service between Delhi and Lahore has been restored. Similarly, another bus route has been opened between Sirnagar and Muzafarabad. There is a need to reopening old Sindh-Rajasthan/Sindh-Kutch land route, provided the visa system strictly observed with the purpose of avoiding a flood of discontented Muslims from India and Bangladesh migrating to Sindh. Train and bus services at Lahore-Delhi route should play daily instead of twice a week.

6. *Establishment of Trade-links between India and Pakistan*

India and Pakistan are contiguous to each other. There is a great deal of similarities between the life-styles of their people. Indian products can be easily consumed in Pakistan and vice versa. Despite these complementarities, trade between the two countries is not sufficient. According well-known Pakistani political-economist, Akbar Zaidi, despite political upheavals, India is Pakistan's nineth largest trade partner[9]. However, the volume of bilateral trade can be further increased if smuggling between them is curbed. The import of one country's goods through a third country like Dubai or Singapore should be discouraged. For instance, Indian medicines are available in Pakistan through Dubai and export quality Sindhi mangoes find their way into India via Dubai. These items are not on import list of the two countries. Members of Indian and

Pakistani chambers of commerce and industry visit the two countries. Hopefully, trading list can be broadened between the two countries. Pakistan can sell its surplus electricity to India. The proposed Turkmenistan-Afghanistan-Pakistan gas pipe line can be extended to India as well. India and Pakistan can form a free trade area on the model of America-Canada and Mexico. North America Free Trade Area (NAFTA). The bourgeoning trade relations between India and Pakistan will increase interdependence, which will be helpful for settling their disputes amicably.

7. *Settlement of Disputes*

Last but not the least aspect of India-Pakistan relationship is the peaceful settlement of disputes between them. Without settlements of disputes, durable peace between the two countries cannot be maintained. Thus, it is necessary to address the disputes properly and find out their settlement according to convenience of the people of disputed part of territory. In other words, the criterion for the settlement of the disputes should be based upon the benefit of the people not the territorial entities called states, i.e. India, Pakistan. After all, the states are for the benefits of the people and not the other way round. Pakistan is calling for a "composite dialogue" on all issues including the Kashmir dispute. It is a functional approach to the settlement of Indo-Pak disputes. According to this scheme of things, the atmosphere of the amity can be created by settling the peripheral disputes first and the core afterward. Since Kashmir dispute is the "core dispute" between the parties, its settlement should be addressed last. Three other disputes from the periphery to core scale are: The Sir Creek Maritime Boundary between Sindh and Kutch/Gujarat; proposed Wulhar dam over the Jhelum River in the Indian administered Kashmir Siachen Glacier, the un-demarcated boundary in extreme north. In the past, some sort of understanding between India and Pakistan had been reached. Now peace process can be revived and these minor disputes can be solved easily.

The Settlement of Sir Creek Maritime Boundary will be easy only according to the well established principles of international law of sea. The settlement of this dispute will save thousands of the fishermen families from Sindh and Kutch from the hardship which they face at the hands of the navies of the two countries. Since the waters are not demarcated, fishermen go to the other country un warned and get arrested. They languish in the jails of Karachi and Bhuj for years without committing any social crime. Thus, there is a humanitarian need to settle the Sir Creek maritime dispute on the humanitarian basis. The Wulhar Dam and the Siachen Glacier issues can be settled under the same spirit of accommodation. Thus, the settlement of the peripheral disputes will enable India and Pakistan to establish sufficient confidence building measures between them and prepare the ground for the resolution of the Kashmir dispute.

The settlement of Kashmir is a difficult problem between the two states. Any reference to UN resolutions as Pakistan has been doing since six decades appears to be out of the context. The Ground realities should be the yardstick for settlement of Kashmir dispute. People of Pakistani administered Kashmir and the Northern Area are practically integrated with Pakistan. Infact, Northern Areas have been given administrative status of the fifth province of Pakistan, Hindus of Jammu region and Ladakhi Buddhists will be last persons to join Pakistan. As a result of frequent sectarian clashes in Pakistan in which Shias die, Shias from Drass-Kargil area, straddling on the other of the divide, might have little charm for Pakistan. For their convenience, Shias on both sides of LoC, in the northern areas will be interested in a free access to their relatives and friends. They may be content with the concept of "soft borders."

The crux of the trouble and the resultant insurgency is in Kashmir valley. It requires a great deal of effort on the part of the parties concerned and international community for its settlement. There is no denying the fact that conflict in Kashmir is major source of earning for the military establishment of Pakistan, especially the ISI indeed, The justification of their presence and manipulation of Pakistani state apparatus. However, the trouble in the Valley is exclusively due to the cross-border terrorism. Hawkish politicians and hype Medias of the two countries also whip up trouble. Moreover, it has domestic dynamics as well. Kashmiri aspirations paradigm have spirit of accommodation and compassion and that will be the culmination of thaw between India and Pakistan.

Notes and References

1. Interestingly under the American pressure, whenever, a high ranking American dignitary visits Pakistan, a high profile Al-Queda or Taliban leader is captured by the ISI and subsequently handed over to the Americans. For instance, the Taliban second in command, Mullah Abdul Ghani Baradar, and his three accomplices have been captured a when Mr. visiting the US envoy to Pakistan and Afghanistan, Richard Holbrook is in Pakistan. See, Jeremy Page and Zahid Hussain, "Capture of Taliban Leaders Suggests $12bn US Gamble is paying off", *The Times*, (London), 19 February 2010.

2. A.G. Noorani, "Forms of Dialogue", *Dawn* (Karachi), 20 February 2010.

3. Humphery Hawksley, *The Dragon Fire*, (Oxford, Macmillan, 2000), pp. 92-93.

4. Emily Wax, "India, Pakistan vow to 'stay in touch' in first formal talks since Mumbai siege", *Washington Post*, February 26, 2010.

5. V.R. Krishna Iyer, "Dreaming of a chance for peace", *Hindu* (Chennai), 26th February 2010.

6. "Vague Promise to Stay in Touch", *Dawn*, 26 th February 2010.

7. Editorial "Meeting in Delhi", *Dawn*, 26 th February 2010.

8. India has more liberal visa policy for Pakistani academics than vice versa. The Pakistani academics do not have to report at the police stations, whereas, regrettably, the Indian scholars and laureates, especially of Sindhi- origin have to report to the police station wherever they have to go in Sindh.

9. Akbar Zaidi, "Trade & Peace: Are They Linked?" *Dawn*, 15th February 2010.

11

Is Pakistan Chafing USA vis-a-vis China in South Asia?

In this presentation, I will examine the nature of Pakistan-United States relations with reference to the convergence and divergence of their interests in South Asia. Divergences of perceptions and interests between Pakistan and US are many. While it is desirable to reduce these divergences and develop special relationship with the US, it should not be done at the cost of its national sovereignty and good relations with other nations.

India, Pakistan, Bangladesh, Sri Lanka, Nepal, Afghanistan and Bhutan, and the Maldives form a distinct geographical entity called South Asia. Pakistan, India and Bangladesh are also called the "Indian Sub-continent". They are the core members of the area, while, the Maldives, Sri Lanka, Nepal and Bhutan stand on the periphery. The South Asian states have their own socio-economic group, named as the South Asian Association for Regional Cooperation, (SAARC) with headquarters in the Nepalese capital, Kathmandu.

Though South Asia has close links with Southeast and South West Asian regions, it is distinct from both the neighbouring regions by virtue of its political, cultural and historical background. Since it is the home of all great religions and variety of cultures , it is also called the "civilizational area".

South Asia except Afghanistan, and Nepal, was part of the British Empire till the departure of Britain from India coincided by Partition of India in 1947 and it still retains some of the features and problems of the imperial past. India, Pakistan and Bangladesh have similar administrative set-ups and a lot of other things in common. The similarities among these three countries are so great that perhaps no other group of countries in the world can match them.

Like many developing countries, South Asian nations face the problems of national integration and economic development. Above all, due to distrust emanating from the legacy of partition, Pakistan gives highest priority to its internal and external dimensions of security.

Interests of Pakistan in South Asia

Like any nation state, vital interests of Pakistan are protection of its independence and territorial integrity. From its strategic thinker's point of view, Pakistan faces the security with, Afghanistan in the north-west, Taliban insurgency in whole country in general NWFP in particular, and Baloch nationalist insurgency in Balochistan poses additional threat to Pakistan.

There have been three wars between India and Pakistan. The last one of 1971, was almost disastrous for Pakistan in its political and military consequences. The two wings of Pakistan were separated. A united Pakistan was 1:3 in its power ratio with India, now it has been reduced to 1:7.[1]

During the Cold War era, as successor to former British Indian Empire in north-west of the subcontinent, Pakistan showed a keen interest to keep Afghanistan as a buffer zone between former Soviet Union and South Asia. At that time, USA was overtly concerned about real or imagined USSR thrust towards southward in quest for the warm waters of Indian Ocean.

After Russian Military intervention in Afghanistan in 1979, Pakistan faced a number of difficulties. About 3 million Afghan refugees settled in Pakistan causing great strain on Pakistan's meagre resources. Destabilized situation in Persian Gulf due to Iran-Iraq war (1980-88), coinciding with Russian military presence in Afghanistan, exacerbated concern to Pakistan.

There arc no permanent friends and no permanent enemies in international politics. It is a rule of diplomacy that there should not be more than one adversary at a time. If there is more than one adversary, compromise should be made with one of them, preferably the less dangerous one. As late Professor FS. Northedge argues: It is pragmatically necessary for States to improve their relations with former enemies and rivals, if strains are developing between themselves and third States[2].

Pakistani leaders, especially military rulers, perceive India as an adversary. But altered situation in north-west in 1979 onwards, has forced them to adopt a more pragmatic attitude. Arguably, the purpose of offering no-war pact to India in 1982 by General Ziaul Haq, the dictator of Pakistan, was to defuse tension with and Day more attention to the situation on north-west.

Interests of the United States in South Asia

United States is the sole super power or traditionally speaking, a global power. Being a global power, it has world-wide interests and commitments. The regional policies of a global power are more or less subordinated to its global policies.

Presumably, the first and foremost function of a super power in the normal international system is to maintain the balance of power with an adversary. The balance of power is maintained to safeguard the existence of nation state system. It is maintained in a number of ways: for example achieving parity with adversary or undermining his superiority by gaining an edge over him[3]. During the Cold War era, America considered Soviet Union as an adversary and probably preferred, the last method for the management of equilibrium. West Europe and Middle East are generally regarded as the core areas of a global balance of power. Until mid 1990s, South Asia stood at the periphery of power scale. However, the detonation of their nuclear devices by India and Pakistan in 1998, made the area as "the nuclear flashpoint" and one of the pivotal areas of the world.

The Soviet presence in Afghanistan in the 1970s and 80s disturbed the power equilibrium. America as a super power was very much concerned about this de-stabilization of the region, which may go against its worldwide interests. For a while, the maintenance of local balance of power, by undermining the Soviet Union's gains in Afghanistan, was the major interest of United States in this area. To achieve this goal, it gave proper attention to regional politics of South Asia. Presently the heavy presence of Al-Qaueda and Taliban in Pakistan and Afghanistan, is matter of great concern to United States.

India is biggest state of the region and nature of US ties with India largely shape politics of the region. On Afghanistan issue, Indian position is pragmatic. It is in favour of NATO forces to eliminate Islamic terrorism. Taliban. Similarly in the post-Cold War era, India is not against American presence in the Indian Ocean region.

US ties with Pakistan are important to the American strategists in their war against terrorism, because it is the supply route to NATO forces in Afghanistan. Sometime ago, explaining this factor, Dr Peter Lyon argued: ...in these circumstances, only various nations of the South Asian region can provide United States with an opportunity to contain the Muslim militias. US, therefore, is trying hard to bring about a détente in inter-state relations in South Asia[4].

Convergence of Pakistan-United States Perceptions and Interests in South Asia

One can find many similarities of perception and convergence of interests between Pakistan and US. Regional stability and curbing of religious terrorism are their principal common interests. Because of its fragile economy and overspending on defence Pakistan needs economic aid. Only an economically and socially stable Pakistan can resist threat from the militants. US fulfils economic and military needs of Pakistan liberally. Under the Kerry Lugar Law, it has given $7.5 billion for five years.

Normalization of relations between Pakistan and India is interest of US. After Soviet withdrawal Afghanistan in 1989, Pakistan's defence focus largely shifted to the eastern border from north-western border. Pakistan's support to Sikh and Kashmiri insurgents in 1980s also mounted tension with India. In 1999, during Kargil Crisis, when Pakistan's forces penetrated deep into Indian territory in the north and the two countries poised their nuclear weapons against each other, America defused the tension between them. Since then it is playing behind the scene role of a facilitator between them[5]. Continuous tension between India and Pakistan is harmful to United States policies in South Asia. The relaxation of tension between India and Pakistan, gives an opportunity to United States to consolidate its position in the area.

There is a gap between theory and practice of United States attitude towards the outside world. In theory, it still adheres to the Wilsonian views about democracy as a means of attaining peace. In practice, like many Western nations, America has a record of supporting dictatorial regimes in the Third World. Analyzing this paradox in US foreign policy, the political scientist, Karl Deutsch argues:

> Thus, a great power, whose department of defence is under pressure from armed services to establish strategic - naval and air bases in foreign countries... may end up putting its bases into some of the world's poorest and most backward countries, where unpopular and corrupt or oppressive governments may be willing to offer strategic sites for such bases to a foreign power, most cheaply or with the least insistence on the share in the political control. As a result, a great democracy such as the United States, without any necessary deliberate intentions of its leaders, may find it allied around the world with a remarkable collection of backward monarchies, authoritarian regimes and military or civilian dictatorship[6].

Though Zia and Musharraf military regimes in Pakistan stated that they did not grant bases to US, yet because of prevailing Afghan situation, US got bases in Pakistan and as a quid pro quo, military rule and violation of human rights were condoned by the United States. Civilian government of Pakistan, which came to power in 2008, because of its weak base, continues with the same policy vis-a-vis United States.

Divergence of Pakistan-United States Perceptions and Interests in South Asia

Pakistan's nuclear programme has been disapproved by United States. Both Carter and Clinton administrations took tough measures against Pakistan and US aid to it was suspended. However, once again after 9/11, considering "Pakistan as a non-NATO ally", the Bush administration restored aid to Pakistan. But Pakistan is perceived with suspicion as a "potential nuclear proliferators" and a state whose nuclear weapons may fall into the hands of terrorists. This is one of the reasons that unlike the India-US Civilian Nuclear Agreement of 2008, United States is reportedly reluctant to strike a similar agreement with Pakistan pass similar nuclear technology to it and recognize Pakistan as a nuclear state[7]. This is one of the contentious issues in US-Pakistan relations.

After 1971 war, power ratio between India and Pakistan drastically changed. America apparently recognizes this change. Pakistan on the other hand, is unwilling to accommodate itself to the Indian predominance. This is another issue of disagreement at least in public, between United States and Pakistan. Pakistan intends to be hyphenated with India and implicitly insisting on parity with it, which is not acceptable to United States.

United States bourgeoning relationships with India appears to be a matter of concern for Pakistan, which is perceived as an alliance between the US, Israel and India aimed at encircling and defanging Pakistan. On its own, Pakistan is rapidly cultivating a web of relationships with China. China has built a deep-sea port at Gwadar, province of Balochistan, in the proximity of Persian Gulf. It is reported that Pakistan has given docking facilities to the Chinese Navy at Gwadar and China has also installed surveillance facilities to monitor Indian and American military activities in the Gulf and Central Asia.

After an oil rich and modesty populated Qatar, with second highest growth rate of 8.6 per cent per annum and yearning to be the largest economy of world[8], energy hungry China plans to build an all weather road and railway line connecting Gwadar with the Chinese city of Kashgar in its Muslim majority province of Xingjian. It is one of the largest suppliers of military hardware to Pakistan, which includes four F-22 frigates, four early warning aircrafts, tanks and eight

China-Pak joint fighters (JF-17/ FC).[9] China has heavy investment in Pakistan's industrial sector, specially in power generation sector and mining industry[10]. In addition, China does not follow American line of sanction against Iran, over latter's nuclear programme[11]. Since China has common borders with Pakistan, the latter cannot afford to annoy it. Thus, on China, United States and Pakistan have divergent perceptions.

Undoubtedly, Pakistan and the United States have different power capabilities and geo-strategic interests in the world. Obviously their interests in South Asia are not totally identical. Making a balance sheet of convergences and divergences of their interests, one finds more points of divergence. Interests of Pakistan demand reducing the points of divergence. However, Pakistan does not have to be a coup follower of the US. It should follow a policy of firmness on some matters but show flexibility on others. Several steps can be taken in this direction.

America is a democratic state. It respects democratic nations in the world. Democratic India receives a higher degree of respect than a military dominated Pakistan. Restoration of genuine democracy in Pakistan, improves the Pakistani image in the US and its problems receive a more sympathetic treatment.

Normalisation of Relations with India

A policy re-orientation is needed towards India. Despite ups and downs, Pakistan has persitently pleaded dialogue with India. Successive civilian governments in Pakistan have tried to restrain ISI and Army to stop insurgency in India which includes J&K. This policy should be vigorously pursued and the fear that India would undo Pakistan should be given up. Americans also feel that disintegration of Pakistan is not in the interest of India. The latter can not absorb Pakistani provinces in a new Indian Empire.

India and Pakistan share a great deal of cultural heritage. They have similar administrative institutions. If some fields of common interests are marked out, joint ventures can be started. Along with political, a non-political and functional attitude is also required towards India. Cultural exchanges, visits by academics and flow of tourists will help bringing two nations closer to each other. The theory of functionalism argues that when non-political problems are solved and people are brought together, it will be easy for governments to solve their political problems. Good neighbourly relationships India will help Pakistan to reduce its military expenditure and acquire greater flexibility in its dealings with the extra-regional powers.

While it is desirable to reduce the points of divergence between Pakistan and US, it is equally desirable that on issues that touch Pakistan's sovereignty and vital interests, Pakistan should pursue its own course. Pakistan must maintain good relationships with other countries. In this respect, the former West Germany can serve as a good example. During the Cold War period, though it was a front line state and member of NATO, it pursued a policy of the Ostpoltik (eastern politics) with the former East Germany and détente with Russia. It defied US sanctions against construction of Siberian gas pipeline. Thus, despite its "special relationship" with US, former West Germany pursued an independent course towards Russia in order to safeguard her national interests. West German policies towards its eastern part and Russia payed dividends. Ultimately in 1989-90, former East Germany reunified with West Germany and once again the two German states like 1870, merged into a single Germany (*Deutschland*). Pakistan should do the same. It appears that on its own, India follow West Germany's example in dealing with Pakistan, which at the moment, may be its difficult neighbour, because of the military's overbearing influence there. However, because of some mischief makers, the whole Pakistan should not be perceived as a nasty neighbour.

In the final analysis, Pakistan should be an ally of the sole superpower, nevertheless, such an alliance should not be at the cost of either Iranians, Chinese, Russians and any other country or people of the world.

References

1. *The Military Balance 1981- 82* (London: The International Institute for Strategic Studies), pp. 76-86.

2. FS Northedge, *The International Political System* (London: Faber and Faber 1976), p. 266.

3. Inis Claude Jr, *Power and International Relations* (N.Y:, Random House 1962), pp. 14-16.

4. Peter Lyon, "Pakistan's Current Relations with Three Great Powers", *Journal of South Asian and Middle Eastern Studies*, p. 14.

5. Strobe Talbot, *Engaging India, Diplomacy, Democracy and the Bomb* (New Delhi: Penguins, 2004) pp. 155-169.

6. Karl, W. Deutsch, *The Analysis of International Relations* (N.J: Prentice Hall 1978), p. 91.

7. Saed Shah, "Pakistan Pushes US for Nuclear Technology Deal", *Guardian*, 23rd March 2010.

8. "Top Growers", *The World in 2010: The Economist Intelligence Unit*, (London: 2010) p. 97.

9. "Central and South Asia: Pakistan", *The Military Balance 2009*, p. 330.

10. Maqbool Ahmed and Nasir Rahim, "Treasure Denied", *The Herald*, March 2010, pp.

11. "U.S. Foreign Policy: Containing Iran", *The Economist,* 13th March 2010, p. 28.

(This is the updated version of a conference paper, "Pakistan-US Relations in South Asia" published in, ed, Rais Ahmed Khan, *Pakistan-United States Relations*, Area)

12

Shift in Pak-US Policy after USSR Demise

Napoleon Bonaparte, a great French General, who shook the status quo in the late 18th and an early 19th century Europe, said : It is geography which makes the history. This dictum is aptly applicable to the relationships between different states even today. Even national interests, the main determinants of security and foreign policy of a state, are defined in terms of geographical setting of that state in the region and in world.

History of Pakistan-United States relationship, which started at the time of the creation of Pakistan and passed through several phases, is also principally shaped by their geostrategic settings. United States is a global power with worldwide political, economic and strategic interests. Its relationship with any state or region of the world, is determined by consideration of its national interests. Post-1971 Pakistan, principally a South Asian state, is located at the tri-juncture of South Asia, Middle East and Central Asia. United States deals with Pakistan at any given time, keeping in view the position of Pakistan vis-a-vis the former's global perspectives. Pakistan, on its part, being much smaller than its traditional adversary India, attempts to muster military and diplomatic support of members of the international community in general, United States in particular. Both Pakistan United States, during different periods of time, have dealt with each other with different expectations. The focus of this chapter is on Pak-US, relationship during the post cold war era *i.e,* a period, which started in 1989-90. It also attempts to investigate the problems lying ahead for these two states in 2000s.

Pak-US Relations during the Cold War Era

Professor Fred Halliday of the London School of Economic, divided the cold war era into two phases.[1] During the first phase (1945-1970), world politics was shaped principally by the pattern of rigid bipolarity or intense rivalry of former USSR (Soviet Union) and United States. In this period, considering the Soviet Union as a threat to the free world, United States pursued the policy of containment, which was ultimately aimed at "mellowing down", a euphemism for disintegration of the Soviet Union. Because of Pakistan's geostrategic location vis-a-vis the Gulf and Afghanistan, it was coopted as a partner in the cold war strategy.

In the 1970s, an era of understanding between the Soviet Union and the United States, generally referred to as detente, began. During this period, Pakistan eclipsed in US policy calculations. Due to Pakistan's nuclear programme, which it launched in reaction of the similar Indian programme, economic and military aid was suspended by Carter Administration in 1978. So much so, that while visiting Tehran and Delhi in September 1978-9, Jimmy Carter declined to visit Islamabad.[2]

The second phase of the cold war era began in the late 70s when President Carter made a 3 per cent increase in the US defence budget and adopted an proactive policy towards Soviet Union by creating a rapid deployment force to be stationed in the Gulf.[3] The cold war took a new serious turn, when out of fear of turmoil in Iran and its possible repercussions on its under soft belly in Central Asia, the Soviet Union entered into Afghanistan in December 1979.[4]

Soviet Union's invasion of Afghanistan by United States, where from 1980 onwards, President Ronald Reagan was in the saddles; was perceived as an invasion against the free world and an attempt to disrupt the sea lanes in the Gulf and to occupy oil fields in Gulf region. Ronald Reagan reinvigorated US policy of containment and ultimate disintegration of Soviet Union, as formulated by George Kannan, a senior Kremlinologist, in the 1940s. Dubbing Soviet Union as an evil empire, Ronald Reagan pursued the policy of rolling back of the communism under his famous, Reagan Doctrine which he formally proclaimed in 1985.[5]

Soviet Union's invasion of Afghanistan revitalized Pakistan's strategic significance in the American game plan and a new warming up of Pakistan-United States relationship. Sanctions against Pakistan were lifted. It received US $3.2 billion aid to refurbish its armed forces. According to General Jahandad Khan, a close colleague of General Zia-ul-Haq, Pakistan reached an understanding with United States over the crucial issue of Kashmir and its nuclear programme.[6] On its part, Pakistan set up training camps for Afghan guerrillas, who called themselves as Mujahideen. Besides the refugee camps, Madrassahs (religious schools) became the military training centres for Afghan warriors.[7] An amount of about 2 billion U.S. dollars was funnelled into Afghanistan through Pakistan.[8] Afghan guerrillas received the most sophisticated US weapons including anti-aircraft stinger missiles and British made blue pipe missiles. All such weaponry was channeled through Pakistan. America appealed its Muslim allies, especially Saudi Arabia and Egypt, to send their volunteers to Afghanistan for fighting against Russians in the name of *Jihad* fighting against Russians in the name of *Jihad* (holy war). One of these volunteers was the Saudi millionaire Osama Bin Ladin, who not only himself went to Afghanistan but also put his money at the disposal of Mujahideen. During Zia era, a process of Islamization of the country and indoctrination of armed forces on the religious lines[10] also began, with the purpose of establishing an Islamic system of government in Pakistan.

Till mid eighties, United States got Soviet Union engaged mainly on two fronts: the proxy war in Afghanistan and the arms race taken into space by launching the so-called "Star War Programme" by putting nuclear weapons in the space which were aimed at the Soviet targets, with a staggering economic cost. Soviet Union was also facing turmoil in Eastern Europe, especially in Poland, Hungary and East Germany. When Mikhail Gorbachev became the head of the Soviet Union in 1985, Soviet war weariness in Afghanistan, its economic collapse and ideological failure were in sight. It was under these circumstances that Mohammad Khan Junejo, Prime Minister of Pakistan, signed the famous Geneva Accord with Afghanistan. This Accord, which had the American blessing, provided for the Soviet withdrawal from Afghanistan until 1990.

After the fall of the Berlin Wall and reunification of Germany (1989-90), Soviet Union started falling apart. When the Soviet collapse became imminent, America arguably reset its priorities with regard to Afghanistan and Pakistan. By the end of cold war, Pakistan lost its importance in US strategic calculations. Once again, economic and military sanctions were imposed on the pretext of its nuclear programme.

Pak-US Relationship in Post Cold Era

From 1990 onwards, because of the change in United States global priorities, difference of perceptions between Pakistan and the United States again began to damage their relations. These differences have broadly been related to the following areas :

A. Pakistan's nuclear programme

In order to avoid a nuclear war or the spread of nuclear weapons in the developing world, where the command and control structures generally remain shaky; United States has been advocating the policy of non-proliferation. It insists other states to sign and ratify the Comprehensive Test Ban Treaty (CTBT) of 1996 and Non-proliferation Treaty of 1969. Since the Indian nuclear test of 1974, United States knew that both Pakistan and India were embarked on their respective Secret Nuclear programmes. It insisted both of them for accession to these non-proliferation treaties. India never says no to these treaties but puts a condition that unless the United States itself accedes and ratifies the CTBT and reduces its stockpiles, it will not adhere to the treaty. Pakistan's position is almost similar. It insists that it cannot sign the treaty unless India does so. Thus, argument goes on between India and America, on one hand and Pakistan and the United States on the other.

Previously, India and Pakistan were perceived by United States as nuclear thresholds or clandestine nuclear powers, but nuclear tests of the two countries, carried out in 1998, removed any US doubts about their status. It stopped their economic aid. Japan and other donor also stopped aid to Pakistan. In the year 1998, Pakistan received an aid of 440 $ millions from the World Bank. If it had not tested the nuclear devices, Pakistan's total allocation would have been 1.20 billion dollars.[11] Thus, detonation of nuclear devices hit Pakistan more than India, because of the latter's bigger foreign exchange reserves and higher industrial output.

Pakistan has not signed the Non Proliferation Treaty so far. Its proximity with the Middle Eastern Muslim countries is also a concern for the United States, which feels that Pakistan could transfer its nuclear technology to the Muslim States. Thus, Pakistan's nuclear weapons are considered more alarming by the United States than the Indian nuclear weapons which are less likely to be transferred to any other region of the world.

The missile race between India and Pakistan is also a matter of concern for the United States. Both the countries have acquired a capacity of hitting the targets up to 2000 kilometers. In other word, India and Pakistan can hit each other's cities with both conventional and nuclear payloads, fitted into their missiles.

In August 1999, India pronounced its nuclear doctrine of "minimum credible nuclear deterrence". According to it, in case of a war, India will not use nuclear weapons first. However, the nuclear weapons will be fitted into its sea, air and land based missiles, planes and submarines.[12] American experts such as Professor Rodney Jones has advised Pakistan neither to jump into a new nuclear arms race nor to declare any doctrine of its own.[13] Ignoring the American advise, General Musharraf, announced his own policy of "minimum nuclear deterrence".[14] This policy seems to be a counterpoise of Indian nuclear doctrine. This sort of anti-non-proliferation policies of both India and Pakistan would widen bridge between them, on the one hand, and with the United States on the other.

In 1919, League of Nations was the brainchild of the United State but it itself did not join it. Yet USA appealed other states to join the League. Similarly, although American Senate has rejected the CTBT, US Administration puts pressure on other states to accede and ratify CTBT. In the case of not doing so, U.S. aid is either stopped to them or its amount curtailed. Thus, Pakistan's nuclear and missile race with India remains an irritant in its relations with United States.

B. Kashmir

Pakistan and the United States perceive Kashmir dispute from different perspectives. From Pakistani point of view, Indian administered Kashmir should accede to Pakistan. For the last 64years, Pakistan's diplomatic and military efforts have been directed in this context to the settlement of Kashmir issue. As mentioned earlier, bedsides economic aid, Pakistan has attempted to seek America's military and political support for the settlement of Kashmir dispute. Without settlement of the Kashmir issue, Pakistan cannot visualize any meaningful improvement of its relations with India. US on its part, sees Kashmir as a serious problem between India and Pakistan, but advises Pakistan to solve it with India on the bilateral basis. Pakistan, however, prefers a third party involvement. Forces of two countries are usually in high state of alert at the line of control to meet any eventuality.

According to Cooley, ISI diverted US. weapons meant for Afghan Mujahideen to Kashmiris, after the Soviet withdrawal from Afghanistan in 1989. This was done by the ISI without the knowledge of United States[15]. Supply of these weapons, in the words Jaswant Singh, former minister of external affairs of India turned scholar, intensified the insurgency in the valley.[16] Pakistan claims to be supporting the Kashmiris morally and politically only.

Because of the heavy Indian causalities in Kashmir, New Delhi has been accusing Pakistan of supporting the fighters. In 1990, India and Pakistan were once again at the verge of a war. As the then US administration knew that the two countries were clandestine nuclear powers and any conventional conflict between them could escalate into a nuclear war; it sent its emissaries to both countries for de-escalating the tension.[17] In May 1999 once again, a high degree tension arose between India and Pakistan, when India accused Pakistan of sending infiltrators on the other side of line of control. America supported the Indian stand and urged Pakistan to defuse the tension and called for the withdrawal of its regulars.[18]

US chief of the Central Command, General Anthony Zenni, visited Pakistan and called for restraint. A similar message was conveyed to the Indians through American ambassador in Delhi. It was feared in United States that as a reprisal to crossing the border by Pakistan backed fighters, if Indians crossed the line of control, a conventional conflict could escalate into a nuclear war. So, they tried to de-escalate the tension between the two countries. Kashmir was considered "a nuclear flashpoint in South Asia". But America declined to equate it with Kosovo and East Timor, which called for its active intervention.[19] Prime Minister of Pakistan, Mr. Nawaz Sharif, visited Washington in July 1999. The former President Clinton upon called him for withdrawal of Pakistani troops from the other side of the line of control in Kargil. He did so. Pakistan's new ruler, General Musharraf, had also unilaterally withdrawn troops from the international borders with India. But the tension still remained high in the India-Pakistan relations. America cannot impose its will on these nuclear powers. At the most, it could use influence over them for an amicable settlement of the dispute. In 2001, when terrorists attacked the Indian parliament, India blamed Pakistan for adding and abating them and tension rose to a high pitch when Indian troops were mobilized to the war position. Similarly when on 22nd November 2008, members of *Lashkar-i-Tayeba,* which is an ISI trained group of Pakistani commandos, killed more then 160 Indians in Mumbai, there was a war hysteria in India which was avoided by pressure from the International Community on both sides but the tension mounts still very high on this issue because Pakistan refuses to extradite the mastermind of the attack, Hafiz Saed, and other perpetrators.

C. Resurgence of Islamic Fundamentalism

19th Century British Prime Minister and statesman, Lord Palmerstone had said: there are no permanent friends and eternal enemies in politics. Nature of the relationship between states is determined by their national interests at a given time. As discussed earlier, America in 1980s, encouraged the setting up of training camps for Afghan Mujahideen inside Afghanistan as well as in Pakistan. It also appealed its Muslim friends to send volunteers for fighting war in Afghanistan. Appeal of *Jihad,* quest for adventurism and charm of Afghan women[20] attracted many volunteers from Pakistan and Arab world to join the *Jihad* in Afghanistan.

After withdrawal of Soviet troops from Afghanistan in 1989, US priorities changed. Infighting between different Afghan factions was not in the US interests. So, it withdrew its support to Afghan Mujahideen.

Most of Arab volunteers also returned to their countries, with an idea that after collapse of Soviet Union, it was United States, which was enemy of Islamic world. Pro-American governments in Egypt and Saudi Arabia became the main targets of these new zealots, who called themselves Afghans. America itself became their target. In 1993, the World Trade Centre in New York was bombed. There was another bomb blast in Okalhama city in 1995. The foot prints of these bombers were traced back to Afghanistan. In 1995, American Embassy was bombed in Islamabad. In 1996, American barracks in Saudi Arabia were attacked by the Islamic zealots. In 1997, 4 employees of Union Texas Company were murdered in Karachi. Next year, US embassies in Kenya and Tanzania were bombed. These bombing were allegedly sponsored by Saudi-millionaire Osama bin Ladin, who is now living in FATA of Pakistan. America had asked Taliban to extradite Osama for trial. But they refused. Similarly, Pakistan had expressed its inability to influence Taliban, who are widely believed to its brain children.

Initially, it was hoped that the Taliban will open trade routes to Central Asia, which would benefit the American multinationals. This hope was not realized. In 1997, President Khatami became the head of Iran. He offered to open a dialogue with the West. And after a long time in 1998, King Fahad of Saudi Arabia attended the Islamic Summit in Tehran. Saudi-Iran rapprochement also temporarily diminished the Taliban's significance for Saudi Arabia and correspondingly, for the United States. Iran was already at odds with Taliban, because of the alleged massacre of Shia minority in Afghanistan in 1997. Thus, a new grouping of states consisting of Iran, India and America emerged against the Taliban.

India strongly accused Taliban for training Kashmiri insurgents. Thus, a convergence of relationship developed between America and India over the Taliban whose predecessor Mujahideen, were the creation of ISI and CIA. In August 1999, there was a high lend meeting between Karl Underforth and Martin Idayk in Delhi with his Indian counterparts, to curb terrorism in South Asia.[21] Taliban were accused of cultivating opium and exporting heroin to the outside world through Pakistan. According to a UNDP Report,[22] the production of opium had doubled up to 4600 tones in 1999. Terrorism and narco-terrorism are perceived by free world as major threats. Afghanistan under Taliban is their main exporter. Against this backdrop, the UN Security Council in October 1999 imposed sanctions on Afghanistan.

In Pakistan itself, different religious groups, such as *Lashkar-i-Tayeba, Sipah-i-Sahaba, and Harkaktul Ansar* have created the problem of law and order by promoting religious and sectarian intolerance. Most of these groups have training camps in FATA. Prime Minister of Pakistan was forced by internal and external circumstances to pressurize Taliban to stop their training camps.[23] He had sent his then aide, the former chief of ISI, to Kabul for that purpose.

General Musharraf gave an impression to the world he was a Kamalist i.e, a modern Muslim who abhors fundamentalism. Then US ambassador, William Milam, hoped that Pakistan, which enjoy, a great deal of influence over Taliban, would exercise influence over then to help removing terrorism from the region.[24] The moot point is, how far General Musharraf succeeded in influencing the behaviour of Taliban? Maulana Samiul Haq of Jameet ul Ulma-i-Islam (JUI) threatened the Chief Executive of dire consequences, if he implemented the US agenda in Pakistan's internal and external politics.[25] Maulana's word certainly carried some weight, which Musharaf's regime found hard to ignore. Maddrassahs retained their privileged position in the country.

Fundamental American interests in South Asia are promotion of peace, stability and winning war on terror in Afghanistan and FATA in Pakistan. Peace cannot be imposed from outside. America has to help democratic forces in the region, which were repeatedly undermined by military coups and their aftermaths are still felt by the present civilian government of President, Asif Ali Zardari. Stability in South Asia will contribute to the stability in the world. America as the sole superpower has come up to this expectation by supporting the democratic forces.

References

1. Fred Haliday, *The Making of the Second Cold War,* Second Edition, London: Verso, 1989.

2. General KM Arif. *Working with Zia: Pakistan's Power Politics 1977-78.* Karachi: Oxford University Press, 1995.

3. *Ibid.*, pp. 11-15.

4. *Ibid.*

5. *Ibid.*

6. Jahandad Khan, *Pakistan : The Leadership Crisis,* (Karachi: Oxford University Press, 1999).

7. Peter Mersden. *Taliban.* (London: Zed Publishers, 1998).

8. Fred Halliday. *Third World: An Essay in Soviet-American Relations.* (London. Radius. 1989) pp. 77-78.

9. John K. Cooley. *Unholy Wars: Afghanistan, America and International Terrorism.* (London: Public Press, 1999) pp. 222-223.

10. Stephen P. Cohan. *The Pakistan Army.*(Karachi. Oxford University Press, 1998).

11. *Dawn.* 22 September, 1999.

12. Rodney Jones, "Minimum Credible Deterrence," *Dawn,* 14 September, 1999.

13. *Ibid.*

14. *Dawn, 2* November, 1999.

15. John K. Cooley, *op.cit.,* p. 7.

16. Jaswant Singh, *Defending India.* (Bangalore: MacMillan India Limited, 1989), pp. 150-153.

17. Seymour Hersh, "On Nuclear Edge : A Report At Large", *Heritage,* 19 March, 1993.

18. *Dawn,* 16 June and 9 September, 1999.

19. *Ibid.*

20. *Herald,* August 1999.

21. Cited in Afzal Mohamud, "Indo-U.S. Entente". *Dawn*, 5 September, 1999.

22. *Dawn,* 11 September, 1999.

23. *Dawn,* 7 October, 1999.

24. 19 October, 1999.

25. *Dawn,* 9 August, 1999.

(The earlier version of this conference paper was published under title," Pak-U.S. Relationship in the Post-Cold War Era' in *Pakistan Journal of American Studies*, Vol: 17, Spring & Fall 1999, No 1&2. By the Study Centre for American Studies, Quiad-i-Azam University Islamabad).

13

Refined Teaching Methods in International Relations

Teaching of any subject is to disseminate knowledge to the students about it. Thus, teaching and learning go hand in hand. Undertaking research or supervising it also emanates from teaching. Thus, teaching is the basic tool of passing on knowledge to the students of any discipline. Before discussing how International Relations, a social science, should be taught particularly in Pakistan, one has to discuss *what* is to be taught? And *why* it is to be taught. These are interrelated questions and will be addressed accordingly.

It will be more appropriate if it is discussed what is the subject matter of International Relations? According to any textbook definition, whether new or old, International Relations is a discipline that discusses the problems, which lead the states and people to conflicts and wars and how conflicts can be mitigated and harmony among them brought about.[1] The very discipline of International Relations was introduced in the United States and the United Kingdom in 1920s to discuss causes of war and finding ways to avoid it. Since the world is divided between states and the number of states is proliferating not reducing, the institution of the state was and is vital if not no exclusive focus of study of International Relations.[2] And it remains almost the same even today.

Change of Circumstances and Indigenization of Discipline

The theory of International Relations and an overall nature of the subject, change according to the changed political, social, economic and cultural circumstances, which affect the behaviour of the state and non-state actors operating in the international system in given circumstances. After the post-Cold War era (1990s onwards), the vital concepts of "national security" and "national interests" are also taught in a different manner. Previously, much emphasis was on the "national interest", which were in many cases "governmental interests" and the "military aspect" of statecraft. But as just mentioned, the scenario is rapidly changing in the post-cold war era. The study of International Relations is markedly shifting from the "state-centric approach" to "people centric approach". And the negative and positive implications of globalization on the individuals and groups are also investigated.

National Security and National Interests

In Pakistan, due to political instability and frequent bouts of dictatorship, "the national security" was interpreted with major emphasis on its military dimension. Now it has begun to be taught from a different perspective. Thus, security is interpreted in the terms of human welfare from where the concept of "human security" is emerging, which has more relevance to developing states like Pakistan.[3]

Over the period of 63 years, the country has been directly or indirectly ruled by military, which has siphoned of much of the national budget in the name of national security vis-à-vis defence against "Indian threat". In addition, armed forces have helped themselves with national exchequer by building their own industrial and real estates and vested interests.[4] Thus, while teaching the concept of "national security", one has to pay special attention to its human dimension. Welfare state is an institution that exists for the benefit of its citizens. The citizens are at the disposal of the state only in totalitarian states.

Generally speaking, "national interests" are interpreted by policy-making elite, epically the foreign office, which is a component of establishment. Think-tanks, academia, press and civil society also offer their interpretations of "national interests". However, in Pakistan, practically speaking, interpretation of "national interests" and "national security" is done by real and permanent policy makers of Pakistan, the Army and intelligence agencies, especially the ISI. Again, most of the Islamabad based think-tanks are allegedly funded by the ISI.[5] These think-tanks interpret "national interests" in such a manner that it suits the GHQ. Arguably, the Foreign Office in these circumstances is a "post office" passing and receiving dispatches to and from different embassies. However, we have a vibrant media and a vocal civil society keeping a check on the military suited interpretation of "national interests".

There is a difference between what Barry Buzan calls "the regimental or governmental interests from the national interests".[6] We the academics, being members of civil society should teach these vital concepts of "national security" and "national interests" according to our conscience. Let us not be mouthpieces of the establishment or the whosoever party is in power.

State-Society Relations

Pakistan is ethnically and religiously a heterogeneous state. Many of our domestic tensions are interlinked with security and foreign policy concerns and emanate from these tensions. In addition, we cannot shelve these differences. In other subjects in general and theory of International Relations in particular, we should have also to teach state-society relations,[7] focusing on different segments of society and how to bring about harmony between them. It is the national cohesion, which makes a state weak, or strong.[8] It makes a state dependent or independent in the pursuit of its internal and external policies. The ethnic and religious dimensions of Pakistani society should be taught in our syllabus.[9]

The Political Dimension of Islam and Pakistan

Islam has special significance in our society and correspondingly, a degree of influence on the policy-making processes. Islamic states are our kindred states with whom we are supposed to have special relationship because of our ideological inclination. Unfortunately, most of the Muslim states are ruled by the dictators and autocrats.[10] These unpopular regimes, especially in the Middle East, are patronized by the sole superpower for its insatiable urge for oil and other strategic natural resources. Now it has become crystal clear that in 2003, Bush and Blair attacked Iraq to occupy principally, its oil fields and maintain a strategic position vis-à-vis the Iran, Syria and Afghanistan, not because of either destroying weapons of the mass destruction nor receiving a word from God to launch invasion for facilitating the advent of Lord Jesus Christ on the earth, as many neo-con and Evangelists believe.[11]

After the end of cold war, flames of Islamophobia are fanning in the West, which got added dimension after 9/11. Frontier province of Pakistan (nowadays called Khyber-Pakthnkhaw) and the adjoining the FATA are considered bastions of terrorist brand of Islam, where all sorts of *Jihadis* are based and trained.[12] Pakistanis are usually regarded as the terrorists.

In order to remove this negative impression of Pakistan. The Higher Education Commission of Pakistan has rightly designed a course, entitled "Islam and International Relations", in the syllabus of International Relation[13]. However, the central focus of the course, should not be on the interpretation of Fiqah and Hadith but on the causes of resurgence of political Islam, its impact on world and the reaction of the Industrialized Western democracy.[14] In addition, the argument for and against, Samuel Huntington's theory of "The Clashes of Civilizations" should have been the main focus of its study. Impartial and valued works of late Professor Fred Halliday of the London School of Economics (LSE) and Robert Frisk of the British newspaper, *The Independent,* should have also been included in the syllabus of this subject.[15]

War on International Terrorism and Pakistan's Role

United States in the 1980s exploiting the vulnerabilities of the Zia regime, turned Pakistan into huge training centre for Mujahideen fighting the Soviets in Afghanistan at home, of 3 million Afghan refugees and conduit of drugs to the world. Similarly, after 9/11, because of the unpopularity of Musharraf regime and his resultant dependence on US backing, in the name of war on International Terrorism, Musharraf government was bombing its own citizens in FATA and Waziristan. It also implicitly allowed the NATO forces to hit the targets within Pakistan. Ironically, US weapons to be used against *Al-Qaida* and Taliban are instead, being used against the Baloch tribesmen. Some of these weapons are even diverted to the eastern command, bordering India.

Domestically, explosion in cities, attacks on cantonments and on dignitaries, most conspicuously the assassination of Benazir Bhutto, leader of Pakistan Peoples Party, in December 2007, sectarian violence, and gang warfare between the student wings of different political parties, have become an everyday phenomenon in our country. All this extremism is the result of

Pakistan's military alignment with the United States in the name of initially fighting the communists, now America's own creation, Taliban and *Al-Qaida*.

In order to appreciate and explain the phenomenon of terrorism, its implications and measures to eliminate it, a course entitled "Political Terrorism" has been designed under the auspices of the HEC. Unfortunately, the pioneering study of Professor Paul Wilkinson[16] is missing from the course document on this subject, which along with late Professor Fred Halliday's works on this topic should be included in it.

Pakistan and Climate Change

Global warming and climate change have added new dimensions to our food and health security concerns. It has made us vulnerable to natural disasters. It affects our individual and collective lives, political and economic choices which we are supposed to make.[17] Nineteenth and twentieth centuries were the age of scrambling for petroleum, just to keep the engine of industrialized west running. Twenty-first century according to some experts may be the age of war for water within the state and between states arising out of global warming.[18]

Like other glaciered regions such as North and South Poles and the Antarctic, due to the overall depletion of the Ozone layer and correspondingly a marked increase in temperature, glaciers of Himalayas range, where main sources of the South Asian Rivers are located; are melting fast. This phenomenon gives birth to untimely rains, floods and droughts. Pakistan in general, its southern province Sindh in particular, as lower riparian of the Indus River System emanating from the High Himalayas, faces water scarcity and consequential food shortage. Conversely, due to heavy raining in Ladakh region in India, northern areas and Khyber Pakhtunkhwa in Pakistan, which are the catchments areas of the Indus Rivers, Sindh is witnessing the super most floods of more than a century. About 20 million persons have become homeless in Pakistan and 14 millions only in Sindh. Thousands of people have lost their lives and the crops have been washed away. The Country faces a disaster and the climate change is one of its catalysts.

In 2008 unfortunately, fungus infected our wheat crop throughout South Asia. Since then we are much short of the stock for feeding our populations. According to Jacques Diof, Director General of United Nations Food and Agriculture Organization, Pakistan and 35 other states face acute food shortage and the food crisis may lead to wars and riots.[19] This scarcity of food is directly connected to the rising heat and untimely raining. deforestation taking place on both sides of River Indus are also increasing the volume of heat in the atmosphere.

Rapid urbanization and industrialization, especially the Carbon Dioxide emitted by vehicles, refrigerators and coal-power stations play havoc with our Ozone Layer, which protects our atmosphere from the intensive heat. In addition, the deforestation of the mangrove forests in the coastal belt of Karachi, the capital of Sindh and economic hub of the country, and destruction of the natural habitat of Dingi and Banddar Islands and small Island near Hawks-bay on the Karachi coast, have been sold by the City Government of Karachi, Port Qasim Authority and former Sindh Government to a Dubai based consortium Emmer Group. This international consortium wants to build the Island, cities like Dubai. However, tempering with the nature, according to many experts will make Karachi vulnerable to Tsunami like hurricane, earthquake and intensive flooding, because Karachi, located in the seismological fault-line.[20] Thus, there is a dire need of examining the after-effects of these man made greed-based security concerns for us. It should also be examined how any disaster should be prevented? In addition, how the negative effects of the global warming can be minimized even within national borders with the collaboration of other signatories of Kyoto Protocol on global warming in 1997 and Copenhagen agreements.

Overview of the Rest of Syllabus of I.R.

Rest of subjects offered by the HEC in syllabus of International Relations, such as, diplomatic history, area studies, International Political Economy, International Law, International Institutions, Strategic Studies and Peace Studies, etc are quite good. Their study will help a student in understanding the intricacies of the current trends of international politics. However, Theory of International Relations should retain its principal position as a compulsory subject in the Discipline of International Relations and from time to time it should be revised incorporating global trends and our own problems in it.

Techniques and Methods of Teaching International Relations

How International Relations as a discipline should be taught? And how the teaching methods can be improved?

Lectures and Seminars

There is no substitute of classroom lecturing. In the West, a course is divided, for instance in England, in a term of ten weeks, a subject is divided in ten topics, if it is a half weight course. If it is a compulsory course, like *Theory of International Relations* with different names, then it takes twenty topics or the two terms. Weekly one-hour lecture is delivered on it by the subject teacher. Then a similar number of seminars are held on that course. In these seminars, presentation is given by the students and its different dimensions are discussed by them. Some teachers encourage students to write book-reviews related to a particular topic or topics. I still remember the three reviews done by me for Professor Michael Donelen of the LSE in mid

70s. These reviews were on E. H. Carr's *The Twenty Years Crisis,* Michael Waltzer's *Just and Unjust Wars,* and, Louis Hankins *How States Behave.* In these reviews topics such as the relationship between power and morality, moral aspects of war and normative aspect of International Relations were discussed. This study still helps me in teaching the theories of International Relations. In the West, at the end of these seminars, the teacher gives his or her comments and suggestions to the students to improve it. Sometimes, the improved versions of that seminar paper delivered by a BSc or a MSc student are published in the professional journals like the LSE-based Journal, the *Millennium.*

A compulsory course for MSc is taken by all students. But seminars on it are organized by a number of teachers (including doctoral students) interest in the same subject. Every student has an opportunity to present his or her views on the topic. Thus, the subject is thoroughly grasped by students.

The practice may be same in Europe and North American Universities. However, as for as most of our universities in Pakistan are concerned, no such seminars are arranged. In contrast, lectures of 50 minutes duration are delivered and the last ten to fifteen minutes are left for questions from students. Their comments are rarely invited in such a short duration. Sometimes, lecture is just delivered from the obsolete material and no chance is given to students to ask the questions or they are even discouraged to do so. In order to bring our teaching standards at par with good universities of the world, student participation in subject seminars should be introduced and encouraged in Pakistani universities.

Multi-Media Devices

It is a positive development that the teachers in the subject lectures and the speakers in the general lectures are using multi-media devices. By showing pictures, or presenting statistics, combined with narration, they make lecture quite interesting and informative. After the presentation, question answer session follows, which inculcates a great deal of knowledge. Usage of multimedia devices should be encouraged in our universities.

Conference/Workshop Culture

It is a good practice that the International Relations Department of Karachi University from time to time organizes the workshops and seminars on different topics, where not only members of the faculty but scholars from other Universities and aboard express their views. Sometimes, leading retired diplomats also participate in these seminars and share their view on a particular topic. In addition, senior students also give presentations, which boost their analytical capacity. Quaid-i-Azam University does the same. Other universities also, casually organize similar events. Sometimes, participation is on the basis of contribution of a scholar to his or her field of inquiry, but in many cases, it is by nomination of higher authorities of the guest University. It is quite ironic that in some universities, same speakers give general lectures on any topic on the earth. In some public universities, this sort of "professional seminarian" is frequently invited on public exchequer for reasons best known to the university high-up. This luxury should be stopped. Only world class scholars should be invited so that students and the young faculty may be benefited from their presence.

Inter-University Student Participation

The participation of students from other Pakistani universities in national and international conferences and workshops at the host university should be highly appreciated. If the HEC or another funding agency or the sending university bear their travelling expenses and the host university provides them with local hospitality. This inter-university cooperation both at faculty and student level will be quite helpful to make International Relations a popular and valuable subject to the students, who plan to have the future in academia, civil services and the media.

Launching of Association International Studies

Organizing a professional conference like, "The State of International Relations in Pakistan", by the Department of International Relations of Karachi University, is a good opportunity for discussing various dimensions of the discipline in Pakistan. The Chairman, Dr. Moonis Ahmar and his colleagues, as well as students and Karachi University administration should be congratulated on it. I hope it will lead to the establishment of Pakistan International Studies/or International Association. This sort of association is over due as Dr. Rasul Bakhsh Rais has mentioned in his paper published somewhere.[21] On the pattern of the British International Studies Association (BISA), the Pakistan International Relations Studies should hold its annual meetings. It may start with a general body meeting and then specialized sessions and a concluding session. In all these sessions besides experts, the student participation from the host and other universities should be encouraged, where the major problems which the country faces and how they should be conceptualized should be discussed.

Recommendations to the Higher Education Commission and Foreign Office

This association should make its own recommendations to formulate a curriculum for the BSc and Master levels and send it the HEC for consideration, which has already formulated syllabus for the students of international relations in 2006. Two the of members of its committee, Dr. Alqama (a Kent University Ph.D. holder and Dr. Mansoor Kundi) have done nice work. If Dr. Rasul Bakhsh Rais and Dr. Tahir Amin and a few other well known scholars, instead of nominees of different chairperson, selected on the criterion of patronage, would have been co-opted in the committee, certainly it would have produced a better document.

The recommendations of such academic conferences or workshops or the professional associations, specializing in

International Relations should also be sent to the Foreign Office for policymaking considerations. After the installation of a civilian government, one can hope that the Foreign Office will be quite active in the orientation and implementation of foreign policy. Like any foreign ministry of a democratic state, it will give due consideration to the informed opinion in the policy making processes.

Regional and International Collaboration

Luckily, Dr. Imtiaz Ahmed, a leading scholar of International Relations from Bangladesh is with us. His presence is a good omen for launching the Pakistan International Studies Association. We live in a larger world. Because of our similar higher education systems, South Asian states, India, Bangladesh and Sri Lanka, are our natural partners. Jawaharlal Nehru University, (JNU), Jamia Milia Islamia, Delhi, Centre for South Asian Studies Rajasthan University, Bombay and Calcutta Universities in India; Dhaka University and Bangladesh Institute of Strategic and International Studies, Institute for the Study of Ethnicity of Sri Lanka, which is an independent body, not affiliated to any university, or the Regional Centre for Strategic Studies (RCSS) Colombo, can be amongst among our partners in developing the South Asian version of International Studies. Coordination with scholars from these countries will enable us to make our teaching and research more effective.

Many of participants in this conference will be certainly in touch with their alma maters and other leading institutions in the West. Let us have coordination with the leading institutions like Harvard, the MIT, Oxford, Cambridge and LSE in teaching and doing research in International Relations. Hanns Seidal Foundation or any other donor agency may be among the source of funding for organizing these events whose beneficiary will be ultimately our youth. If our youth is properly educated, we can resolve all of our problems such as international terrorism and sectarianism and provincial disparities or disparities of wealth among own citizens. By doing so we can build a better image for Pakistan. The International Community, especially the funding agencies will certainly support us in this endeavour.

In a developing country like Pakistan, where civil society is striving hard to liberate the state from the shackles of the military generals, intelligence agencies, bureaucrats, political mountebanks and opportunists and their external patrons; United States Academics of the discipline of International Relations should play an active role in developing a theory and designing the syllabus, which must retain its Western origin but explain our problems according to our needs. Collaboration with colleagues in different universities of the country, South Asia, and the world at large, will enable us to teach and undertake research more effectively. That will serve the very purpose of establishment and evolution of an interdisciplinary subject which emerged around 80 years ago in the West and which may help students to mitigate causes of conflict in the world and promote harmony within the states as well as between them.

References

1. Charles Reynolds, *Theory and Explanation in International Relations* (London: Martin Robertson, 1973), pp. 1-29.

2. Chris Brown with Kirsten Ainley, *Understanding International Relations,* Third Edition: Revised and Updated (Basingstoke: Palgrave: MacMillan, 2005), pp. 5, 66-67.

3. Khadija Haq, *Human Development in South Asia 2005: Human Security in South Asia,* Mahbub ul Haq Human Development Centre (Karachi: Oxford University Press, 2006).

4. Ayesha Siddiqa, *Military Inc. Inside Pakistan's Military Economy* (Karachi: Oxford University Press, 2007).

5. This point was succulently raised by Mr Jaspal in his paper "Linkages Between International Relations and Strategic Studies: A Case Study of Pakistan", presented at the conference "The state of International Relations in Pakistan", held on 26-27 March 2008 at the Department of International Relations, University of Karachi. Mr Jaspal pointed out that that General Ayaz Jamshed, the Director of the Institute of Regional Studies is nominee of the GHQ through the President. He further said that there is no transparency in the appointment of the heads of Islamabad-based institutes such as the Institute of Strategic Studies, the Institute of Regional Studies, and the Institute of Policy and Research (IPRI). Their heads are Formally the nominees of the President and the intelligence agencies are their principal referees for the appointment procedure.

6. Barry Buzan, *People State and Fear: An Agenda for International Security Studies in the Post-Cold War Era* (Sussex: Harvest Whetsheaf, 1991), pp. 57-96.

7. Bill Macsweeney, "Review Article, Identity and Security: Barry Buzan and Copenhagen School", *Review of International Studies,* Vol. 22, No. 1, January 1999, pp. 81-82.

8. B. Buzan, *op. cit.*

9. The works of Anthony Smith and Erick Hobswam need to be included in a chapter on ethnicity. For instance, Anthony Smith' book, *The Ethnic Origins of Nations,* (Oxford, Basil Blackwell, 1988), and Erick Hobsbawm' chapter in his book, "Nations and Nationalism in the New Century", in his book, *Globalization, Democracy and Terrorism,* (London: Little Brown, 2007), are superb studies in the filed of ethnicity.

10. Noam Chomsky, *Imperial Ambitions: Conversations On The Post-9/11, World,* (New York: Metropolitan Books, 2005, pp. 42-65, and Tariq Ali, and David Barsamian, *Conversation with Tariq Ali: Speaking of Empire and Resistance* (London: The New Press, 2005), pp. 93-123.

11. Rod Liddle, "And God Said: Yes Tony, Invade Iraq-If You Want to That is", *The Sunday Times* (London), 6 April, 2008.

12. "Terrorists Operating on Pak-Border: US", *Daily Times* (Karachi) 18 April, 2008.

13. "Islam and International Relations", Revised Curriculum: 2006, International Relations Higher Education Commission of Pakistan, Islamabad, 2006, p. 33.

14. *Ibid.*

15. Fred Halliday, *Islam and the Myth of Confrontation: Religion and Politics in the Middle East*, (London: I.B. Tauris, 1995); F. Halliday. "The Clash of Civilizations? Sense and Nonsense. In *Islam and Global Dialogue: Religious Pluralism and the Pursuit of Peace;* edited by Boase, R. Ashgate, 2005, p. Chapter 7; F. Halliday. The BBC and the Kilroy-Silk affair. In *Muslims and the News media:* edited by Poole. Elizabeth. I. B. Tauris, 2006; F. Halliday, The contradictory legacies of Ayatollah Khomeini: the Iranian revolution at twenty. *Ayatollah Khomeini and the modernization of Islamic Thought,* edited by Tapper. R. Centre for Near and Middle Eastern Studies. School of Oriental and African Studies, 2000; F. Halliday. 9/11 and Middle Eastern studies past and future: revisiting ivory towers on sand. *International affairs* 80, No. 5 (2004). pp. 953-962; F. Halliday. "Islamophobia" reconsidered. *Ethnic and racial studies 22.* No. 5 (1999), F. Halliday, It's time to bin the past. *The Weekly Observer* (London), 30 January, 2005, and Robert Frisk, for instance: "Even I question the truth about 9/11", Daily *The Independent,* Saturday, 25 August, 2007

16. "Politics of Terrorism", *Revised Curriculum: 2006, ibid,* p. 32. *Paul Wilkinson, Terrorism Vs. Democracy: The Liberal States Response revised second edition* (New York: Routlege, 2006).

17. Karen M. Mingst, *Essentials of International Relations,* Third Edition (London: W.M. Norton & Company, 2004), p. 280.

18. John Gray, "Those Who Control the Oil and Water Will Control the World", *The Observer,* 30 March, 2008.

19. *Dawn,* (Karachi), 14 April, 2008.

20. Maqbool Ahmed, "Islands in the Storm", *The Herald,* November 2006, pp. 30-31, Moosa Kaleem, "Operation Wipe Out"; *-ibid,* pp. 32-33. Naseer Memon, "Climate Change and Vulnerability of Sindh Coast," *Economic and Business Review: Dawn,* 14 April, 2008.

21. Rasul Bakhsh Rais, "Teaching of International Relations in Pakistani Universities", in Inayatullah, Rubina Saigol (eds.), *Social Sciences in Pakistan: A Profile,* Council of Social Sciences Pakistan (COSS) (Islamabad: Council of Social Sciences, 2005), pp. 9-30.

(This is an updated versionof the paper, "Teaching Methods of International Relations in Pakistan" in ed, Moonis Ahmar, The State of *International Relations in Pakistan* Karachi : the University of Karachi Press, 2009.)

14

Academic Freedom in Pakistan

Academic freedom of expression has always been suppressed by military regimes in Pakistan. This state of affairs has adversely affected the academic system, specially social science research. Those who disagree with the official line on national and international matters have to face the threat of dismissal, harassment and denial of permission to go abroad for attending conferences. As a result, there is no substantial original thinking and there is no excellence in research in the social sciences.

The faculty of thinking and rationalization makes human beings superior to animal species. Human beings think about themselves, their families and their surroundings. They have the sense of right and wrong and from where the concepts of morality emanate. They come up with criticisms and suggestions on changes in their surroundings and the world at large. That is why freedom of expression has been recognised as one of the important components of the universal declaration of human rights.

Although freedom of expression is guaranteed to every individual by the UN, it is restricted by political system of a particular state at a particular time. Totalitarian regimes orbit around one person or a clique. Any alternative view about that system, is severely crushed. Freedom of expression was strictly forbidden in Nazi Germany and communist USSR. So it was in China till recently.

In the Muslim world including Pakistan, mullahs being the beneficiaries of the status quo, have misinterpreted Quranic injunctions about "the obedience to the ruler". According to this misinterpretation, any ruler, whatsoever corrupt, incompetent and unjust, is to be obeyed by the citizens living within his realm. This misinterpretation of Quran has led to the stagnation of Muslim societies, resulting in violation of human rights and rampant violence, including terrorism, within their bounds and the world at large.

Since its entry into the western sponsored military pacts in the 1950s, political system of Pakistan has been directly or indirectly dominated by the military and its intelligence agencies, which attempt to make it a controlled society and suppresses dissent. Universities are also being run under this mould of thinking. Bureaucracy acts as the junior partner of military establishment. Many retired generals and bureaucrats have been appointed as vice-chancellors by different military dictators over the years. Mediocre academics, working as vice-chancellors, are yes-men of the establishment.Intelligence services have been pervasive in campuses.Lectures are overheard and nonconformist views are considered anti-state activity. Natural sciences are promoted and social sciences are neglected, because the former, in the words of Stephen Cohen, a leading American scholar on south Asian affairs; create human robots in the service of military-industrial complex.[1]

Pakistan has a tradition of appointing non-academic vice-chancellors, for political reasons. This category of vice-chancellors has a deep sense of its unsuitability for the job. In order to overcome it, they may try to project themselves as extra-tough guys. Over dependence on the government, promotion of a crony culture and hobnobbing with blackmailing union leaders, paradoxically are not their pillars of strength, but sources of vulnerability.

Those academics who disagree with the official line on national and international issues, or raise a voice of dissent against the policies of an autocratic vice-chancellor, have been harassed and dismissed from the job, irrespective of their excellence in their respective field of enquiry.

In 1959, barrister Imdad Ali Kazi alias Allama I.I Kazi, was the vice-chancellor of Sindh University. He was a good scholar, but a problematic personality - an intolerant man with strong sectarian tendencies, who ultimately committed suicide. Taking full advantage of Ayub regime's martial law, he dismissed professors like Jameel Wasti and Ghulam Murtaza Kazi alias "Gandhi", because they refused to recognise him as their "Imam". During the military action in East Pakistan (March-December 1971), five teachers of the same university were charged with anti-state activities. But immediately after the Dhaka debacle, they were acquitted for lack of evidence. In the ill conceived list of the so-called "1,300 corruption and mischief making officials", four teachers of Sindh University were sacked in 1972. As a matter of fact, two of them from the political science department, were not only good scholars but also persons of impeccable integrity. The department never recovered from their loss.

In the mid-1970s Sheikh Ayaz, a poet of high stature and a symbol of Sindhi nationalism, but non-academic, was appointed as the vice-chancellor of Sindh University. His appointment was aimed at converting the current of Sindhi nationalism into Islamic socialism of Pakistan Peoples Party.

He was an utopian, idealising Stalinist Russia, where the first secretary of the Communist Party presided over the politburo and purged the "reactionaries". In Sindh University, his imaginary politburo members were second rate teachers and petty bureaucrats, who mastered the art of sycophancy and were beneficiaries of his stewardship. He assigned the role of "reactionaries" to the critics of his non-academic and lavish style of management. Indeed, his main critic was an alumni, of London School of Economics, Professor Ilyas Abro about whom a mention has also been made in chapter thirteen,

Meanwhile by coincidence, Zulfiquar Ali Bhutto, had inducted Sheikh Ayaz as the vice-chancellor. He was overthrown in 1977 and hanged in 1979 by general Zia-ul-Haq. Pragmatism propelled Sheikh Ayaz to wear the military uniform and eulogise Tara Masih (the hangman of Bhutto). But the tide turned against him. Seven teachers who he had sacked earlier were reinstated. Professor Abro became the vice-chancellor and proved himself one of the ablest headers of the institution. But colossal damage was done to the university. The "misfits" appointed by Sheikh Ayaz had become seniors and played havoc with the university.

Any head of state by virtue of his title as the president, acts as the chancellor of Quied-i-Azam University, Islamabad, according to its charter. In this capacity, General Zia, (on the yardstick of "loyalty to salt") appointed a mediocre as its vice-chancellor and decorated him with covetous award, *Sitare Imtiaz.* (The Star of Distinction). Proving his fidelity, this vice-chancellor sacked three academics who were against military dictatorship in the country. Ultimately the faculty threw him out.

Province of Punjab is the power wielder in federation of Pakistan, Department of political science of Punjab University has been the hotbed of contesting liberal and conservative ideologies with countrywide implications. Hassan Askari Rizvi, who worked in this department, was a visiting scholar at Columbia University in late 1990s. In his book, *Military, State and Society in Pakistan,* Rizvi observed that in Pakistan, military was behind political instability. Military has corporate interest in politico-economic fields of the country, which it does not want to surrender to any civilian authority.[2]

When Rizvi returned from Columbia in 2001, General Arshed Mahmood was the vice-chancellor of Punjab University. There was an unavoidable clash between the two mindsets. One believing in power and regimentation and the other in free discussion. In this contest, the scholar preferred to leave the university. General won the battle at the expense of the institution.

In 2001, the military government of General Musharraf, appointed Mazharul Haq Siddique, a retired top civil servant, 66, as vice-chancellor of Sindh University.[3] Because of the prolonged control of syndicate, university was controlled by a non-PhD teacher-leader, a *Bhuttar* (feudal).[4] Siddique's age factor and corresponding indecisiveness, gave an extra leverage to *Bhuttar*. He became the dean of three faculties and chief planning officer-cum-chief engineer, awarding scholarships and contracts. The university lurched into his fiefdom and the vice-chancellor became its titular head.

Reacting to this deplorable state of affairs, four academics, including an alumnus of a top British-university, wrote an open letter highlighting implications of this feudalism in the university. In normal circumstances, *Bhuttar* would have issued his rebuttal and the allegations would have been refuted by the administration. But undermining academic values and threatening academic freedom, letter writers were charge-sheeted and administration appeared to be bent on sacking them. Mercifully, Sindh High Court granted stay order to these academics. Ultimately Musharraf's draconian law under which these teachers were charge-sheeted, was repelled by parliament in 2010. However, even if these nonconformist academics were not sacked, they underwent a lengthy process of harassment, denial of permission to attend conferences abroad and isolation at the campus. Because of such draconian measures, most of academics in Pakistan, do not express their views freely. For instance, only a few of them questioned the rationale of Pakistan going nuclear in 1998, or its misadventures in Kargil in 1999. The net result of this suffocation is that, there is no substantial original thinking and correspondingly, there are no excellent research works, especially in social sciences. Regrettably, none of the Pakistani universities ranked in the Top 200 Asian Universities, let alone the Top 500 Universities of the world.

Therefore, in order to bring Pakistani universities at par with world-class universities, the creation of a research culture which is rooted in academic freedom; is a must. That itself depends on having a genuinely democratic set-up in the country.

References

1. Stephen Cohen, *Pakistan: The Idea of State.* Pakistani edition. (Lahore: Vanguard Publishers, 2004). p. 284.

2. Hassan Askari Rizvi. *Military, State and Society in Pakistan, (Besingstoke:* MacMillan, 2001.

3. In Pakistan, there are nine retired generals and civil servants out of 47 vice-chancellors of the public sector universities. All these retired officials and government officers including Siddique have been given extension by the government. He got his fourth consecutive extension as the vice-chancellor of Sindh University till 2013, but due to resistance from the teaching community, he was sacked in 2010. The only exception to this procedure of extension appears to be Captain Usman Ali Isani, former vice-chancellor of Quaid-i-Azam University, Islamabad,

who reportedly refused to endorse the Model University Ordinance 2002, which gave powers to the government for sacking any academic at any time without mentioning any reason to him.

4. *Bhuttar* retired in June 2005, but the syndicate, executive body of the university and the bureaucracy are still dominated by his cronies. Through him the intelligence agencies interfere in the University. Thus, like the Zia legacy in Pakistan, the *Bhuttar*'s legacy continues in the University of Sindh.

(This paper in its original form was published as entitled "Academic Freedom in Pakistan", in *The Economic and Political Weekly of India, (EPW)* Mumbai, 24th December 2005. It is reproduced here by te courtesy of the *EPW*)

PART - IV
TRIBUTE TO EDWARD SAID

15

The State of Higher Education in Pakistan

Because of apathy of Pakistan's successive governments towards its education, public sector universities are not up to the mark and their jobless graduates resort to extremist activities. If the declining standards of higher education are not controlled, they can pose threats to Pakistan's viability and correspondingly to the international community. Thus, civil society, government and international community must address this problem seriously.

One of the yardsticks of prestige of a state in international society is the standard of its universities. Besides its military and economic clout, American universities, particularly, Ivy-League such as Harvard and Stanford, contribute enormously to the American stature. Their graduates by controlling the American institutions indirectly shape the world events. It can be said equally about the 'Top Ten Universities of England especially Oxbridge and the London Colleges.'[1] Despite decline of its power, Britain is still proud of its educational institutions.

Graduates of its top universities rule Britain and many other countries. In the case of developing countries, their universities play a vital role in their development and survival in some cases when some analysts perceive them as failed states.[2]

The London Times senior *commentator*, Bronwen Maddox, sees modern education as the biggest holes among the political life and social fabric of Pakistan.[3] Dr. Atta ur Rahman, former Chairman of Higher Education Commission of Pakistan, the agency that funds public sector universities of the country, regretted that none of Pakistani universities was included in the list of '500 Top Universities of the world.'[4] Standards of the higher education are so poor that in 2007, only 4 percent of the candidates passed competitive examination for civil services. Because this poor performance of the university graduates, Irfan Hussain, a retired civil servant and now educationist apprehended that country will be without good civil servants in future.[5] In the higher education sector, things have yet to improve during the civilian dispensation (2008 onwards). This deterioration is so alarming that according to Professor Stephen Cohen, the American expert on South Asia "it casts shadow over too bright future of Pakistan."[6]

This paper attempts to study the state of affairs and find solutions to improve it. It is divided into five sections: first, government-university relationship, second university administration third faculty, fourth student factor and fifth society's attitude towards universities. Public sector universities, which are supposed to educate principally the underclass youth for their future careers, are the focus of this investigation.

Government and Universities

Political system of a country and quality of its leadership play key roles in running of state machinery as a whole including universities. In 2010, Pakistan is 63 years old. For 32 years, out of these 63 years, military dictators have ruled it directly. During remaining period, including the present civilian government, armed forces and intelligence agencies, especially the Inter-Services Intelligence Agency (ISI) and Military Intelligence (MI), have remained the main power wielders behind the scene, in all public spheres including the universities. This confession was made by former ruler of Pakistan, Musharraf in an interview to a private television channel[7]. The UN commission probing the murder of Benazir Bhutto confirms the similar assertion.[8]

Theoretically speaking, universities are autonomous bodies, but for all practical purposes, an army-agencies monitored troika of the central-provincial governments and Higher Education Commission runs them. Federal Ministry of Education makes an overall education policy of the country. A former Education Minister, retired General Javed Ashraf Kazi was an ex ISI chief. He was accused of receiving kickbacks as Railways Minister and had aptitude for managing the education ministry.[9] A civilian federal education minister, Mir Hazar Khan Bijarani, a feudal chief, was more interested in looking after his tribal affairs than running his ministry. So far, he is on record for not speaking a single word about the National Education Policy to be implemented in 2010. However, he has rightly suggested dissolving the Higher Education Commission of Pakistan about which, a mention will be just made.

As will discussed later, ironically, the present Oxford educated education minister, Sardar Asif Ali Ahmed, appears to protect legislators with alleged fake degrees from disqualification in a row with the Higher Educational Commission and the Election Commission of Pakistan. Thus, education ministry receives less attention than it deserves. After armed forces, education ministry is the biggest employer in the country. Thus it is considered to be the recruitment office for the educated youth. Otherwise, its performance is abysmal.

The Higher Education Commission (HEC) is the second regulatory authority controlling universities. Besides funding public sector universities, it monitors their syllabus and formulates rules for their functioning. The President appoints its Chairman and Executive Director. Its former Chairman, Dr Attau Rahman was reportedly a close relative of General Musharraf. The present Chairman of HEC, Dr. Jawed Leghari was supposed to be a Zardari man. But demonstrating this credibility on the issue of fake degrees, he has proved that he is, his man. So far Dr. Leghari has asserted that the President's sister and two vice-chancellors have fake degrees. But the HEC as a whole, is filled with retired military officers or their relatives. It is reportedly tinted with nepotism, inefficiency, corruption. One of its Director-General has been caught of having a fake Ph.D. The HEC is also accused of lacking a clear vision and a bureaucratic approach to academia. It is also believed that HEC plans to emulate American system of education in the country without adequate resources.[10] Thus, it cannot play an effective role in checking declining standards of education.

At the provincial level, provincial governors are chancellors of universities under their respective jurisdiction. They appoint vice-chancellors and other senior officials. Chancellors symbolize the status of universities. A chancellor should be the man of vision and calibre. Before becoming the Vice-Chancellor and Chancellor of Oxford University, Lord Curzon, was viceroy of India. Its present Chancellor, Sir Chris Patten was last Governor of British colony of Hong Kong. He was also the European Union's Commissioner on foreign affairs. Sir Patten has huge administrative experience, which he utilizes even for a symbolic position as the Chancellor of Oxford University. Similarly, Dr Radhakrishnan and Dr Zakir Hussain were vice-chancellors of Indian universities before becoming the Presidents of India. Present Indian Vice President, Mr Hamid Ansari, is a career diplomat and specialist on West Asian affairs. He was Vice-Chancellor of Aligarh Muslim University also.

The case of chancellors of the public sector universities of Pakistan appears quite opposite. Ironically, by virtue of being self-appointed presidents, Zia and Musharraf were Chancellors of the premier Qaud-i-Azam University (QAU) and twelve other federal universities. President Asif Ali Zardari with unknown educational background is the Chancellor of these federal universities. The chancellor of ten universities of NWFP is retired General Awais Ghani. Similarly, the Chancellor of four universities of Balochistan, Nawab Zulfiquar Khan Magsi, is a feudal. Chancellor of eighteen universities of Punjab is a PPP leader. Above all, Governor of Sindh the Chancellor of eighteen public sector universities of the province. Dr Ishrat-ul-Ibad is leader of Mutahida Quomi Movement, (MQM), a political party widely alleged of terrorism, land grabbing, drug mafia and money laundering[11]. Dr Ibad himself is implicated in the murder of philanthropist and chancellor of Hamdard University, Karachi, and late Hakim Seed.[12]

A chancellor supervises universities through a cell in Governor House, headed by his Special Secretary. It is widely alleged that Chancellor's secretariat, in collusion with the MQM and intelligence agencies, runs the universities of the Sindh. Seemingly, instead of monitoring the standards of teaching and research of the universities, maintenance of the law and order is their top priority. This objective can be achieved, sometimes, by allowing university administration to co-opt some unscrupulous teachers and *Bhatta Khor* (extortionist) students.

It is the vice-chancellor who is head of a university and should be symbol of its prestige. He/she is both its academic and administrative leader and ought not to be a retired general or a bureaucrat, as the vice-chancellor of Sindh University used to be till June 2009, despite public outcry.[13] Secondly and more significantly, according to Cambridge historian Ayesha Jalal, in order to make Sindhis incompetent, establishment allows dropping of standards of education in Sindh.[14] Presumably, the appointment of non-academics or academically mediocre as vice-chancellors, which Sindh University is usually having, will be instrumental in implementing this policy. They lack leadership qualities, self-confidence and standards of education will fall with their appointment.

University Administration

University administration means vice-chancellor downwards. Role of Pakistani vice-chancellors has been just discussed. Here the role of his subordinate officials is evaluated. Pro-vice-chancellor, registrar, controller of examinations and director of finance, are main officers of the administrative set up of a university. In West, these positions are filled by advertisement. Karachi and QAU universities advertise these positions, but in many universities these officials are appointed by the vice-chancellor.

If registrar is a person of integrity and experience, he will enjoy the confidence of his subordinates. On the contrary, if a dummy and dishonest person is given this job, he will presumably, receive dictates from intelligence agencies. Thus, functioning of the administration will be badly affected and consequently, university as a whole will suffer. An institution like Sindh University is the case in point, where repeated reappointment of retired registrar-cum-security officer, is reportedly a protégée of the agencies. Because of inefficiency and arcane method of working, teachers and staff constantly demanded his removal. But he is in the saddle and contributes to the malfunctioning of University.

If a teacher is given an extra academic additional duty like the controller of examinations or the inspector of colleges or director of transport as in the case of Sindh University, he will be more interested in these duties than performing academic duties, because these are vistas of minting money. Similarly, if officials like directors of finance or planning are appointed on the basis of nepotism, as example of Sindh University indicates, the institution will become financially and morally bankrupt. Ultimately its educational standards will suffer badly.

Teaching-cum administrative set up

Another group of the administrative set-up comprises departmental and faculty heads, *ie,* chairpersons, directors of centres/institutes and deans. Basically, they are the academics themselves. Their principal function is teaching, doing research and supervising it. For their additional charges, they get allowances, perks, and elevation to the highest administrative grade 22. These additional charges are for a fixed period. These academic cum-administrative heads look after their respective departments/centres and faculties.

In Pakistan, vice-chancellors appoint departmental heads, directors of centres and deans, whereas in marked contrast of the West, these vacancies are filled by either election or advertisement. After completion of three years of their tenure, departmental heads in the West get one year's Sabbatical Leave to overcome their losses. Here in Pakistan, many chairpersons, directors, and deans get one tenure after another and do a great deal of lobbying for it. Whole exercise promotes the culture of sycophancy.

Addiction for the additional charges does not stop here. Many Pakistani university teachers usually feel proud on the number of additional charges they hold. More a person holds additional charges, more important and powerful he or she is supposed to be in the university hierarchy. The case acquisition of additional charges is common in all Pakistani universities, though their number varies from place to places. Sindh University probably could be cited as an example of highest concentration of additional charges in few parsons. A non-PhD. teacher was concurrently the dean of three faculties, chairman of two most important committees. In addition, he was dealing with scholarships and construction works. His associates have had up to three additional charges each plus membership of syndicate and executive body of the University. Preference for these additional charges badly affects the performance of their wielders on lecturing and research commitments. The Federation of Pakistani University Teachers has suggested that not more than one additional charge should be given to any teacher. These additional charges should not be considered as criteria for the special grade 22.15 But no action has been taken in its regard by the universities.

Faculty

Third pillar of the university system is its faculty *ie* the academics. There are three main functions of the academics: first, teach and train the younger generations in their respective disciplines. Secondly, undertake research. Thirdly, supervise research of their students. The faculty plays these crucial roles for maintenance of high standards of education. Thus, it should be the role model of teaching, scholarship, and integrity.

Teachers are appointed among the best candidates, having necessary qualifications for that position. Apparently, this universal criterion is applied in Pakistan also, but in realty appears to be different. Besides talented candidates, sycophants also get appointed as lecturers in grade 18, having right connections in university administration, its selection Board and syndicate.

After their appointments, many lecturers use universities as launching pads for passing competitive examinations. Others make inroads in the governmental departments through political entry. One university teacher went for grade 15 jobs in Water and Power Development Authority. Many such teachers, stuffed in a university concern is making money by grafting, doing invigilation duties in affiliated colleges, and tabulation in examination department, which in some places, is called "Dubai" because of minting money by issuing forged mark sheets or even awarding bogus degrees.

There is a second category of academics, which select the academia out of conviction. They perform their principal duties of teaching and research diligently. Indeed, some of them speak truth to the power, if necessary. Unfortunately, their number is small. However they are role models for academic community. Undoubtedly, late Professor Hedley Bull of Oxford University, who saw his doctoral guide supervising even on his deathbed, can be a role model. There are a few dedicated Pakistani academics as well. Political Scientist, late Dr Niaz-ul-Haq of Sindh University, joined academia after resigning from covetous civil service. The historian, late Prof. Riazul Islam of Karachi University, a Cambridge educated scholar, declined to become vice-chancellor of Karachi University for completing a book. Presently, Dr Tariq Rahman, an excellent Linguist at the QAU, is among these rare scholars, who give top priority to research and remain in public sector universities instead of living abroad or to a private university for lucrative salaries. Because of their dedication to work, union leaders are sometimes not happy with them and the administrations usually give them a cold shoulder. Outspoken social scientists like Dr Hassan Askari, are disliked both by state and university administration. Despite difficulties, this small group of scholars, tirelessly produce high quality research and contributes enormously towards the rating of their respective institutions. For improving standards of university education, in the words of Professor Abdul Wahab, Vice-Chancellor of Mohammed Ali Jinnah University, Karachi, this sort of persons with an appropriate mindset, values, motivations and attitudes should be selected for the academia.[16]

Supervision

Besides teaching and undertaking research, another crucial job of the faculty is supervising research. Indeed it is, a difficult task. It requires passions, proper training. Pakistan is deficient in proper supervisors. Before early 70s, universities sent their faculty abroad for doing PhD to good universities such as Oxbridge and LSE, etc. After doing their PhD, these academics were groomed researchers and good supervisors. Mid 70s onwards, cultural scholarships were also awarded for doing Doctorates in non English speaking countries, where research students learn a local language of host country and also got degrees. With few exceptions, like Dr Mubarak Ali Khan, the well known historian, who did doctorate from Germany, past and present recipients of degree on cultural scholarships are no match to PhD holders from elite western universities. The HEC seemingly encourages doing PhD from good universities. But at the same time, in order to get tuition fees concession, it encourages universities for signing agreements with average British universities for sending their research students there. Thus, for making a strong pool of scholars, university teachers should be sent to these top universities.

There is another method of doing the doctorate by obtaining it locally. Usually these 'indigenous PhDs' are unsatisfactory and lacks transparency. In many cases, the supervisors themselves are 'ghost authors' of the thesis. Amazingly, some of them enjoy the status of HEC distinguished professors. They have every facility to produce plagiarized PhD, although the HEC passed laws to eradicate plagiarism.[17] However, the influential supervisors or their research students violate it at their will, with the help of unscrupulous examiners or self-seeking members of Advanced Studies and Research Board, the body of universities that monitors the standards of research or vote-catching members of the syndicate.

As a formality, PhDs are evaluated abroad. Nevertheless, in a number of cases, these examiners are average academics of Pakistani origin. Late Dr Riazul Islam, reportedly opposed the appointment of Pakistani expatriates as examiners in a session of Academic Council of Karachi University, but nobody listened to his sagacious voice in the country, where expediency, gets precedence over principles. In one case, a Pakistani expatiate, working in a British university, which according to the *Times* index, is below Thirty[18], the expatiate being a friend of the spouse of the candidate and already having his vacations in Pakistan, gave his report in less than a month, which is unusual by British standards. Credibly and scholarship of an examiner depends upon the status of his work place. Good universities always appoint the top faculty. Conversely, if a person works in an average university, his level of scholarship and credibility may not be so good.

In order to meet the scarcity of supervisors, HEC has hired Foreign Faculty. This programme has its loopholes. In a list of 450 supervisors, most of them are expatriate Pakistanis, who are mainly the runaways. Surprisingly, one of them was the Imam of an Ottawa mosque. Another lot is from the former Soviet bloc and Bosnia Herzegovina, for whom English is the second language, whereas it is the medium of instructions and expression in Pakistan. Only three British scholars joined the faculty. There are two Pakistanis from Harvard and Columbia respectively.[19] The salary of a hired faculty member is confidential. But according to reliable sources, an expatriate Pakistani, with zero teaching experience, got about Rs. 500000, ($6089) per month, whereas some Pakistani professors, having doctorate from London and post-doctorate from Oxford, draw the salary of Rs. 72000 ($877) PM. Appointment of foreign faculty has created resentment among the Pakistani scholars, who either are going to other countries or private sector universities with better salaries.

In order to keep Pakistani scholars happy, HEC has introduced tenure-track system, which offers relatively higher salaries, but it has its own pitfalls in Pakistan. The contract of a teacher can be cancelled if he or she is not on the good terms with the chairperson of department. Thus, the teaching community has rejected it. Hoodbhoy suggests correctly that in order to meet the deficiency of supervisors, instead of deserted Pakistanis, Bangladeshi and Indian scholars, having roots or connections in this land, should be hired on preferential basis[20]. A good faculty is guarantor of bright future of Pakistan.

Students

Students are fourth pillar of university system. Universities are established for them. Teachers are supposed to teach them and administration is supposed to provide them with the best facilities for completing their studies. In Pakistan, mainly the underclass students get their education in the public sector universities. Many graduates of these universities do not get jobs in the private sector; in tough competition with well connected and well educated graduates of private universities. Apart from substandard teaching, a host of other factors such as the admission procedure, living conditions, transport facilities, unsatisfactory reading and internet facilities and a defective examination system, affect the performance of these students.

Admission Procedure

Good universities of the world usually give admission on two bases: school leaving certificate and the suitability of an applicant for a particular subject by interviewing the candidate[21]. Pakistani universities also followed this procedure for a long time. Nowadays, choice of 10 subjects is given to a candidate. A quiz competition type entry test is conducted by admission offices of universities. In many cases students are placed not in the department of their choice. If there is Honours system, after completing their second year, these unhappy students get their second year converted into the pass degree and go either to another university or another department/ institute of the same university. Thus, many departments do not receive or could keep good students. The History Conference held in Karachi University in April 2005, rightly demanded reintroduction of the old admission procedure with modifications.[22]

Accommodation

About 70 percent of the Pakistani population still lives in the rural areas. Correspondingly, majority of university students hail from there. They require university accommodation, which is cheaper and convenient. Unlike the advanced countries, admission is not given according to the availability of the accommodation. Number of admissions has multiplied three fold during last ten years, but no commensurate accommodation has been offered. Thus, there is an acute shortage of accommodation.

In places like Sindh University, two students are supposed to share a double room till 3rd year. However, these rooms are crammed up even with six students. These rooms look like jail barracks.[23] Because of overcrowding, studious students suffer. Because they cannot study and sleep properly. Thus, the admission number should match the accommodation facilities. Similarly, adequate transportation facilities should be provided to students commuting from campuses to down town.

Ban on Student Unions

Freedom of expression and freedom of assembly are among the basic human rights. Intellectual life flourishes on the campus when students and faculty enjoy these rights. Students are most sensitive part of society. They take interest in the national and international issues. The best platform for expression of their views on these matters are student unions, which also train politically active students for future leadership of their respective countries. They also produce future intellectuals. Oxford Union is called the nursery of British Parliament. Many of its former members, such, Gordon Brown, Bill Clinton,

Benazir Bhutto, became leaders of their countries. Cambridge and LSE unions groom progressive intellectuals and philosophers. Thus, the student union is must for an intellectual life of a university.

Before the advent of the Zia regime (1977-1988), student unions functioned in universities, which were represented by student wings of different political parties. During their general body meetings, there was exchange of arguments between students. But all these heated debates ended by offering positive suggestions for the welfare of the university.

Considering students as a threat to his tyrannical rule, Zia took a draconian action of banning their unions. Students were snatched of their platform for expressing their views. In addition, intelligence agencies armed the anti-Bhutto elements affiliated with some religious and ethnic parties. Criminals were freely lodged also in hostels. Now on, for settling their issues, students instead of using the force of argument resorted to the argument of force. When Zia regime felt that jinnee was out of bottle, it erected walls and deployed rangers, paramilitary force at campuses. But their presence did not make any marked difference. Karachi, Sindh and Punjab Universities give semblance of battlegrounds between different armed gangs of students pitted against each other. In Karachi, the pro-MQM and Jameet-i-Tulba backed students were dagger drawn at each other. In Sindh University, two factions of the Peoples Party and different groups of the Jay Sindh Students Federation were, at each other's throat. In Punjab University, not only Jameet and PPP fought gun battles but the Jameetis reportedly killed a professor. On all these occasions, paramilitary force, the Rangers was silent spectator. On the contrary, sometimes, they manhandled faculty members, as the case of Dr Riaz Ahmed of Karachi University demonstrates.

Civilian government announced to lift ban on student unions. The Government gave Dr. AA Nayyar, of Sustainable

Development Policy Institute, Islamabad, this task to solicit views about the issue in universities. He gave report for lifting the ban through legislation but so far nothing has been done. Thus, continuation of Zia's policies of ban on students unions, and consequential shot between student factions and deployment of Rangers continue. It perpetuates an atmosphere of suffocation and insecurity on the campuses which is quite harmful to the student community, as well as civil society.

Unsuitable Examinations System

Examination system at different public sector universities appears to be out of tune with the realities of our country and time. In 1972, Karachi and Sindh Universities, took two seemingly unrealistic decisions: First, switching from English, they made Urdu and Sindhi languages, respectively as the mediums of instruction. Secondly, they introduced semester system. These decisions proved harmful for higher education system in Pakistan.

Previously, students studied the standard book on any particular subject. Now their majority look for third rate books written in English, Urdu and Sindhi, having no match with the authentic texts. Ironically, some books were written for seemingly cheating purpose in the examination. For instance, in the discipline of International Relations, there is an author of about half a dozen books. Each chapter of these books is of two and a half to eight page size. Because of personal and political connections of the author, his such in low quality books are used at least three universities of Pakistan. Regrettably, these substandard books were included in the syllabus approved by HEC till 2005. Thus, being Urdu and Sindhi mediums alongside, substandard English textbooks have done enormous harm to higher education of the country.

The semester system works in those universities, where its basic requirement, such as the teacher-student ratio of 1:10

is maintained and library and internet faculties are adequate. It is an internal arrangement, in which the subject teacher conducts examination. QAU was first institute that adopted the semester system. Because of fulfilment of requirements, it works well there. However, it is dysfunctional in most of other universities, which lack its basic requirements.

In addition, semester system blocks the external assessment. Under the old system, scripts in English were assessed by anonymous outside examiners. Down to 1971, it was difficult for west Pakistani students to approach an examiner in former East Pakistan. The semester system made easy for students to approach the examiner by flattering or bullying him. Thus, the vernacular languages combined with the semester system have led to an overall deterioration of the higher education system.

Thanks to internet, good students are well versed with English. They insist on adopting English as the medium of expression. Moreover, many students prefer an anonymous outside assessment of their scripts instead of the semester system. Therefore, a modified version of the old system should be adopted in the public sector universities of Pakistan. Preferably, arrangements should be made under the auspices of the SAARC, under which our universities should send their graduate and the post-graduate scripts to external examiners of top regional universities on reciprocal basis.

Civil Society

Here, civil society means educated class, people's representatives and the media. It owes a great deal to the universities. Universities transmit knowledge to it. On their part, they expect support in maintaining their independence. This societal support to universities is necessary in a country, which is directly or indirectly dominated by the armed forces, intelligence agencies, corrupt bureaucracy and indeed, the obscurantist Mullahs.

After 2008 elections, attitude of public representatives in National and Provincial Assemblies and Senate has markedly changed towards education. Good education is considered to be a guarantor of national survival,[24] and who temper with it ought to be punished. Former Chief Justice of Pakistan, Hamid Doggar was called to standing committee of the National Assembly to answer his complicity in marking scam of his daughter's intermediate examination. Nawaz Sharif the leader of Muslims League, expelled several of his party central and provicial legislaters for producing the false degreee which filing their election documents. So far, no such a purge has taken in the PPP. Although the doubts are being cast about the authenticity of the Master Degree of a sister of President Asif Ali Zardari.

Sanads (certificates) issued by *Madrasas* are equivalent to a university degree. This decree facilitated many Mullahs to win the 2002 elections and become Musharraf's coalition partners, who tacitly promoted Talibanization process. Now there is revulsion against the *Sanad* holding legislators. But the HEC policy has yet to be repelled.

Much before, politicians and intellectuals have expressed their concern on educational issues. The *Dawn* gives space to articles contributed by Irfan Hussain and Zubaida Mustafa on the issue of plagiarism and other related topics. One can hope that the concern of civil society about falling standards of education will compel the government to arrest it.

It has been argued above that overbearing influence of intelligence agencies in all walks of life, including institutions of higher learning, is the principle cause of markedly declining standards of higher education. Higher education is one of the essential ingredients of viability and prestige of a state in the world. Qualified youths are its assets; otherwise, they could contribute to its status "a failed state", posing threat to the international community. Pakistan's higher education offered by public sector universities has reached to such a low ebb that if its further deterioration is not checked, the results will be horrendous for the state, because of Pakistan's geo-strategic location. Thus, in order to tackle this problem, government, society and international community, should join hands.

The first and foremost step to bring about improvement in the public sector universities is, to make them free from the interference of the intelligence agencies. Officials of HEC and Governor Houses, especially in Sindh and Balochistan, having alleged links with the agencies should be removed. Similarly, retired army officers and bureaucrats who act as vice-chancellors, registrars, security officers or even controllers of the examinations, having reportedly connections with the agencies, should be purged.

Special attention should be given to the appointment of the vice-chancellors. They should be excellent scholars with proven integrity, because they are the persons who provide leadership to universities. Good vice-chancellors do not need to bribe teachers by assigning more than one additional charges. Additional charges will not be a criterion for elevation to the special grade-22. Similarly, the good vice-chancellors will appoint their registrars and other officials in their own image. Universities will be having efficient and upright administrations, which will contribute to serving teaching and student communities. It will result in raising the standards of education. In addition, vice-chancellors of scholastic nature will promote democratic culture in universities by respecting the right of freedom of expression of teachers and students.

Teachers should be selected as discussed earlier, on the criteria of their mindset. Their PhDs will stand quality not quantity test. In order to do so, they should be encouraged to receive their degrees from the elite universities of the world. For four years commencing from 2005, the Fulbright Scholarship Programme has earmarked US$150 m for Pakistan is the biggest of its own kind. And USAID has granted a five year $100 million educational aid to Pakistan, which will be tripled three years later[25]. Similarly, the British Council has also increased its scholarships. In addition to the Commonwealth and British Council Scholarships, from 2005 onwards, Pakistani students have so far received 49 Chevening Fellowship.[26] It is good number, but because of the traditional links with Britain, there should be more scholarships for the Pakistani youth, especially from less developed areas of the country. SAARC scholarship also can help a great deal in increasing the pool of good teachers in Pakistan. The South Asian University, established in Delhi in 2007 can also help Pakistan in training its academics for higher degrees.

The lifting of the ban on students union is over due. If it is lifted, students will express their views freely, which will help reduce graphically the gang warfare among the student factions. Thus, restoration of unions will also eliminate goonda elements (musclemen) from the student community. Political activity within universities will be peaceful. This will be greatly helpful to improve the standards of the higher education.

Under a new education policy, admissions ought to be given to students on their aptitude and availability of facilities such as accommodation, library, laboratory and internet. Rangers should be removed from the campus because they are an extra-burden on them. They harass male students, stare at girls and sometimes misbehave with teachers. Students will be treated with dignity by university administration, so that they become good citizens in future.

Legislative bodies should keep their eyes on the performance of universities through their education standing committees. Similarly, performance of civil society in monitoring the functioning of public universities is necessary and its scope should be widened. There is need for increased interaction between members of the student community, parents, academia, university administration, government functionaries, journalists and other intellectuals, so that universities should remain focus of their common attention.

According to Professor Cohen and other commentators, future of Pakistan appears to be uncertain27, A raw lot, produced by public sector universities will be one of the catalysts of its demise. Conversely, a pool of highly skilled work force, principally produced by same institutions, will contribute enormously to its development and viability. One should remember that development of the human resources is the best form of defence than vice versa. In final analysis, by joint efforts of government, academia, civil society and the international society, Pakistani higher education will markedly improve.

References

1. The British newspapers yearly publish the rating of the British Universities, *The Guardia Higher Education* gives its own rating which is respected all over the world. See for instance, "Cambridge Tops 2010 University League", *Guardian,* 11 May, 2009.

2. The Foreign Policy Magazine in its index of the "Failed States" has put Pakistan on 10th number of 60 such states. One of the indicators of its failed status is its poor public services which encompasses education. *Foreign Policy,* June, 2009. And also see Selig Harrison, *Pakistan: The State of Union: Special Report April 2009:* Centre for International Policy, Washington D.C., 2009, p. 25.

3. Bronwen Maddox, "President Pervez Musharaff Pays Higher Price for a Little Time", *The Times,* 11 September, 2007.

4. Dr. Atta ur Rahman, "Higher Education in Pakistan: A Silent Revolution," Higher Education Commission of Pakistan Advertisement Supplement, *Dawn* Karachi, 28th September 2007, Shangai Jiao Tong University, (SJTU) had done for first time the Academic Ranking of the 500 Top Universities of the World, in 2004 which is being updated yearly but Pakistan's ranking remains the same. In 2008, the Lahore University, a private institute was included in the list of "500 Top Universities".

5. Irfan Hussain, "Rent-a Mongoose", *The Daily Times, (Lahore)*, 1st October, 2007.

6. Stephen Cohen, *The Idea of Pakistan,* (Lahore: Pakistani edition, Vanguard Publisher, 2005), pp. especially 243-247.

7. *Daily Times,* 14 October, 2008.

8. "UN. Blames the Musharraf Government for Benazir Bhutto's Murder", *Dawn*, 16th April 2010.

9. Masoud Ansari, "Criminal Negligence" *News line, (* Karachi), August 2005, p. 75.

10. Pervez Hoodbhoy, "The HEC Project", Letters, *Dawn,* 28 July 2005, and Nasir Jamal Khattak, "Don't Fix It If It isn't Broke", Education Page, *Dawn,* 23 September, 2007.

11. Moosa Kaleem, "May 12: A Script Gone Away", *Herald,* Karachi, June 2007, pp. 64-73.

12. MS Korejo, *A Testament of Sindh: Ethnic and Religious Extremism: A Perspective,* Oxford University Press Karachi, 2002, pp. 120-121.

13. A Former Student, *"Reappointment* of the VCs", *Dawn,* 26th June, 2009 And "Teachers Bodies Want SU VC Removed". *Dawn,* 9th July, 2009.

14. Ayesha Jalal, *Democracy and Authoritarianism in South Asia,* Cambridge University Press, 1995, pp. 230-231.

15. *Dawn,* 14th September, 2007.

16. Professor Abdul Wahab, "Reforming University Education", *Dawn: Higher Education Gazette,* 17th June, 2009.

17. Dr. Shamsul Haq and Dr. Noman Ahmed, "The Plagiarism Plague", Education page, *Dawn,* 12 August, 2007.

18. *Guardian,* 11 May, 2009, *op.cit.*

19. "Faculty Hiring Prgoram" http://www.hec.gov.pk/InsideHEC/Divisions/HRD/FacultyHiringPrograms/Pages/Faculty Hiring Programs. aspx, last acceded on 25th May 2010.

20. Hoodbhoy, *op.cit.*

21. Jessica Shepherd "10,000 Fewer University places than Expected", *Guardian : Higher Education,* 24 May 2010.

21. "History Conference in KU Demands Refurbishing the Higher Education System" *Daily Times,* 21 April 2005.

22. Personal Observation of this author.

23. Sabiha Mansoor, "Faculty Development in Higher Education-1-11", *Daily Times,* 25th-26th May 2010.

24. Cited in *Ibid.*

25. "British Envoy calls for Strengthening Educational Links", *Dawn,* 21 May 2010.

26. Cohen, *opcit.*

PART - V
HIGHER EDUCATION IN PAKISTAN

16

Sectarianism: A Threat to South Asian Security

Religious fundamentalism or extremism has two principal forms in South Asia. One them is Sectarianism, which can be defined as a phenomenon in that an individual, or a group of individuals, adhering to any particular cult or a sect of a religion, develops a feeling of self-righteousness and adopts an attitude of intolerance towards other sects of the same religion. Here, sectarianism is used for achieving the political objectives of imposing one's own denomination by force on the other sects. Communalism is also quite a similar phenomena of this extremist nature in which an individual, or a group of individuals, hates other groups and uses violence in the name of religion for the attainment of political objectives[1]. Sectarianism and communalism operate as divisive forces within their given societies by increasing tension within their different sections. Sometimes, these intra-state tensions find expressions in the inter-state pressures, increase the vulnerabilities of a given state vis-a-vis other states and raise the level of regional and global insecurity.

South Asian societies are heterogeneous in their characteristics. There are religious, sectarian, caste, class and ethnic cleavages within them and correspondingly within the regional states. Forces of sectarianism and communalism pose a serious threat to integrity of these states. The purpose of this study is to analyze the causes of emergence of sectarianism and communalism in South Asian states, their implications for national and regional security and also remedies to control their adverse effects.

Because of diverse nature of their societies, most of the South Asian states, face one or other form of sectarianism/ communalism. Sri Lanka, since its inception as a sovereign state in 1948, faces tensions between mainly Buddhist Sinhalas and Hindu Tamils, sometimes irrupting into a separatism and insurgency in north and east of the country. From time to time, Bangladesh has witnessed tension between Muslims and non-Muslims, both Hindu and Buddhists either in its heartland or in the hill tracks. India and Pakistan, two principal countries of the region, face a serious threat to their security from forces of sectarianism and communalism, which increases the level of tension in their mutual relationships. In earlier chapter, we have dealt with the adverse effects of sectarianism on human security in Pakistan, in this chapter we will dwell upon communalism in India and its effects on the society and state of India and the South-Asian Security as a whole.

Emphasis on Education and Morality

At primary and secondary school level, the emphasis of education should be on morality instead of divisive issues. In Pakistan, during the classes of religion or Islamic studies, Muslim and non-Muslim students are separated from each other. Muslims take Islamic studies, whereas, non-Muslims take civics. Muslim pupils are further sub divided into *Sunni* and *Shia* sections. Most of the schools do not have a *Shia* teacher for

Islamic studies. So *Sunni* and *Shia* pupils are handled together. As just mentioned, highly charged teachers teach issues who are usually too parochial in their frame of mind. Net result of the divisive teaching is emergence of feeling of bitterness amongst the *Shia* students. Whether it is combined class or separate classes for different sects, both generate resentment, antagonism, and bigotry. Thus, in order to overcome the feelings of divisiveness at primary and secondary school levels, joint classes of ethics should be held for *Shia* and *Sunni*, Muslim and non-Muslim pupils, where the teaching of social and moral issues should be taught.

Popularization of the Teaching of Mystics

Instead of religious controversies and dogmas, teachings of the South Asian mystics, such as Shah Latif Bhittai, Bulleh Shah, Baba Guru Nanik Sahib, Das Kabir, Tulsi Das, and Dadoo should be incorporated in the curricula at the schools levels as it used to be taught in the pre-partition days. These saints preached unity and love of humankind and devotion to God. Their message was not confined to any particular sect or religion. To mellow down the influence of sectarianism and communalism, teachings of these saints should be popularized by the media. In order to control bigotry, sectarianism and communalism, this sort of curriculum may be introduced in South Asia as a whole.

No Coalition with Criminals

Mainstream political parties of Pakistan, in wider interests of the state, should learn a lesson from the Indian political scene. In May 1996 elections, fundamentalist BJP emerged as the single largest party. Considering it as a threat to national cohesion, the left wing and small parties, under the leadership of Deve Gowda formed a National Government. After Gujarat riots in 2002, the BJP was rooted out, a Congress led coalition government came into power in Delhi in 2004, and it won for second time in 2008. By contrast, in Pakistan the sectarian parties, especially Sipaha-i-Sahaba of Sunni/Wahabi denomination, are heavily infiltrated by criminals. They are sometimes elevated to political position. Sheikh Hashism Ali, a leader of Sipaha-i-Sahaba, nominated in 8 murder cases, became a minister of Punjab during 1993-94.[2] Rana Sanaullah , the law minister of Punjab still hobnobs with the Sipaha-i-Sahaba leaders. So much so after the Lahore Bomb blast of March 2010, chief minister of Pakistani Punjab, Mian Shahbaz Sharif said to Taliban that since they are allies, they should have at least spared Punjab from their bombing campaign.[3] Such a frank admission of connections with the terrorists cum drug peddling Taliban by chief minister of the largest and most powerful province of the federation, speaks volumes of leanings towards extremisms which is no only dangerous for Pakistan's body politics but badly affects its relationships with all immediate neighours , India, China, Afghanistan and Iran. Thus patronizing criminals and extremists should be discarded in South Asia as a whole.

Person to Person Contact

Person to person contact in South Asia should be increased. The older generation in different countries has created a stereotype image of other communities. This image should be changed by bringing different people from distinct communities together. Visits of academicians, intellectuals, sportsmen and common persons to other country should be encouraged. By following such a strategy, fanaticism will mellow down. If a Muslim-basher like Mr Lal Krisahan Advani of BJP is invited to visit Hyderabad Sindh and if he visits the shrines of Shah Latif Bhittai, and Qutib Shah in Tando-Jahanian in the suburbs of Hyderabad, Sindh, he might give up or reduce his hatred against the Indian Muslims and Pakistan. It is quite interesting that when in June 2005 LK. Advani visited his birthplace, Karachi, and met his Sindhi and Paresse friends, he expressed deep regrets over his role in the demolition of Babri Masjid,

Gujarat riots[4], and eulogized Jinnah as a secular leader. But when he returned to Delhi and found himself isolated. Only thus, by bringing the people of different communities closer to each other, a stage could be created for a conducive environment in South Asia.

Emphasize on South Asian Identity

In the making of foreign policy, due consideration should be given to the South Asian identities of our respective states. This proposition is particularly applicable to Pakistan, where different governments have been insisting upon the Middle Eastern and Central Asian identities of the country. From the beginning of the Cold War era in the late 1940s, which coincided with the partition of India and the endemic Indo-Pak rivalry, successive Pakistani rulers have been wrongly insisting on their Middle Eastern identity, which was not correct. Pakistan is an active member of SAARC. Again on the pretext of the search of security against India, after the disintegration of the Soviet Union and the resultant emergence of Central Asian Republics (whose population is mainly Muslim), quite a few intellectuals, fundamentalist political parties, especially, the Jammat-i-Islami and retired generals, are persistently emphasizing on Pakistan's Central Asian character. Surprisingly, the liberal intellectual, Senator Aitazaz Ashen, in his illustrious treatise on the Civilization of Indus Valley, argues that the Indus man is more close to his fellow Muslim Central Asian cousin than the neighbour from the plains of Ganges.[5]

Undoubtedly, Pakistan is physically adjacent to both the Middle East and Central Asia. Yet its major mooring is in South Asia. It shares its river system with India. The two states have common cultural heritage. Their forces are principally deployed against each other, which also creates a negative but unavoidable linkage between them. Thus, consequently, Pakistan's identity, and correspondingly, foreign policy should be principally oriented towards South Asia.

Improving relations with India, should be the top priority of Pakistan's policy makers. On their part, the Indian policy-makers should consider their country as one among the equals in South Asia. The improvement of Indo-Pak relations will be conducive in curbing the trends of communalism, fundamentalism and sectarianism at intra-state level and good neigbbourly relations at the inter-state level in South Asia.

References

1. Asghar Ali Engineer, "The Gujarat Carnage: Causes and Consequences", in eds, Lancy Lobo and Biswaroop Das, *Communal Violence and Minorities*, (Jaipur: Rawat Publications, 2006) p.127.

2. Aaimar Ahmed Khan, "Playing with Fire," *The Herald (*Karachi:, September 1996) p. 78.

3. "C.M. Shahbaz Wants Taliban to Spare Punjab" *Dawn,* 16th March 2010.

4. "Advani Visits His Birth place: Mahota Palace:", *Dawn*, 6th June 2005, and Kawish (Karachi edition, Sindhi, 6th June 2005).

5. Aitazaz Ahsan, *The Indus Saga* (Karachi: Oxford University Press, 1996), pp. 125-126.

(This paper is the revised and updated version of an earlier paper, entitled "Sectarianism: a threat to South Asian security", published The *Indian Journal of Secularism,* the Centre for Study of Society and Secularism, Mumbai) Vol. 2, No. 4, January-March, 1999.)

17

The Root of Indo-Pakistani Discord

It is a deplorable state of affairs that India and Pakistan since their independence, despite many historical, cultural, ethnic and linguistic affinities, have had little success in normalising their relations as good neighbours. In 24 years from 1947 to 1971, they thrice plunged into war.

At the heart of discord between them is a legacy of suspicion. India and Pakistan have failed to overcome the spectre of suspicion which has been haunting communal discord since the 1930s. Each country has a negative image of other and is suspicious of its motives. In the past, India had considered Pakistan, in league with the United States, to be interested either in Balkanizing India further or destabilizing it. Pakistan considers secularism as Hinduism in disguise, directed at swamping the Islamic features of Indian society and reabsorbing Muslims into the Hindu flock. The ruling class in Pakistan wrongly believes that political parties striving for greater provincial autonomy are led by secular leaders who are foreign agents.

Apart from the Indian philosophy of secularism, Indian democracy posses an additional threat to Pakistan's military rulers or military oligarchy. They feel that expansion of travel and trade with India would expose them to the public at home. Pakistani rulers are considerably upset by the programmes of Indian television, which highlights cultural similarities between the two countries and propagate benefits of democracy. Pakistan's rulers would like to jam these programmes, but this is not technically feasible.[1] Moreover Pakistani ruling elite does not encourage exchange of literature in social sciences and continues to restrict the exchange of ideas between two countries. Thus, the past suspicions, along with their respective ideologies, kept India and Pakistan apart from each other.

Anomalous Borders

As a result of hurried partition in 1947, India and Pakistan have neither natural borders nor defensible frontiers. This state of affairs compels them both to deploy bulk of their troops against each other. Troop mobilizations even for regular exercises sometimes create panic on the other side of border, bringing two countries to the brink of war. The perpetual troop deployment has created a war psychosis, with the two countries regarding each other as 'traditional enemy'. These negative perceptions block the process of normalization between them.

Another anomaly of the border is that people of same stock, speaking same languages, straddle across it. These peoples have a natural interest in developments taking place across the border, where their kith and kin and old time friends live. This combination of interest and nostalgia for the other side of the border, creates problems for both governments. If the Sikh Yatrees (pilgrimis), in whose ranks extremists also penetrated, extend hospitality to their co-lingual Punjabi Muslims, including the then dictator of Pakistan (1977-1988) General Zia himself, the Indian authorities took notice of the cordiality.[2] On the other hand, if some Sindhi members of Congress (I) press Indian government to supported demands for restoration of democracy in Pakistan or asked All India Radio to increase broadcasting of Sindhi programmes, Pakistan government was quick to denounce such action as interference in its internal affairs. Recriminations about interfering in each other's internal affairs and the massing of troops against each other stem from the nature of borders between the two countries.

Kashmir Dispute

Kashmir dispute between India and Pakistan could not be solved either politically or militarily. Pakistan's military attempts to integrate the entire valley could not pay dividends in 1948 or 1965. Under the Simla accord of 1972, governments of Zulfiquar Ali Bhutto (ZAB) and Indira Gandhi worked out a modus vivendi over Kashmir, pledging not to alter the status quo by use of force and to seek a final settlement by negotiation.

The Simla accord survived until military coup in Pakistan in 1977. Since then, Pakistan's position on the Kashmir issue has ostensibly changed, though it has not yet formally repudiated the Simla accord, as demanded by the rightwing political parties, including then ruling Muslim League. Pakistan's leaders have frequently visited Pakistani administered part of the valley, where they made inflammatory speeches. The issue was once again being raised by them at international forums, in contravention of the Simla accord. In the Indian part of Kashmir, National Conference, headed by Dr. Farooq Abdullah, formed a coalition government with Congress (I). Despite Abdullah family's pronounced charisma, the Islamic fundamentalists, who wish to join Pakistan, were/are active in the valley. Indian government squarely blames Pakistan for encouraging the Kashmiri separatists. These charges were vehemently denied by Zia regime, but India, perceiving the gap between General

Zia's words and deeds, remains convinced that Pakistan was interfering in the Indian administrative part of Kashmir. The matter remains one of the major irritants in Indo-Pakistani relations.

Nuclear Programme

In 1974, India detonated nuclear devices near the Pakistani border. Indian claims to be testing nuclear capabilities for peaceful purposes only, were not believed by the Bhutto government. Convinced that India had gone nuclear, it determined that Pakistan too must follow suit. With reported financial assistance from Libya and other Arab countries, it ordered Pakistani scientists to make an Islamic bomb.

United States took serious notice of Pakistan's intention to go nuclear, stopping all aid to it. It is also widely believed in Pakistan that the Carter administration gave its blessing to General Zia's military coup against Bhutto government in order to thwart Pakistan's nuclear programme. But the military takeover in Pakistan did not in fact affect the programme. On the contrary, exploiting President Reagan's Russophobia and his wish to see the Russians bogged down in Afghanistan, General Zia expedited Pakistan's nuclear programme and refrained from signing the Non-Proliferation Treaty. In an interview with the Indian journalist, Mr. Kuldip Nayyar, Dr. Qadir the brain behind Pakistan's nuclear programme, hinted that Pakistan possesses the bomb, which could be used in its defence. Subsequently in 1998, India and Pakistan manufactured nuclear weapons. Their respective nuclear weaponry has increased the possibilities of an accidental nuclear showdown between them.

Great Debate

Pakistan's nuclear programme aroused a great debate in India. The Indian government announced its intention to reassess its (professedly) peaceful nuclear programme. In other words, in response to Pakistan's clandestine nuclear programme, India has started its own weapon-oriented programme. Pakistan's rulers expressed their concern over the Indian nuclear programme. But their offer of inspection of each other's nuclear installations was turned down by India considering it a propaganda ploy designed to divert the world's attention from Pakistan's own nuclear programme.[4]

If Pakistan had signed the Non-Proliferation Treaty unilaterally, as suggested by many of its friends, including the former American ambassador to Pakistan Dean Hinton, India would have been placed under enormous pressure to do so as well. Pakistan's decision to pursue the nuclear programme single-mindedly, has instead opened a new era of arms race in the sub-continent. It remain to be seen whether the introduction of nuclear weapons will make deterrence credible between the two powers. General Zia was probably in a better position to answer this question.

Domestic Instability

The Indian sub-continent is a heterogeneous area culturally, linguistically and religiously. These diversities do not make difficult the maintenance of a central unified administrative system in the region. Centrifugal tendencies have as a result always been strong in both India and Pakistan. Diversities have given birth to the issue of provincial autonomy, which has a great deal of impact on Indo-Pakistani relationship.

Although the founders of modern India were aware of the multi-ethnic character of their country and believed in the principle of unity within diversity, they sensed a separatist flavour in autonomy demands and saw foreign hands behind them. Pakistan is blamed by India for unrest in the north-east areas of Indian union. India has always accused Pakistan of stirring up trouble in the Indian part of Kashmir.

Sikh Problem

The Sikh problem in the Indian Punjab was originally a demand for increased quantum of the Punjab state autonomy within the Indian union. It led to its becoming a separatist movement. Some extremists were pressing for the creation of an independent Sikh state of Khalista (the land of pure) something akin to Pakistan. Rajiv Gandhi contend that 90 per cent of the Punjab's terrorism problem would disappear if the Pakistani role were eliminated. Thus, along with United States, Pakistan was accused by Indian authorities of encouraging separatism in India.

The problem of provincial autonomy in Pakistan has wider implications for Indo-Pakistani relations. Because of numerical superiority of Punjabis in armed forces and bureaucracy, the province of Punjab has enjoyed a dominant position in Pakistan. As far as center-province relations are concerned, Punjab insistence on centralization of power has upset the small provinces, especially Sindh and Balochistan. Punjab is seen to be using its military-cum-bureaucratic muscle to impinge on their resources. In response, the small provinces have been insisting on an increase in provincial autonomy. The Punjabi oligarchy has resisted these demands. It has revealed a willingness to deal with an iron hand with what it sees as secessionist movements or anti-state activities. The most effective form of government to protect vested interests of Punjabi oligarchy appears to be military dictatorship.[7] This form of government in Pakistan has horrendous effects on Indo-Pakistani relations.

Diversionary Tactic

Military rulers of Pakistan, being unpopular in the country in general and in the provinces other than the Punjab in particulars, have repeatedly raised the spectre of an Indian bogey or have indulged in activities hostile to India. The main purpose of these policies is to divert attention from the problem of provincial autonomy. General Ayub Khan, for example, used to accuse India and Afghanistan of fomenting trouble in Balochistan and the North West Frontier Province. But in 1965 he sent infiltrators to Indian Kashmir. His misadventures in Kashmir ended in the Indo-Pakistani war of 1965.[8] Another dictator, General Yahya, resisted handing over power to the Awami League, which had an overwhelming majority in former East Pakistan, now Bangladesh. His subsequent military action resulted in separation of East Pakistan. Similarly, General Zia's overtures to the Sikhs and Kashmiris and his complaints about Indian interference in Sindh province are chief reasons for the present unhappy state of affairs between India and Pakistan.

Continuation of military rule in one form or another depends, upon the maintenance of one of the largest armies in the world. Such an army can be justified only on the grounds of an external threat. Policymakers in Pakistan have been acting in such a way that the clash of interests or continuation of tension with India becomes inevitable. To put it in another way, continuation of conflict with India serves the vested interests of Punjab oligarchy in Pakistan.

Pakistani Tactics

Tension with India is heightened in a number of ways :

By seeking military parity with India. This objective is to be achieved by the acquisition of the latest United States weapons and the forging of an alliance with the United States and China. From India's viewpoint, Pakistan's military ties with extra-regional powers bring super-power rivalry to South Asia, where India intended to establish its own pre-eminence. In response to Pakistan's military ties with the United States, India hardened its attitude on bilateral matters and sought closer co-operation with the former Soviet Union. Pakistan's military treaties with United States provided India with the pretext for alliance with friendly countries.[9] The conclusion of Indo-Soviet treaty of 1970 was a response to US Secretary of State Kissinger's secret trip to China, arranged via Pakistan. If India refuses to criticize the Russian occupation of Afghanistan, it is a reaction to United States' supply of sophisticated weapons such as F-16s and AWACS to Pakistan. India believes these weapons will be used against it.

- Pakistan's nuclear programme is a part of its quest for its nuclear parity with India.

- General Zia's exchange of pleasantries with Sikhs and utterances about Kashmir. These led India to the belief that Pakistan, in a alliance with the United States, is embarked on a campaign to destabilize India.

- Zia regime's reluctance to increase volume of trade and travel between the two countries and its delaying tactics led to avoid the reopening of the Khokhrapar route, between Sindh and Rajasthan. These actions convince Indian authorities that regime in Pakistan was not really interested in the improvement of relations between the two countries.

The Punjabi oligarchy domination of decision making processes in Pakistan is one of the main reasons for discord between the two powers. This group of policy makers, principally, comprised of military officials and intelligence agencies formulates policies in such a way that tension with India is bound to continue. This situation would have certainly improved, if smaller nationalities were given equal representation in the decision making process of Pakistan. Meanwhile, the military power at the disposal of Punjabi oligarchy and Reagan administration's support for it makes this an unlikely prospect. In consequence, there was no major improvement in Indo-Pakistani relations.

References

1. *Dawn* (Karachi), 8 August, 1986.
2. Rajeendra Sareen, 'Diverged Indo-Pak Perceptions', *Tribune* (Chandigarh), 9 September, 1986.
3. H.V. Hodson, *The Great Divide* (London: Oxford University Press, 1985), pp. 427-503.
4. Dawn, 1 May 1987.
5. 'A survey of India', *Economist,* 9 May, 1987.
6. For a detailed account of the tug of war between the Punjab and other provinces see Gowher Rizvi, 'Pakistan: The domestic dimensions of security', in Berry Buzan and Gowher Rizvi (eds), *South Asian Insecurity and the Great Powers* (London : Macmillan, 1986), pp. 60-87.
7. Amenah Azam Ali, 'Punjab: The Silent Majority', *Herald* (Karachi), May 1987, pp. 57-70.
8. Major-General Sher Ali Khan, 'The 1965 War Led to the Bengal Crises', *The View Point* (Lahore), 4 September, 1986, pp. 21-2.
9. Anita Inder Singh, 'Super-power Complex and South Asia', in Berry Buzan and Gowher Rizvi, p. 213.

(This paper is the revised and updated version of an earlier paper, entitled; "The Root of Indo-Pakistani Discord", in *The New Zealand International Review*, Vol: XII.No:4, July-August 1987, Canberra, 1987. This is its updated version)

Index

U

V